Absentee Ownership

and its

Discontents

Critical Essays
on the Legacy of
Thorstein Veblen

Absentee Ownership and its Discontents
Critical Essays on the Legacy of **Thorstein Veblen**
edited by Michael Hudson and Ahmet Öncü
with a foreword by William M. Dugger

Book cover and page design: Ertuğrul Karabulut
Cover graphic: Millions of acres in Iowa and Nebraska for sale on 10 years credit by the Burlington & Missouri River R. R. Co. at 6 percent interest and low prices. Buffalo, New York, commercial advertising printing house (1872).
Credit: Library of Congress Printed Ephemera Collection (Public Domain).

ISBN: 978-3-9814842-7-4

Absentee Ownership
and its Discontents

Critical Essays on the Legacy of **Thorstein Veblen**

edited by **Michael Hudson** and **Ahmet Öncü**
with a foreword by **William M. Dugger**

ISLET

FOREWORD

Radical Critic of the Competitive Order: Veblen's Place in Modern Economics

William M. Dugger

Leading Modern Economists

Thorstein Veblen, Adam Smith, Karl Marx and John Maynard Keynes are the leading modern economists. Smith, with his invisible hand doctrine, led the way in supporting a competitive order. He argued that when individuals compete, empathy and sympathy limited the harm most individuals do to others. He did allow that a system of justice was needed to restrain those lacking in moral sentiment. Mostly, however, competition would restrain individual self interest and guide it toward the common good as if by an invisible hand.

Marx was the leading opponent of capitalism. He argued that it was based on the exploitation of the working class by the capitalist class and that increasingly severe realization crises would finally destroy capitalism. Keynes was the leading reformer of capitalism. He argued that it could be saved from depression (realization crisis) by appropriate government management of effective demand.

Veblen, however, is a unique outlier amongst the four leading economists. He opposed the competitive order. He disagreed with Adam Smith, and insisted that the case of America showed conclusively that competition inherently led to conspicuous consumption and waste as well as industrial sabotage and international conflict. The competitive order could not be reformed by an improved system of justice or by monetary and fiscal stabilization policies. It had to be replaced with a cooperative order. He took a broader view than the others, except perhaps for a broadly interpreted Marx. Veblen went far beyond capitalism, seeing it as only one of many variants of the competitive order. Capitalism was a destructive class system. Veblen stood with Marx on that.

Both were critics of capitalism. Not just capitalism but competition itself was the poison pill, according to Veblen. Marx's target was capitalism, a smaller target than Veblen's competitive order. Veblen critiqued the entire competitive order, not just the recently emerged capitalist variety. Using the evolution of the competitive order in America as a case study, he showed that it was not just capitalism that was destructive and that there was not just one aspect of it that could be reformed. Instead, the whole competitive order, in whatever variety, should be replaced by a cooperative order. Veblen's place in economics is to remind us even today that replacement is the great need of modern civilization, if it is to save itself alive from its current institutional order.

The Poison Pill of Competition

Using "the case of America," Veblen showed that competition is not limited to certain kinds of behavior. It has not been and cannot be limited to changing the price or the quality of a product sold in the market. It has not been and cannot be limited to the market. It spreads to all behaviors in the social order. Such behaviors include -but are not limited to- production, consumption, learning, religious devotion, internal governance and international relations. Competition is a pill; when swallowed, its effects spread everywhere.

Adam Smith argued that the pill's effects were mainly limited to production and the market, although competition could even improve the motivation of religious personnel. Most importantly, he argued that the competitive pill's effects were beneficent. Competition improved motivation and directed individual activity toward the common good—the invisible hand. On the other hand, Veblen argued that an impartial case study of America showed that the competitive order played out very differently. The effects of competition were malignant rather than beneficent. Competition did not play out as a merely individualistic system of checks and balances, where the self interest of each individual was limited (checks) by the self interest of other individuals and then guided (balances) into channels provided by the market prices offered by still other individuals. Instead, competition encouraged alliance, conspiracy, and collective struggle—industrial sabotage, conspicuous consumption and international conflict. Veblen found that organizing and fighting the competition or changing the rules to one's advantage were the imperatives in competition. That was the case whether in economics, politics, international relations, or wherever.

Veblen found three major ways to win a competition in any sphere of life. One was to improve your performance so that it was better than that of your competitors. The second way was to harm your competitors' performance so they would perform worse than you. The third way was to change the nature of the game to gain an advantage.

Once changed, winners had a vested interest in the new rules. Veblen found that in actual practise, in the American case in particular -"in the nature of the case"- as he often put it, the first way did not predominate. Instead, competition pushed individuals to form alliances with whoever they could, in order to strengthen their common defensive and offensive maneuvers against the other competitors. Their organized action was most effective against whoever did not succeed in organizing against them. The actions (also the "reform" of the rules) were not guided as if by an invisible hand to serve the common good, but were guided by the organized hands to serve the interests of those who controlled the organization. When the interests so organized were able to get the state to defend their organizations (corporations) and their interests in them with new legislation, new judicial precedent and constitutional amendment, they became absentee owners of vested interests. When they had assembled enough absentee ownership to make it matter in the competitive struggle, they became the substantial citizens that made up the national establishment. Said establishment then acted over and against its own underlying population and also over and against the opposing national establishments participating in the international competition between nation states.

Veblen A Century Later

Veblen's work possesses lasting scientific credibility and persuasive political power. Scientifically, his theory of the competitive order in the large has turned out to be empirically and historically correct. Modern society's variant of the competitive order has turned out to be spiritually, domestically and internationally malignant. Peace has seldom threatened to break out. Instead, arms races and alliances have left competing national establishments increasingly armed to the teeth and engaged in violent confrontations. For their parts, the domestic economies of the combatants have suffered through more than a dozen business cycles (so-named by Veblen's student Wesley C. Mitchell) and have fallen into two deep crises: The Great Depression and now The Great Recession.

The Veblenian critique calls for anger, but not despair. On the political front, his critique of the competitive social order has helped move three generations to take political action against it: first the New Dealers of the 1930s and 1940s, next the counterculture youth of the 1960s and the 1970s (including me) and now the egalitarian protesters of the New Millennium. So far they have failed to replace the competitive order. The stakes have increased after each failure.

The Big Fix

Veblen knew that the future is contestable. The competitive order may be replaced by a cooperative one before we destroy ourselves. But the obstacles are formidable. The competitive struggle has run long enough in America that the winners and their descendants have succeeded in pushing their vanquished opponents backward and in propelling themselves forward so far that the winners no longer have to compete to stay ahead. They can absent themselves from the struggle entirely and still remain on top. They can devote their efforts to inflating themselves and deflating everyone else with conspicuous consumption and conspicuous leisure. Their invidious distinctions disable everyone else with envy for the great and spite for the small.

The absentee owners/leisure class members can continue to win without running because they can start at the finish line. They have become absentee *winners* because they have become absentee *owners* with enough pecuniary substance to remain at leisure while others run till they drop. The absentee owners and their descendants also have become substantial citizens who use their national establishments to make and enforce the rules of the game as needed to ensure their freedom to maneuver. Today they are the 1% who take their share from what the 99% produce and use the national establishment to defend the usurpation through the justice system and extend it into other countries through the globalization process.

The American case showed Veblen a century ago that *The Fix Is In*. Once in, *The Fix Has Stayed In*. That is what the case should show the rest of us as it continues to play out. The competitive order keeps the fix in place while appearing not to do so. The ostensibly democratic national establishment still defends the substantial citizens and the advancing state of the industrial arts still raises the GDP in spite of the absentee owners with their vested and newly vesting interests and their industrial sabotage.

Tulsa, July 14, 2016

PREFACE

The Global Financial Crisis since 2008 has left in its wake the most severe economic downturn since the Great Depression. Governments and entire national economies have been sacrificed to save the financial sector and its major clients. Bailing out banks, bondholders and Wall Street brokerage houses – the institutions whose mismanagement, over-lending and outright fraud led to the crash – has widened economic polarization and caused fiscal strains.

This has led many countries to reconsider the character of macroeconomic management and behind it, the body of economic and political theory guiding today's societies. What seemed at first glance to be a systemic policy failure of mainstream economics is coming to be seen as not so much a failure as part of an orchestrated class to protect financial wealth and its allied *rentier* sectors. Economic policy has passed out of the hands of elected democratic government to central banks and other government agencies controlled by financial planners and the *rentier* class behind them. Their post-crisis management has enabled these interests to gain control of a large swath of the public domain of debtor countries, along with industries and real estate in the creditor nations themselves.

The *Communist Manifesto*'s classic dictum that "the executive of the modern state is nothing but a committee for managing the common affairs of the whole bourgeoisie" no longer seems to be an exaggeration, but it may be updated to describe modern governments above all as committees to subsidize and rescue the banking and financial sector, which has become the manager and central planner of today's global economy.

The effect is to curtail industrial capacity, subordinating the forces of industrial capitalism to an extractive (and increasingly concentrated) financial superstructure consolidating its power by bank loans, bond and stock ownership – turning the rest of society into debtors, renters and buyers of monopolized goods and services.

What remains in dispute is just who comprises the today's ruling class and where its policy program is leading. The present collection of essays trace how Thorstein Veblen described the way in which the mid-19th century's industrial capitalism was becoming centered on what today is called the Finance, Insurance and Real Estate (FIRE) sector. Each author in this volume discusses the character of today's capitalism, and how and why the capitalist class remains politically dominant despite the fact that it repeatedly fails to fulfill the requirements of economic leadership it claims to fulfill. Together, these papers contribute to a better understanding of "capital in the twenty first century," to use the phrase that has become popular following Thomas Piketty's best seller.

Veblen made numerous contributions to a diverse set of fields. Not surprisingly, he has been considered by some to be an economist and by others a sociologist. To others he seemed broadly to be an anthropologist, political or cultural theorist. The authors of the current collection view him as a critic of "the established order of business," continuing in the tradition of classical political economy to analyze the often dysfunctional modern world that, in his mind, required a restructuring.

Unlike today's neoclassical economics, classical political economists distinguished between earned and unearned income, that is, the types of income accruing to productive and unproductive labor and investment respectively. The labor theory of value found its counterpart in the "rent theory" of prices. This distinction between intrinsic cost-value and market price (with economic rent reflecting the margin of price over value) provided a basis for analyzing the ownership of wealth and other special privileges to extract income without creating real value by producing goods and services.

The policy conclusion of this classical approach was that material wealth adding to overall well-being could be augmented only by productive investment. By the same token, a subset of unproductive *rentier* property and financial claims was extractive rather than productive – and hence, was a form of economic overhead, not real wealth. This was the essential theme of classical rent theory, which Veblen continued at a time when the economics mainstream was denying the distinction between rent extractors and industrial investors.

Pursuing the logic of classical rent theory, Veblen investigated the consequences of concentrating ownership in the hands of an evolving capitalist class. He described "absentee ownership" as the "latest stage of capitalism" and "the new order of business" at the outset of the twentieth century. "It may be said, of course, and perhaps truthfully, that the absentee owners of the country's industrial equipment," he wrote, "come in for a disproportionate share of the 'national dividend,' and that they and their folks habitually consume their share in superfluities; but no urgent moral indignation appears to be aroused by all that."

This class of absentee owners comprised a new aristocracy. Like their feudal counterparts, they did not directly manage the means of production or other assets, which took on the form mainly of corporate bonds and stock. Real estate investment was largely for speculative purposes to obtain price gains, while the stock market likewise aimed increasingly at making purely financial gains.

For Veblen, absentee ownership as the latest stage of capitalism consisted of three pillars: "the mechanical system of industry, the price system, and the national establishment." This tripartite social organization was centered on the financial sector, whose major business concern was to create industrial monopolies while gaining control of national politics. Veblen called these monopolists and political deep state the "vested interests." The credit system was the core of the financial sector, which was employed to gain unearned income on behalf of these vested interests.

The result was bifurcation between the super rich absentee owners and the underlying population, whose survival has increasingly come to depend on credit, *i.e.*, debt on the liabilities side of the balance sheet. In Veblen's words, capitalism in the form of absentee ownership works in such a way that "the country's assets should, at a progressively accelerated rate, gravitate into the ownership, or at least into the control, of the banking community at large."

In view of Veblen's argument that engineers would play a major or even the most progressive role in society, this book is significant largely because it is the product of an international conference on Veblen's legacy organized by the Chamber of Electrical Engineers of Turkey in 2012 in Istanbul. It is hard to imagine such an attempt by an engineering association in any other country. We therefore are grateful to Chairman Cengiz Göltaş of the 43rd Board of Governors of the Chamber of Electrical Engineers of Turkey, and to all other members of the 43rd Board for their support of the conference. Our thanks also go to Chairman Hüseyin Yeşil of the 44th Board of Governors and all other members of the 44th Board and Chairman Orhan Örücü of the Center for Continuing Education of the Chamber of Electrical Engineers for their support and interest in our project. And for their continued assistance throughout the project we would like to thank the Chamber members Oylum Yıldır and Emre Metin.

We would like to extend our heartfelt thanks to Sidney Plotkin for generously sharing his fine expertise with us in the preparation of the conference, Veblen, Capitalism and Possibilities for a Rational Economic Order, Istanbul, Turkey, 2012. We also would like to thank all the people who delivered papers or acted as moderators and chairs of sessions. In inviting some speakers, Sabri Öncü played a critical role. We are grateful to him for his valuable contributions to the success of our conference. Finally, we would like to express our genuine thanks to Ertuğrul Karabulut for his meticulous work in designing the cover and preparing the book for publication.

Michael Hudson and Ahmet Öncü
New York and Istanbul
August 14, 2016

CONTENTS

Thorstein Veblen: An American Economic Perspective

Michael Perelman

Introduction

Blessed with both insight and style, Thorstein Veblen has become more relevant than ever, given current conditions. Neoliberalism in both economics and politics is enjoying a stranglehold on society. Its arrogant supporters blithely dismiss any information that might contradict their rigid dogma and treat all who would challenge them with contempt. To make matters worse, the neoliberals also dominate the media and academia, making respectful or even intelligent debate virtually impossible.

Information about corporate behavior was not readily available, but intrepid Progressive journalists, often called was muckrakers, were revealing the unconscionable practices of the great corporations, which wielded state power to take advantage of against workers, bilked investors, and bled government resources with the aid of an army of corrupt politicians. Even without the muckrakers, public opinion was hostile to the obvious widespread corporate and political malfeasance.

Nonetheless, challenges to corporate behavior had little effect. Even after the election of 1892 when the anticorporate Populist Party won a great victory in Congress, their political influence then quickly evaporated, partially because their leaders' rural roots. Their lack of polish and sophistication opened them up to ridicule. Consequently, the titans of business were able to enjoy immense power and influence, immune from any unpleasant consequences of their corrupt behavior.

Given these conditions, what then would be the most effective way for Veblen to convey his perspective to the public? Adopting a conventional style of academic writing would have been an exercise in futility. To do so would entail working within the norms of a system, which he had already rejected. But how could Veblen carry on a successful dialogue when he rejected out of hand the core beliefs of those whom he labeled, The Vested Interests, especially when he perceived a gap between rationality and reality so wide that suggesting reasonable policy changes would be pointless.

Instead, Veblen perfected a unique style of criticism: blending ridicule, irony, and satire, made more distinctive by a humorous application of an archaic vocabulary. This approach allowed him to bring attention to his critique at the same time his humor had the potential to make corporate power seem more vulnerable to public dissatisfaction.

Veblen's critique, however, went much deeper than the work of the muckrakers, who merely intended to show how government officials and the captains of industry were violating the norms of society. For Veblen, those norms were also defective.

Despite the obvious technical progress that was occurring around him, Veblen dismissed the popular notion that society was undergoing a thorough going modernization. Instead, he insisted that omnipresent vestiges of primitive culture still exercised powerful influence within the culture of a supposedly modern society. A truly flourishing society required transcending the dysfunctional consequences of the institutional arrangements that this atavistic culture produced, including a grossly inefficient application of modern technology.

In the end, Veblen, like Marx before him, practiced "ruthless criticism of all that exists." but Veblen directed his merciless criticism at the material and cultural defects of capitalism rather than the existing social relations underlying capitalism. Veblen's approach may well have been the most effective means of calling attention to the shortcomings of capitalism. His cultural critique is unparalleled in the English speaking world, with the possible exception of John Kenneth Galbraith, who managed to translate much of Veblenesque analysis into a more popular style.

Cultural Criticism

Typically, the terrain of criticism tends to be cultural. Critics often present themselves as arbiters of good taste in the worlds of literature, art, fashion, or even food. Perhaps to fend off criticism from those who might question their right to adopt such a lofty position, critics must pay close attention to the style of their work. One favorite technique for critics is to ridicule their detractors in an unexpected way, often by means of, as Veblen would say, "invidious comparisons."

More often than not, the ambition of the critic is to become accepted by the world, which is the presumed object of criticism. Iconoclastic critics, such as Veblen's, are different. They proudly stand apart from the subjects of their criticism because they have no need to adopt a pretense of superiority or to crave acceptance by the community that they criticize.

Veblen, however, was not above making unflattering comparisons, often showing similarities between primitive behavior and his modern targets. In making such portrayals, Veblen benefited from an enormous inventory of source material because of his wide interest in other cultures.

For example, to learn about Icelandic culture, he spent many summers on an island inhabited by immigrants from Iceland. He began boarding with one of these families, with the proviso that they would converse with him only in their native language. He soon became proficient enough that he translated *The Laxdaela*, a tenth century Icelandic saga. The translation must have been very well done:

> Astonished at the sensitivity with which Veblen had rendered The Laxdaela Saga into English, an incredulous University of Wisconsin philologist inquired of the book's publisher, B. W. Huebsch, whether Veblen was "by any chance himself an Icelander else, as an economist, how comes it he can read this speech of the twilight of the Gods?" (Bartley and Yoneda 1994: 603)

Veblen included an introduction with the observation that the earlier Viking practice of seeking material gain "by force and fraud at the cost of the party of the second part" was actually much the same "as the national politics pursued by the statesmen of the present time" (Bartley and Yoneda 1994: 596; Veblen 1925: vi, ix).

Veblen's most famous comparison was between the behavior of contemporary robber barons and the cultural practices of primitive societies, especially with regard to conspicuous consumption. He juxtaposed the great robber barons of his day flaunting their wealth with the potlatches of the Northwestern Native Americans, who demonstrated their importance by destroying great amounts of wealth in public bonfires. Although later anthropologists found fault with Veblen's acceptance of the conventional portrayal of the potlatch, the comparison still served to make the robber barons look ridiculous.

Ironically, in their conspicuous consumption, these economic aristocrats often also acted as cultural critics. They did so through their pecuniary rather than their literary powers. They advertised themselves as arbiters of civilized culture by building cultural cathedrals for musical performances or the display of art. In this way, they could hope to win respect by imposing their taste on society at large. For example, they chose to finance symphony halls to promote an alternative to the opera, which they disdained as a crude form of popular culture. Instead, they favored the production of large symphonic works, featuring famous conductors. The role of the conductor, imposing discipline on a large number of musicians with their distinctive responsibilities, bore an unmistakable resemblance to the important responsibilities of the captain of industry (Perelman 2011: 291-294).

Veblen's satiric treatment of the titans of the Gilded Age resembles Jonathan Swift more than Karl Marx, except that Swift relied on fictional anthropology rather than Veblen's modern research. *Gulliver's Travels* parodied the culture of the British Royal Society by portraying it as the Grand Academy of Lagado where the scientists worked on ridiculous and even vulgar projects. Veblen must have been drawn to Swift at an early age.

As a student, Veblen, obviously influenced by Swift, delivered "A Plea for Cannibalism" (Dorfman 1940: 31), suggesting a close parallel with Swift's *Modest Proposal* for selling the flesh of babies for food. In that work, Swift was railing against the inhumanity of the British exploitation of Ireland, by ridiculing the application of political arithmetic. To make that point more emphatic, Swift supported the supposed economic rationality of his project by using Irish data from the early economist William Petty.

Thorstein Veblen in the Context of the Real Industrial Revolution

Veblen's style and subject matter reflected the prevailing economic conditions of the time. He began writing in the aftermath of what might be seen as the Real Industrial Revolution. The rapid technical progress that occurred in this period stands in stark contrast to much more modest developments that took place during the earlier period, popularly known as the Industrial Revolution. Suddenly, huge factories appeared that could take advantage of both a newfound capacity to far more effectively harness the power of fossil fuels to meet a burst of demand created by the military needs of the Civil War.

This new technology, which should have been of great advantage, created no end of problems for the captains of industry. Each new technical development called for larger economies of scale, swamping the market with ever more commodities, which drove down prices below the cost of production. Business faced a choice of either folding up or responding with more even modern technology. However, this new technology would compound the problem of falling prices because the new capital goods were generally designed to operate on an even greater scale, further swamping the market.

What was happening stood in sharp contrast to economic theory, as well as the presumption that capitalism was the natural bearer of progressive modernization. This contrast should have been obvious even to students in elementary economics; however most academic economists, steeped in the theology of market efficiency, failed to grasp a basic problem. Competition, that wondrous fuel of market efficiency, tends to drive prices down toward the cost of producing one more unit. But with huge fixed capital costs, the expense of producing another unit was trivial. In other words, the organic composition of capital was experiencing explosive growth and capitalism was self destructing, so much so that the period after 1873 became known as the Great Depression until after 1929, a later burst of destruction claimed that title.

Key to that earlier depression was a wave of dramatic railroad bankruptcies that took down much of the rest of the economy. Railroads were the key economic sector at the time. Despite repeated bankruptcies, railroad investment exceeded aggregate investment in manufacturing in every decade from 1850 to 1890. Between 1850 and 1880, railroads represented twice as much aggregate investment as the entire manufacturing sector (Sweezy 1954: 532). Despite the major investment in manufacturing that followed, until 1904, the book value of capital in the railroad industry still exceeded the aggregate capital invested in the entire industrial sector (United States Department of Commerce. Bureau of the Census 1975: 684 and 735).

The Morgan family had represented the interests of hapless British bondholders. After having been previously burned by their investments in Latin America, they sought security in American railroad bonds, only to suffer another round of losses. In Charles Dickens' *Christmas Carol*, the miserly Scrooge suffered a series of nightmares, the first being the discovery that he had invested in U.S. railroad bonds.

J. P. Morgan tried without success to get the railroads to voluntarily cooperate rather than to continue to fall victim to what business at the time called destructive competition. He would have the railroads to agree not to compete by cutting prices, but, sooner or later, one of them would go off on its own by lowering prices to get an advantage over its competitors. Competition would break out again, resulting in another wave of bankruptcies.

Exasperated, Morgan took matters into his own hands, buying U.S. railroads and consolidating them in order to reduce competition. Soon consolidations swept across industry after industry, often led by Morgan himself. People commonly referred to this process as Morganization. The most dramatic example came after Andrew Carnegie began building a railroad to take his coal from Tennessee to Pennsylvania. Fearing that Carnegie, who had a long history working for the Pennsylvania Railroad, might expand more dramatically into the railroad industry, Morgan bought up the gigantic Carnegie Steel operation, along with several other steelmakers, to form United States Steel. Once protected from the ravages of competition, Morgan's cartels and those inspired by him were freed from the compulsion to modernize. Instead, they could be operated like banks, which only had to look at their balance sheets with one exception. Additional profit without additional investment was possible if the workers could be driven harder while keeping wages in check.

Over and above the attraction of diminishing competitive pressures, the corporate consolidations offered an opportunity to bilk those who were foolish enough to buy stock based on the misleading information supplied by the financiers who promoted the consolidations.

The transcontinental railroads took center stage in terms of corruption, fraud, and inefficiency. Richard White just published a magnificent twelve year study of the development of the transcontinental railroads in the United States. He devoted years to archival study of the railroads, including the personal letters of the railroad magnates. His conclusion is absolutely Veblenesque:

> The best way to understand the transcontinentals' simultaneous failure as businesses and success as sources of individual fortunes for insiders is to regard them not as new businesses devoted to the efficient sale of transportation but rather as corporate containers for financial manipulation and political networking. They employed rational managers, but they were led by financiers. The financiers made money through subsidies, the sale of securities, insider companies for the construction of the railroads themselves, and land speculation. Each funneled corporate resources into private pockets. To do this, they needed considerable political aid and protection. (White 2011: xxvii)

Morganizing Economics

A new conception of economic theory was taking root during the late nineteenth century. Anyone seeking high quality postgraduate education at the time would be likely to go to Germany. Soon a wave of talented American economists returned from Germany steeped in German economic theory. Germany, unlike the United States, was a country without a rich resource base, yet the German economy grew very rapidly, while resisting the lure of *laissez faire*. German development relied on a powerful system of higher education, which created new scientific knowledge in close collaborations with the giant cartels that controlled much of the German economy.

These economists returning from Germany were not radical but their understanding of economics was closer to J. P. Morgan than Adam Smith. They formed the American Economic Association to act as a counterweight to the prevailing academic economics, but over time, both they and their organization made their peace with the mainstream. However, they had imbibed in training not dissimilar to that of Marx. While rejecting Marx's politics, they could be respectful of his economics.

For example, Arthur Twining Hadley, an early president of the American Economic Association as well as Yale University, wrote to a friend that, "while far from agreeing with him (Karl Marx)," he accepted that his work had a "higher scientific aim than almost any work on political economy in the last half century" (Hadley 1879). Elsewhere he observed:

> The socialists are justified in asserting that there is an inconsistency between our political doctrine of equal rights to pursuit of happiness for everybody, and the facts of the industrial world, as we see them about us. (Hadley 1896: 94)

Writing during the first Great Depression, Hadley's German training allowed him to recognize that the shibboleth of *laissez faire* ideology prevented economists to recognize the self destructive nature of modern capitalism. Nowhere was this tendency toward self destruction more obvious than with the railroads, which were repeatedly going bankrupt. He addressed this problem in his most important work, Railroad Transportation:

To so great an extent were the economists able to point out the evil results of mistaken legislation, that in the popular mind the teaching of economics has become synonymous with the effort to reduce the activity of government to a minimum. The phrase *laissez faire* ..., which was the motto of the physiocrats, has taken an exaggerated hold on the public imagination, and has been regarded as a fundamental axiom of economic science, when it is in fact only a practical maxim of political wisdom, subject to all the limitations which experience may afford. (Hadley 1896: 12)

Nonetheless, he observed:

All our education and habit of mind make us believe in competition. We have been taught to regard it as a natural if not necessary condition of a healthful business life. We look with satisfaction on whatever favors it, and with distrust on whatever hinders it. We accept almost without reserve the theory of Ricardo, that, under open competition in a free market, the value of different goods will tend to be proportional to the cost of production. (Hadley 1903: 69)

Hadley's study of railroads brought him into contact with a capital intensive world (in other words a high organic composition of capital), which bore no resemblance to the simplicity of Ricardo's model of perfect competition:

... the size units of capital is so large that free competition often becomes an impossibility, and theories of economics which are based upon the existence of such competition prove blind guides in dealing with modern price movements. (Hadley 1896: iii)

Ricardo's theory ... fails, because, far below the point where it pays to do your own business, it pays to steal business from another man. The influx of new capital will cease; but the fight will go on, either until the old investment and machinery are worn out, or until a pool of some sort is arranged. (Hadley 1896: 72)

The consequences can be dramatic because:

It is not true that when the price falls below cost of production people always find it for their interest to refuse to produce at a disadvantage. It very often involves worse loss to stop producing than to produce below cost. (Hadley 1896: 70)

Hadley's lesson from the railroads was striking:

Railroad competition may exist everywhere, somewhere or nowhere. If it exists everywhere, rates are reduced to the level of movement charges (variable costs), and there is nothing to pay fixed charges .... If there is competition somewhere, the competitive point will have rates based on movement expenses, and the others will have to pay fixed charges. This constitutes discrimination. If we have competition nowhere, this either involves a pool, or amounts to the same thing. (Hadley 1903: 142-143)

More generally, "The railroad may serve as a type of modern business. Wherever there are large permanent investments of capital we see the same causes at work in the same way" (Hadley 1903: 72).

Although Hadley was deeply conservative, he saw untrammeled *laissez faire* as being even more impractical than socialism. He even suggested that unbridled competition would lead to the survival of "the unfittest rather than the fittest" (Hadley 1886: 224). For that reason, he concluded that, "To enjoy industrial liberty, it will be necessary to resign the claim to industrial lawlessness; the alternative is socialism" (Hadley 1886: 224-225).

In other words, competition can drive business to continuing production at a loss. Hadley could have added that such losses might also tempt business to modernize, leading to greater production, thereby intensifying the already destructive force of competition. The result was the Great Depression he was witnessing. Like Keynes, Hadley was writing to save capitalism from itself.

Hadley was no outsider. Son in law of a governor of Connecticut, he served as both labor commissioner and head of the Public Utilities Commission in Connecticut. President Taft appointed him chairman of the Railroad Securities Commission in 1911. He was equally successful in the academic world, serving as an early president of American Economic Association (1898-1899). As a professor at Yale University from 1879 to 1899, he taught economics as well as Greek, logic, and German and Roman law. From 1899 to 1921, he was president of Yale. After resigning that position, he became a director of the Atchison, Topeka and Santa Fe Railway.

Veblen and Hadley

Veblen's world overlapped with Hadley's. Veblen studied at Yale while Hadley was a professor. Like Hadley, Veblen was offered the presidency of the American Economic Association, although he declined the (dubious) honor. His book on Germany showed an abiding interest in that country's development. Like Hadley, Veblen was connected with both academia and, tangentially, the railroads, in part because he married a woman who had one uncle, James Strong, who was the college president at the school Veblen attended and another uncle, William Strong, had been the president of the Atchison, Topeka and Santa Fe Railway before Hadley joined the company. His wife's father helped himself by getting William Strong to throw a lot of railroad business his way. He was also planning to use his influence with Strong, to get Veblen a position with the railroad shortly before Strong lost his position, forced out by bankers in the wake of disastrous financial performance. According to White's account:

> Even though many of its enemies were vulnerable, the Atchison by the late 1880s had too many fights on too many fronts .... quite suddenly, ... the Atchison keeled over and crawled from the field. It had collapsed under the weight of paper. Building railroads without much regard for how to pay for them or for the traffic they might carry, neglecting to provide or maintain the equipment necessary to run trains on vastly extended systems, and accumulating large and often disguised debts .... The vast quantities of new stock the Atchison had sold declined in value even as the bonds it sold increased its fixed costs. In 1884, as a much smaller road, it had a reported profit of over $5 million, whereas in 1888, having more than doubled in size, it had a deficit of nearly $3 million. (White 2011: 373)

The discovery of widespread, fraudulent accounting only came later.

Despite Veblen's overlaps with Hadley, his writing style bore little resemblance to Hadley's. Rather than providing a more theoretical analysis of the defect that Hadley objectively identified, Veblen brilliantly described the consequences.

Retrospectively, the marginalized Veblen seems to have chosen an appropriate method of presentation. The academic critique of Hadley and the other German trained economists is largely forgotten. While Veblen's approach has always remained somewhat marginal among academic economics, his work still attracts a lively interest.

Veblen's Economic Critique

Veblen saw academic economics, which prided itself for its modern perspective, as a perfect example of cultural backwardness. Conventional economics offered nothing more than a static theory of efficient equilibrium outcomes. For Veblen, Darwinian evolutionary theory suggested a more scientific perspective.

For Veblen, Darwinian like progress was both slow and irregular (see Tilman 1996, chapter 2). He accepted that conventional microeconomics may have been more or less adequate for analyzing a village economy that relied on handicrafts, but made no sense whatsoever for a modern economy with advanced technology.

Nonetheless, economists presented their work as thoroughly objective analysis, although its unstated underlying purpose was to justify policies that favored *laissez faire*, or, in the case of those daring to move slightly outside of the fold, such as Keynes some decades later, to propose modest measures that would make capitalism function more effectively.

Economists shielded themselves from criticism by pretending that their analysis adhered to the highest standards of scientific rigor by adopting a formalistic approach. They suggested that their method was comparable to that of physics. Toward this end they built their theory upon a foundation of unquestioned axioms, which they discovered through introspection rather than through scientific research.

Most conventional economists had good reason to avoid taking notice of the progression of the railroads from modernization, business failure, consolidation, and then stagnation. After all, the leading universities were dependent upon business donations. Business donors understood that *laissez faire* economics justified policies that promoted their best interests. They did not look kindly upon those who questioned that kind of economic theory.

In contrast, the public remained critical of economists who gave their support to a system that had proven defective. In addition to the bad standing in public opinion, the transcontinentals were the justifiable target of the most militant labor conflicts that the country had ever experienced. Of course, the railroads, backed up by the state's military powers, had a decided advantage in the conflict.

In response to the antagonism to the railroads, economists had a ready answer. John Bates Clark, once Veblen's teacher, won acclaim for producing the most sophisticated version of conventional economics at the time one which supposedly proved that workers' share of wealth and income was both moral and just.

Just as Veblen both exposed and ridiculed the obvious irrationality, avarice, and dysfunction of the time, he published a detailed critique of Clark's economics, mercilessly ridiculing the sacred axioms of economic theory. Most famously, Veblen rejected economists' key assumption that capitalism created a progressive civilization in which isolated individuals behaved rationally, immune to any social influence. Beyond boldly distancing himself from conventional economics, Veblen went further, charging that economists' "work was as devoid of scientific merit as it was of social equity" (Tilman 1996: 27). In a hilarious passage chock full of pseudoscientific jargon, Veblen mocked economists' notion, describing their:

> ... hedonistic conception of man [as] a lightning calculator of pleasures and pains, who oscillates like a homogeneous globule of desire of happiness under the impulse of stimuli that shift him about the area, but leave him intact. He has neither antecedent nor consequent. He is an isolated, definitive human datum, in stable equilibrium except for the buffets of the impinging forces that displace him in one direction or another. Self imposed in elemental space, he spins symmetrically about his own spiritual axis until the parallelogram of forces bears down upon him, whereupon he follows the line of the resultant. When the force of the impact is spent, he comes to rest, a self contained globule of desire as before. Spiritually, the hedonistic man is not a prime mover. He is not the seat of a process of living, except in the sense that he is subject to a series of permutations enforced upon him by circumstances external and alien to him. (Veblen 1898: 389-390)

In effect, Veblen was accusing economists of basing their justification of a market economy on arbitrary assumptions of how the people behaved, whereas he preferred the opposite direction of causality in which economists would study the complexity of human behavior in order to learn about the economy.

Obviously, Veblen's understanding of capitalism sharply differed from economists' fantasy about the invisible hand, in which the market benignly serves as a network of information, which alerts rational businesspeople about opportunities to profit in a manner that promotes the social good. Little thought need be given to those who might be inclined to cheat because the market will punish those who deviate from social norms. Presumably, informed consumers will quickly learn of malfeasance, depriving businesspeople of the opportunity to take advantage of others.

Instead of the individualistic rationalism presumed by the economists, Veblen saw a capitalistic world that had not yet managed to shed primitive cultural norms. These residual norms promoted social behavior that was both pervasive and dysfunctional. For Veblen, even the supposedly super rational economists had not shaken off the irrational remains of primitive culture. For example, Veblen began his discussion of Adam Smith by addressing Smith's "animistic bent" (Veblen 1899: 396).

The gap between real technical evolution and imagined social and cultural evolution led to an interesting contradiction. As a result of its delayed evolution, economic theory developed a theory appropriate for a primitive village, while foolishly presuming that the society it intends to analyze has evolved to a point of extreme rationality. In reality, the management of modern industry still bore many elements of barbarian culture. Given the prevalence of these stubborn barbaric residues in capitalist society, future evolutionary progress was unlikely to occur either smoothly or rapidly.

Veblen was not alone in comparing great magnates with barbarians. Charles Francis Adams, Jr. and Henry Adams, Grandsons and great grandson's of the two presidents Adams, published a searing critique of the railroad business, *Chapters of Erie*. Already in the first paragraph, we read:

Pirates are not extinct; they have only transferred their operations to the land, and conducted them in more or less accordance with the law; until, at last so great a proficiency have they attained, that the commerce of the world is more equally but far more heavily taxed in their behalf; than would ever have entered into their wildest hopes while, outside the law, they simply made all comers stand and deliver.

Charles Francis Adams, the railroad reformer, later became the president of the Union Pacific. In that role, he insisted that he was above the industry's norm. Although he was not above resorting to bribery, to his credit, he may not have engaged in the some of the other illegal practices common to the industry. However, in looking at the business culture at the time, one might be justified in assuming that all are guilty until proven innocent.

Veblen was particularly disgusted that capitalism was unable to efficiently exploit modern technology. Veblen clearly understood however, the defect in competition that Hadley had identified. For Hadley, the disorder in the railroads was the result of rational responses to an irrational system. Veblen, however, was unwilling to concede such rationality.

In contrast, Veblen seemed to be as disinterested in abstract or structural analysis as he was in the method of conventional economics. Instead, he chose a different tact. He represented capitalism first and foremost as a culture based on primitive instincts, such as predation and emulation; a culture that stood in the way of technical and human progress, without going into much detail about his alternative program.

Obviously, Veblen's idiosyncratic style of criticism made him even more unwelcome in many academic circles. No one should be surprised that, despite his unquestioned abilities, prior to his appointment at the New School late in life, none of his academic employers ever granted him tenure or even promoted him above associate professor (Tilman 1996: 30). Nonetheless, two of the most influential mainstream economists, Lawrence Laughlin and John Bates Clark, held him in high esteem.

Veblen and Efficiency

Because the railroads were the leading edge of modernization in the United States, they throw light on Veblen's economic critique. Here, Hadley's notion of competition, which may exist "everywhere, somewhere or nowhere," becomes relevant. In the West, the transcontinental railroads market competition was nowhere up through the Civil War.

The railroads reached Hadley's "somewhere" stage as they began to penetrate the West, but general competition was not yet a problem. Without competition, railroads could still charge high rates. Even with generous federal subsidies, rates were not high enough to compensate for the excessive waste, fraud, abuse, and incompetence, which accompanied railroad construction. As the network of railways became more crowded, railroads experienced excessive competition. Exit via bankruptcy and takeovers became common. Some of the largest railroads managed to survive by taking advantage of naive investors who supplied them with vital cash infusions. However, investors were not alone in their naivete. The railroads had no idea of their own cost structure. Consolidations helped move competition back toward the somewhere state. At times, they still found it necessary to pay competitors not to compete.

Despite the economic fragility of the railroads, they dominated the stock exchange. The railroads helped to maintain a brisk traffic in the stock market by cooking their books. In addition, they bought and sold stocks to manipulate the market. Stock market manipulation had the potential to facilitate both takeovers and to create a greater illusion of prosperity to make credit easier to obtain.

Although the railroads might not have been profitable, their owners profited mightily. They set up their own shell companies and then contracted with them for construction. By paying double the actual cost of construction, they could funnel money to themselves at the expense of the railroads. Investors were left holding the bag. At this stage, railroads could withhold productive capacity one way or another, while forcing shippers to pay excessive costs.

The railroad operators cheated consumers; the railroads also cheated each other through stock manipulations and other means to disrupt their competitors. Wholesale purchases of politicians allowed the railroads to win huge subsidies, which deprived the government of funds that might have potentially met peoples' needs. Finally, because railroads emphasized subterfuge rather than productive efficiency, their modern technology failed to come anywhere near its potential. Rather than build their lines to meet social and economic needs, other considerations took precedence, such as the opportunity to improve the value of the owners' private land holdings. Efficiency was also dissipated in wastefully building new lines needed only to forestall the plans of competitors?

While conventional economics instructed the world about market efficiencies, Veblen saw a system that was not merely suboptimal, but absurd. At the same time, business leaders went about proclaiming themselves as the pinnacle of Darwinian selection, which is why Hadley referred to the selection of the unfittest. One of the leading proponents of this Social Darwinism was Veblen's teacher, William Graham Sumner.

Ironically, the economists, who implicitly supported policies that were in line with the interests of these supposedly fittest specimens of capitalism, satisfied themselves with a static theory, which was decidedly un Darwinian. In contrast, Veblen believed that economics should model itself on evolutionary theory, but that social, institutional, and economic evolution was painfully slow, especially compared with the pace of rapid technological evolution.

Rather than acknowledging the evolutionary superiority of the captains of industry, Veblen portrayed them as barbaric, not only in their conspicuous consumption. Their predatory behavior was far more barbaric. Their predation was twofold. First, they preyed on society and, whenever possible, each other. Even more important, their economic sabotage meaning the withholding of efficiency stood in the way of further social, economic, and technical evolution.

Veblen may have been unusually sensitive to the technical deficiencies of modern business. Besides his training as an economist, Veblen was a skilled craftsman and the author of The Instinct of Workmanship. Upon seeing a student was wasting motion in chopping wood, he showed him how to wield an axe more efficiently and was pleased that his lesson succeeded (Dorfman 1940: 498). For him, the price system led to business behavior that was indifferent to matters of either efficiency or larger human needs. Business's attention was wholly directed to increasing profits, which were largely unrelated efficiently organizing productive activity in a way best suited to meet human needs.

To make his point Veblen distinguished between business and industry, where industry was the part of human activity directed toward efficient production.

Conventional economists were unable to understand this disconnect because they had gone out of their way to eliminate any consideration of work, workers, and working conditions. Instead, they emphasized transactions. nsofar as workers were concerned, they were no different from ordinary merchants who sold their wares. Workers' wares were their capacity to work. What employers did with those wares were of no more concern for economists than what consumers ultimately did with the goods that they bought in a store. In this way, economists, assuming that everything operated efficiently, were unable to come to grips with the deficiencies of business.

In response to the dismal capacity of capitalist business to take full advantage of the capacity of modern technology, Veblen published an article, "A Memorandum on a Practicable Soviet of Technicians." This piece first appeared in *The Dial* and then as the concluding chapter in *The Engineers and The Price System* (Veblen 1921).

Veblen's article was not programmatic. He had no particular love for big government. In fact, although he worked in the New Deal and even has been given occasional credit for having inspired the New Deal, he had serious reservations about Roosevelt's program. Instead, Veblen's sympathies lay more with the anarcho syndicalist Industrial Workers of the World. While working for the government, he even recommended that the administration appeal to the Wobblies to help with the wheat harvest. Given Veblen's sympathies, including his reverence for workmanship, Veblen was much less enthusiastic about large scale engineering projects than the idea that responsibility for production be broadly shared; that all workers become engineers of a sort rather than have a small Soviet of Engineers organize work for large numbers of people.

Yet, Veblen himself could envision massive economic transformations. As a good customer of the Sears, Roebuck mail order business, he once suggested that the retail trade, in general, be carried out by the Post Office rather than by innumerable shops and stores in effect, anticipating a system that would be more all inclusive than Amazon today. The reputation of the Post Office was favorable at the time, in contrast to the distaste for the rot of most government agencies. Besides, his intention was technical improvement through the elimination of waste. Shopping would be less time consuming. Retail space could be repositioned, while the personnel in the retail trade could use their time for more productive activities.

In so far as the conflict between engineers and the price system was concerned, a hopeful sign seemed to be on Veblen's horizon: engineers were beginning to professionalize themselves. At their best, engineers represented a culture of rational optimization uncontaminated by the sort of barbaric behavior common among business leaders. The emergence of their new professional engineering societies suggested a possibility of the development of a larger society based on rational principles than might benefit society as a whole, rather than individualistic profit maximization of the predators (Knoedler and Mayhew 1999). Three years after Veblen's death, Technocracy, a movement of engineers who advocated technocratic control briefly came to the public attention. Some credited Veblen's work for the movement, but neither Veblen nor Technocracy were able to influence the capitalist order.

As was usually the case, Veblen's pessimism was more prescient than his optimism. In fact, economists' belief in market rationality has become so extreme in the United States that in many quarters regulations in the financial system are not only unnecessary, but destructive of market efficiency. Somehow, this delusion is taking hold elsewhere in the world.

Sabotage and Goodwill

Veblen emphasizes two characteristics of business enterprise in an uncharacteristic. First, Veblen inverts concept of sabotage, usually associated with the anarcho socialists, with whom he sympathized. For them and for Veblen, the term is described as "the conscientious withdrawal of efficiency" (Veblen 1921: 1); however Veblen took the position that the most significant saboteurs are not radical workers, but respectable business people:

> it is only lately that this ordinary line of business strategy has come to be recognized as being substantially of the same nature as the ordinary tactics of the syndicalists. So that it has not been usual until the last few years to speak of maneuvres of this kind as sabotage when they are employed by employers and their business concerns. But all this strategy of delay, restriction, hindrance, and defeat is manifestly of the same character, and should conveniently be called by the same name, whether it is carried on by business men or by workmen; so that it is no longer unusual now to find workmen speaking of "capitalistic sabotage" as freely as the employers and the newspapers speak of syndicalist sabotage. As the word is now used, and as it is properly used, it describes a certain system of industrial strategy or management, whether it is employed by one or another. What it describes is a resort to peaceable or surreptitious restriction, delay, withdrawal, or obstruction. Sabotage commonly. Sabotage commonly works within the law, although it may often be within the letter rather than the spirit of the law. It is used to secure some special advantage or preference, usually of a businesslike sort. (Veblen 1921: 5-6)

Veblen went on:

> Without some salutary restraint in the way of sabotage on the productive use of the available industrial plant and workmen, it is altogether unlikely that prices could be maintained at a reasonably profitable figure for any appreciable time. A businesslike control of the rate and volume of output is indispensable for keeping up a profitable market, and a profitable market is the first and unremitting condition of prosperity in any community whose industry is owned and managed by business men. And the ways and means of this necessary control of the output of industry are always and necessarily something in the nature of sabotage something in the way of retardation, restriction, withdrawal, unemployment of plant and workmen whereby production is kept short of productive capacity. (Veblen 1921: 7-8)

The legal concept of goodwill dates back to a case from 1580 in which a clothier brought suit on the grounds that a rival had injured him by selling inferior goods with the plaintiff's trademark. In the course of a few centuries, this simple case evolved into a momentous shift in "the meaning of property rights from things to the capitalization of things" (Commons 1924: 264 and 164-165).

This shift becomes most dramatic during the late 19th century, a time when capital goods were replacing labor with breakneck speed. In this regard, Veblen noted:

"Good will" is a somewhat extensible term, and latterly it has a more comprehensive meaning than it once had. Its meaning has, in fact, been gradually extended to meet the requirements of modern business methods. Various items, of very diverse character, are to be included under the head of "good will"; but the items included have this much in common that they are "immaterial wealth", "intangible assets"; which, it may parenthetically be remarked, signifies among other things that these assets are not serviceable to the community, but only to their owners. Good will taken in its wider meaning comprises such things as established customary business relations, reputation for upright dealing, franchises and privileges, trade marks, brands, patent rights, copyrights, exclusive use of special processes guarded by law or by secrecy, exclusive control of particular sources of materials. (Veblen 1904: 139)

Veblen noted the destructive nature of this extended notion of goodwill. In the case of the ancient clothier, one can argue that his goodwill was a public benefit. In the case that his product was superior to that of his imitator, his goodwill might be seen as representing a social good by protecting consumers from purchasing inferior goods. Veblen, however, insisted that the expansive notion of goodwill had no justification whatsoever:

All these items give a differential advantage to their owners, but they are of no aggregate advantage to the community. They are wealth to the individuals concerned differential wealth; but they make no part of the wealth of nations. (Veblen 1904: 139)

One might have thought that the more dramatic role of physical capital in railroads and factories might diminish the relative importance of goodwill. Instead, the opposite occurred. The immaterial property of goodwill grew alongside the rapid accumulation of physical property, in part because the notion of goodwill was expanding.

What could explain this paradox? In a world of simple commodity production, the reward for work would come reasonably quickly. In a world dominated by expensive fixed capital, rewards would spread out over a long period of time. At the time, competitive pressure was destroying the commercial value of investments in long lived fixed capital well before investors could recoup their initial outlays.

Why would investors want to sink their money in failing ventures? The answer is that dishonest bookkeeping especially with appeals to goodwill could create illusions of profit potential, where little, or even none, existed. By hiding losses behind a smokescreen of goodwill, business could pump up the corporation's balance sheet with goodwill in the hopes that such calculations could appeal to investors' willingness to part with their funds.

This illusion often was necessary, because, in many cases, such as the railroads, business ended up relying less on the actual production of useful goods and services than on continual infusions of finance. Veblen's uncle in law, William Strong, was a case in point.

More recently, as business turned away from physical production to the creation and sale of information technologies, the relative importance of goodwill becomes more understandable, but equally destructive. By 2005, intangible assets, including goodwill, accounted for almost half of the value of the total book value of the companies making up the S&P 500 (Serfati 2008:13). The proportion has, in all likelihood has risen substantially since then.

Goodwill began to play an even more important role in the late 19th century, when business was fending off the strong anticorporate mood of the public, business friendly courts began to give stronger legal standing to claims to goodwill. In the process, corporations' claims that government efforts to regulate amounted to a confiscation of goodwill, gained more legal traction.

In this respect, Allgeyer v. Louisiana was a key decision in opening the door for the anti-regulatory power of goodwill. In 1894, the Louisiana Legislature passed a statute entitled "An act to prevent persons, corporations or firms from dealing with marine insurance companies that have not complied with law." The purpose of the statute ostensibly was to prevent fraud by requiring state citizens and corporations to abstain from business with out of state marine insurance companies.

E. Allgeyer & Co. of New Orleans had an open policy with the Atlantic Mutual Insurance Company in New York. The state alleged that Allgeyer violated the law. The Supreme Court unanimously upheld the rights of the business appealing to the 14th amendment, which ironically was intended to protect the rights of the freed slaves.

As Veblen clearly recognized, goodwill represented the power to win more profits than would be the case if market forces would determine the level of profits. In effect, goodwill was a measure of the capacity to diminish competitive pressures. What business called goodwill was, for Veblen, a measure of predatory power, whether the prey would be naive investors or powerless consumers.

Conventional economics had few tools to address the question of goodwill because the law of supply and demand would virtually eliminate profits. Economists got around this unrealistic assumption by assuming that business would earn normal profits, without ever explaining what would determine a normal profit.

The Contemporary Relevance of Thorstein Veblen

For a contemporary economist, Veblen should be more relevant than ever. In Veblen's time, economists were less seduced by abstract theory. Given that environment, Veblen was able to inspire many in the emerging heterodoxical institutionalist school of economics, which had substantial influence in the discipline until the end of the Second World War.

Since then, economic training has emphasized mathematical and statistical tools, mostly with the intention of strengthening the defense of *laissez faire*. In the process, considerations of work, workers, or working conditions fell by the wayside. In addition, concern about efficiency of production became marginalized because economists assumed that market forces would ensure efficiency, even in financial markets. Amazingly, the ongoing crisis has done little to budge economic thinking.

Veblen's approach puts matters up front that are obvious to ordinary people. For example, the absurd blunders and malfeasance of the great financial institutions, which set off the recent crisis, are no secret; however, blunders on such a scale would seem to be virtually impossible according to wisdom dispensed in economics textbooks. Anyone familiar with the dismal job prospects for contemporary college students would be comfortable with

Veblen's discussion about the inability of capitalism to effectively utilize people's skills. Finally, Veblen had the good sense to see how capitalism produces a culture that reinforces the ideological power of capitalism at the same time that it undermines the economy's capacity to meet people's needs through rational methods of production.

Nonetheless, recent outpouring of calls for austerity shows that few economists have a clue about the underlying economic problem. Perhaps, we could take a cue from Veblen himself, who was able to take such shortcomings of his contemporary world in order to ridicule the supposedly scientific axioms of academic economics and to call for a more rational society. Probably none of us will be able to do so with as much with the humor and erudition as Veblen. I would like to imagine that this conference could be a start.

References

Bartley, Russell H. and Sylvia E. Yoneda. 1994. Thorstein Veblen on Washington Island: Traces of a Life. *International Journal of Politics, Culture, and Society* 7 (4, Summer): 589-613.

Dorfman, Joseph. 1940. *Thorstein Veblen and His America*. New York: Viking.

Hadley, Arthur Twining. 1885. *Railroad Transportation: Its History and Its Laws*, 10th ed. New York: G. P. Putnam's and Sons, 1903.

Hadley, Morris. 1948. *Arthur Twining Hadley*. New Haven: Yale University.

Knoedler, Janet and Anne Mayhew. 1999. Thorstein Veblen and the Engineers: A Reinterpretation. *History of Political Economy* 31 (2): 255-272.

Marx, Karl. 1971. (1847). *The Poverty of Philosophy*. New York: International Publishers.

Nabers, Lawrence. 1958. Veblen's Critique of Orthodox Economic Tradition. In *Thorstein Veblen*. ed. Douglas F. Dowd. Cornell: Cornell University Press: 85.

Perelman, Michael. 2011. *The Invisible Handcuffs of Capitalism: How Market Tyranny Stifles the Economy by Stunting Workers*. New York: Monthly Review Press.

Serfati, Claude. 2008. Financial Dimensions of Transnational Corporations, Global Chain and Technological Innovation. *Journal of Innovation Economics* 2 (2): 35-61.

Sweezy, Paul M. 1954. Review of J. Steindl. *Maturity and Stagnation in American Capitalism*. *Econometrica* 22 (4, October): 531-533.

Tilman, Rick. 1996. *The Intellectual Legacy of Thorstein Veblen: Unresolved Issues*. Westport CT: Greenwood Press.

United States Department of Commerce. Bureau of the Census. 1975. *Historical Statistics of the United States: Colonial Times to 1970*. Washington, D.C.: 684, 735.

Veblen, Thorstein. 1891. Some Neglected Points in the Theory of Socialism. *Annals of the American Academy of Political and Social Science*. 2 (November): 57-74. Reprinted in *The Place of Science in Modern Civilization and Other Essays*. New York: B. W. Huebsch.

_____. 1898. Why is Economics Not an Evolutionary Science? *Quarterly Journal of Economics* 12, (4, July): 373-397.

_____. 1953. (1899a). *The Theory of the Leisure Class: An Economic Study of Institutions* New York: Mentor Books.

_____. 1899b. The Preconceptions of Economic Science, II. *The Quarterly Journal of Economics* 13 (4, July): 396-426.

_____. 1975. (1904). *The Theory of Business Enterprise*. Clifton, NJ: Augustus M. Kelley.

_____. 1921. *The Engineers and The Price System*. New York: Huebsch.

_____. 1925. *The Laxdaela Saga*. Translated from the Icelandic, with an introduction by Thorstein Veblen. New York: Huebsch.

White, Richard. 2011. *Railroaded: The Transcontinentals and the Making of Modern America*. New York: W.W. Norton & Co..

Veblen's Institutionalist Elaboration of Rent Theory

Michael Hudson

Simon Patten recalled in 1912 that his generation of American economists – most of whom studied in Germany in the 1870s – were taught that John Stuart Mill's 1848 *Principles of Political Economy* was the high-water mark of classical thought. However, Mill's reformist philosophy turned out to be "not a goal but a half-way house" toward the Progressive Era's reforms. Mill was "a thinker becoming a socialist without seeing what the change really meant," Patten concluded. "The Nineteenth Century epoch ends not with the theories of Mill but with the more logical systems of Karl Marx and Henry George. [1] But the classical approach to political economy continued to evolve, above all through Thorstein Veblen.

Like Marx and George, Veblen's ideas threatened what he called the "vested interests." What made his analysis so disturbing was what he retained from the past. Classical political economy had used the labor theory of value to isolate the elements of price that had no counterpart in necessary costs of production. Economic rent – the excess of price over this "real cost" – is unearned income. It is an overhead charge for access to land, minerals or other natural resources, bank credit or other basic needs that are monopolized.

This concept of unearned income as an unnecessary element of price led Veblen to focus on what now is called financial engineering, speculation and debt leveraging. The perception that a rising proportion of income and wealth is an unearned "free lunch" formed the take-off point for him to put real estate and financial scheming at the center of his analysis, at a time when mainstream economists were dropping these areas of concern.

Veblen's exclusion from today's curriculum is part of the reaction against classical political economy's program of social reform. By the time he began to publish in the 1890s, academic economics was in the throes of a counter-revolution sponsored by large landholders, bankers and monopolists denying that there was any such thing as unearned income. [2] The new post-classical mainstream accepted existing property rights and privileges as a "given." In contrast to Veblen's argument that the economy was all about organizing predatory schemes, this approach culminated in Milton Friedman's Chicago School defense the pro-*rentier* argument: "There is no such thing as a free lunch."

This blunt denial rejected the preceding three centuries of classical value and price theory, along with its policy conclusions promoting taxation of land and other natural endowments,

---

[1] Simon Patten. 1912 (1924). The Reconstruction of Economic Theory. In *Essays in Economic Theory*, ed. Rexford G. Tugwell. New York: Alfred A Knopf: 274. See also Simon Patten. 1899. *The Development of English Thought: A Study in the Economic Interpretation of History.* New York: Macmillan: 339.

[2] On the tendency of post-classical economics to reject the idea of unearned income, see Simon Patten. 1891. Another View of the Ethics of Land Tenure. *International Journal of Ethics* 1 (April). I discuss this doctrinal shift in Michael Hudson. 2011. Simon Patten on Public Infrastructure and Economic Rent Capture. *American Journal of Economics and Sociology* 70 (October): 873-903.

and financial reform. Dropped from view was *rentier* overhead in the form of predatory and unproductive forms of wealth seeking. The post-classical mainstream treats all income as "earned," including that of *rentiers*. Lacking the classical concepts of unproductive labor, credit or investment, today's textbooks describe income as a reward for one's contribution to production, and wealth is being "saved up" as a result of someone's productive investment effort, not as an unearned or predatory free lunch.

This shift in theory has shaped the seemingly empirical National Income and Product Accounts to indulge in a circular reasoning that treats recipients of rent and interest as providing a service, an economic contribution equal to whatever *rentiers* receive as "earnings." There are no categories for unearned income or speculative asset-price gains.

Veblen described the largest sectors of the economy where quick fortunes were made as being all about organizing rent-seeking opportunities to obtain income without real cost. He viewed psychological utility as social in character. In contrast to food or other satiable bodily needs characterized by diminishing marginal utility – *e.g.*, from eating food and becoming satiated – his concept of conspicuous consumption emphasized the insatiable drives to raise one's social status.

The desire for consumer goods was characterized by fads for the most pricey goods as trophies of one's wealth. The result was the mercenary vulgarity of wealthy Babbitts turning culture into an arena for shifting fashion, all to impress others with similar shallow sensitivities.

The largest factor defining status was the neighborhood where one's home was located. Housing was not simply a basic living space as "use value." It established one's position in society, duly enhanced by civic boosterism, public subsidy and infrastructure spending.

To deal with these issues and preserve the critique of *rentier* income, speculation and insider dealing, Veblen helped lead economics into the new discipline of sociology.

The central role of real estate

As the economy's largest asset, real estate was the great popular arena in which to seek speculative gains. Nowhere was this more visible than in small towns, which Veblen found to have had "a greater part than any other in shaping public sentiment and giving character to American culture." The country town was basically a project to puff up real estate prices.

> Its name may be Spoon River or Gopher Prairie, or it may be Emporia or Centralia or Columbia. The pattern is substantially the same, and is repeated several thousand times with a faithful perfection which argues that there is no help for it …

> The location of any given town has commonly been determined by collusion between 'interested parties' with a view to speculation in real estate, and it continues through its life-history (hitherto) to be managed as a real estate 'proposition.' Its municipal affairs, its civic pride, its community interest, converge upon its real-estate values, which are invariably of a speculative character, and which all its loyal citizens are intent on 'booming' and 'boosting,' – that is to say, lifting still farther off the level of actual ground-values as measured by the uses to which the ground is turned. Seldom do the current (speculative) values of the town's real estate exceed the use-value of it by less than 100 per cent.; and never do they exceed the actual values by less than 200 per cent., as shown by the estimates of the tax assessor; nor do the loyal citizens ever cease their endeavours to

lift the speculative values to something still farther out of touch with the material facts. A country town which does not answer to these specifications is 'a dead one,' one that has failed to 'make good,' and need not be counted with, except as a warning to the unwary 'boomer.' [3]

Describing real estate as being "the great American game," Veblen focused on how future prices were enhanced over present values by advertising and promotion. "Real estate is an enterprise in 'futures,' designed to get something for nothing from the unwary, of whom it is believed by experienced persons that 'there is one born every minute.'" Farmers and other rural families from the surrounding lands look "forward to the time when the community's advancing needs will enable them to realise on the inflated values of their real estate," that is, find a sucker "to take them at their word and become their debtors in the amount which they say their real estate is worth." The entire operation, from individual properties to the town as a whole, is "an enterprise in salesmanship," with collusion being the rule. [4]

Retailers in small towns collude to exploit farmers, a practice broken by the spread of mail order catalogues. But monopoly power is achieved most rigorously in local banking. Most loans are for mortgages to inflate land prices. "And the banker is under the necessity –'inner necessity,' as the Hegelians say – of getting all he can and securing himself against all risk, at the cost of any whom it may concern, by such charges and stipulations as will insure his net gain in any event."

Land prices were rising in larger cities as a result of overall prosperity and the easier availability of mortgage financing, while public spending on roads, subway and bus systems, parks, museums and other prestigious activities were organized to enhance neighborhood values. [5]

Veblen's context in the American School of Political Economy and Institutionalism

Veblen wrote in the tradition of the self-described American School of economists. Focusing on technology and the rising productivity of labor and energy-driven capital, its members developed an alternative to Ricardian doctrine. [6] Describing diminishing returns and British class antagonisms as a special case, they focused on increasing returns as the universal wave of the future. I attribute the failure of most historians of economic thought to relate Veblen to this school (or even to acknowledge its existence) to its protectionist policy conclusions.

---

[3] Thorstein Veblen. 1923. *Absentee Ownership and Business Enterprise in Recent Times*: 142ff..

[4] Other contemporaries described how the great American real estate fortunes were obtained by fraud and insider dealing. Gustavus Myers' *History of the Great American Fortunes* (1907-09) focused on John Jacob Astor in New York and the land that Trinity Church vestrymen gave themselves, and how Leland Stanford and his California gang in Congress obtained land grants for their railroads. Frank Norris's 1901 novel *The Octopus* described the railroads' exploitation of California.

[5] Robert Fitch's *The Assassination of New York* (New York: Verso, 1996) analyzed of how real estate elites planned the gentrification of New York City's real estate over the 20th century. Today, the value of New York City real estate exceeds the book value of all the plant and equipment in the United States.

[6] I discuss this School's contribution in *America's Protectionist Takeoff*, which includes a review of how Dorfman misrepresented and misunderstood it.

Liberal historians such as Joseph Dorfman have dismissed this school for describing the United States as an "exception" to the British rule. But the opposite is more accurate. Patten accused British political economy of assuming universal validity for peculiarly British institutions and practices, above all by identifying wages, rent and profits with particular social classes, advocating universal free trade and assuming that all public spending was overhead (as in war spending), not capital investment in infrastructure. The result was that Britain was behind the times, holding on to an intolerantly "monist" (one size fits all) outlook. Patten urged an "economic pluralism" that followed the German historical school – which became known as institutionalism in the United States – in recognizing that economies were organized in a wide variety of ways. [7]

From Patten to Veblen, critics of *rentiers* were so diverse that it would be misleading to refer to them as a "school" as such. Their common denominator was a focus on unearned income and exploitation, which required government policy to reform. Their analytic scope encompassed social institutions, legal and tax systems, educational and public policy priorities headed by subsidies and tariffs. The result was a more complex and also more empirical view than that which characterized the individualistic, abstract and indeed simplistic marginal utility school that was replacing classical political economy from the 1870s onward.

Nowhere was this more the case than in land rent, natural resource rent and monopoly rent. Ricardo described land rent as stemming from diminishing returns widening the margin between high-cost producers (who set the price of food) and low-cost landowners who received the economic rent from rising crop prices. The American School cited progress in chemical fertilizers, mechanized farm production and the development of transport infrastructure as increasing productivity in agriculture as well as industry. Instead of fertility being "original and indestructible" as Ricardo claimed, soil chemistry and capital investment in farm equipment and public support services were turning land into capital, yielding returns in the form of profit.

The Ricardian-Malthusian "Iron Law of Wages" used a simplistic supply-and-demand analysis to imply that population growth and chronic unemployment would keep wages near subsistence levels. American economists developed an Economy of High Wages theory to explain the nation's rising wage levels. Instead of attributing high wages to the "backwoods" availability of free land, Henry Carey pointed out that unless labor was sufficiently productive to sustain higher output, industry could not afford to pay high wages. He attributed the nation's wage levels to technological progress requiring highly skilled labor to operate high-productivity capital. The result was a universal theory of progress, becoming global as higher-paid labor undersold pauper labor – thus forcing laggard countries to join the wave of progress.

Patten's idea that technology was transforming economies from a "pain" to a "pleasure" society led naturally to Veblen's idea of an "instinct of workmanship." Machines were taking over many of the drudgery tasks, freeing human labor for higher, more intellectually absorbing work. Patten and Veblen anticipated Schumpeter in viewing rent as super-profit created by the increasing returns resulting from the advance of science and technology. [8] Lowering costs created opportunities for innovators to earn what Alfred Marshall termed quasi-rents –

---

[7] Simon Patten. 1912 (1924). The Reconstruction of Economic Theory. In *Essays in Economic Theory*: 278f.

rewards for innovation in contrast to income raked off by idle *rentiers*. Gutenberg's innovation of movable type to print the Bible and other books, for example, enabled him to sell them at the same price as competitors using more costly hand copying and engraving systems.

This line of analysis prompted Veblen to describe increasing returns as leading to the monopolies being organized by Wall Street. It was in this financial arena that progress became untracked by monopoly rent used for financial speculation and trust building.

Marshall's generation treated current production and consumption as the "real" economy. Despite the transformative role that finance has played, subsequent mainstream economists treat markets as if most money is paid for goods and services, not real estate, bonds, stocks or other assets. Money and prices appear only as a veil, as "counters." Price changes are viewed merely as replacing pounds with kilograms (or pounds sterling with dollars). Production and consumption constitute the "real" economy, while money and prices – and debt – are only a means of circulating goods and services, not as imposing a debt overhead. Debt is a matter of choice – to consume in the present rather than later, or to invest to make a profit, not as unnecessary "watered costs" or unproductive loans or debts.

Yet all money and credit is debt, after all – and debt determines who gets what, and how income is distributed or siphoned off. By excluding this line of analysis, the mainstream approach diverts attention from the financial speculation and debt overhead on which Veblen focused.

Elaborating the concept of economic rent to focus on unearned fortunes

Writing two decades before Veblen, the journalist Henry George obtained a popular following by denouncing landlords and urging taxation of the land's full rental value. But lacking grounding in classical value and rent theory, he was unable to express his ideas in formal economic terms, and adamantly opposed extending the concept of economic rent to the banking sector. And George soon turned to attacking socialists and other Progressive Era campaigners for promoting reforms other than his Single Tax panacea. Nonetheless, his campaigning inspired fear among landlords, bankers and other *rentiers* that the concept of economic rent would be used to limit their gains. Veblen (along with Patten) fought a rear-guard effort against the new mainstream. While George's followers retained a Ricardian focus on agricultural land, he emphasized financial speculation, recognizing that land rent was being capitalized into mortgages and paid to bankers.

Veblen described how credit was being created for speculative reasons rather than to finance the production of goods and services. Pre-Ricardian political economy had focused on debt and interest (especially James Steuart, Malachy Postlethwayt and Adam Smith). But post-classical economists turned their attention away from the monetary and financial dimension of life, which Veblen termed "pecuniary." Mainstream economics strips away these embedded characteristics.

---

8 Simon Patten. 1902. *The Theory of Prosperity*: 139f.: "Rent is constantly being created by social progress, but in any particular form it is steadily being cut down by the increase in the power of substitution" as businessmen developed substitutes for monopolized goods and services.

Denial of the classical distinction between value and price (and hence, between earned and unearned income) was led by John Bates Clark in the United States, and by a similar "pragmatic" tradition in European supply and demand analysis. From Veblen's perspective this attempt at "universals" trivialized economics. Criticizing business schools for teaching how to make money by creating extractive financial tollbooths without increasing society's productive powers, he found *rentier* interests behind the narrow-mindedness that ignored the predatory character of rent and interest. The emerging "individualistic" orthodoxy had a pro-*rentier* bias, endorsing practices that bled the productive economic core to support a neo-*rentier* class.

To recognize charges over and above the economy's necessary engineering costs, analysis must take into account institutional factors – especially financial dynamics and other *rentier* overhead. There are many ways to embed a given mode of production, and some are freer of *rentier* charges than others. Soviet Russia, America, Japan, Britain and Germany shared a similar technological repertory of power production, automotives, air transport and computer science in the 1970s and 1980s, yet had different property and banking systems, and price regulation for public infrastructure and other monopolies. Land rent, mineral rent, financial returns and monopoly pricing are country-specific and time-specific, and hence find little role in models seeking to depict economics as an abstract natural science on universal principles like physics and chemistry.

By placing rent in its financial context and political setting, Veblen became part of the sociology discipline, consigned to the basement of the social sciences to exclude from the core curriculum discussion about tax reform and other checks or regulation concerning how economic rent was obtained by ownership rights and privileges, monopolies and political corruption.

The rentiers seek to limit the scope of economic analysis to make themselves invisible

The post-classical school accused its institutionalist critics and social reformers of being "anti-theoretical." Geoffrey Hodgson opens his *Evolution of Institutional Economics* by citing representative statements from mainstream economists claiming that institutionalism is more descriptive than analytic, succumbing to a plethora of facts and therefore belonging more to the sphere of sociology than economics. Ronald Coase's complaint that institutionalism "was 'not theoretical but anti-theoretical' has been repeated uncountably by others ...." [9]

The empirical trend among the American School of protectionists economists had a long pedigree going back to Daniel Raymond and Friedrich List (in the time he spent in Pennsylvania in association with Mathew Carey).[10] In 1848, Calvin Colton (a protectionist economic writer close to Henry Clay) wrote that economic generalities applicable to Britain and other European nations were "entirely inapplicable" to the United States. The differences

[9] Geoffrey Hodgson. 2004. *The Evolution of Institutional Economics*. London: Routledge: 3, citing Ronald Coase. 1984. The New Institutional Economics. *Journal of Institutional and Theoretical Economics* 140: 230, and Richard N. Langlois. 1989. What Was Wrong With the Old Institutional Economics (and What is Still Wrong With the New)? *Review of Political Economy* 1 (3, November): 5: "The problem with the Historical School and many of the early Institutionalists is that they wanted an economics ... without theory."

in economic and social structure between the United States and Britain had not "been duly weighed as an element of public economy." Instead of the precepts of British political economy being universal in scope, "public economy has never been reduced to a science, and ... all the propositions of which it is composed, down to this time, are *empirical* laws."[11]

Economics thus found few universally agreed-upon principles to analyze the costs and benefits of protective tariffs, industrial subsidies or privatized versus public ownership or operation. The fact that models of economic rent and the political context for economic policy were ideological opens up discussion of progressive alternatives to British free trade economics and political assumptions rationalizing the status quo as one of (stable) equilibrium.

Taking the lead in developing new general laws for how industry was becoming financialized, Veblen countered the post-classical conflation of rent and interest with profits ("earnings") on three major grounds:

(1) The timeless and decontextualized generalities drawn by the pro-*rentier* logic used circular reasoning to justify the status quo as being natural and in equilibrium. By definition, there was no *rentier* exploitation, even as economies were polarizing. Assuming that every income recipient is paid for a contribution to production implies that the existing distribution of property and mode of financing are optimum. There thus seems to be no need for reform or regulation, either socialist or protectionist.

(2) It is not a virtue for post-classical economics to be value-free. Denying the concept of economic rent as the excess of market price over cost value leads to a conflation of land with capital, rent with interest. Land is treated as a "factor of production," not a monopoly right independent of production, a privilege to put an economic tollbooth in place to extract rent.

(3) Excluding the political dimension of classical political economy is implicitly *laissez faire*. It leaves no role for government – the only power able to regulate and tax land rent and prevent the financial sector from turning itself into an oligarchy. "Free market" opposition to government regulation blocks reforms aimed at bringing prices in line with costs so as to make economies more efficient. "One-size-fits all" generalities lead to Margaret Thatcher's intolerant and censorial assertion: "There is no alternative."

In sum, over-simplicity in excluding discussion of the *rentiers'* free lunch achieves a higher level of abstraction by ruling out concepts that would deem *rentier* income to be unearned and hence unnecessary. All such revenue – economic rent – is "institutional" in the sense that it is not based on the universals of technological costs of production or abstract "supply and demand." Institutions, especially banking and tax systems, are not universal but are historically determined.

Focusing on status quo costs burdened with heavy *rentier* charges implies that an input is worth whatever the buyer pays for it. In practice, this means whatever a bank will lend against its collateral value or income stream. That depends on the terms on which loans are

---

10 In his *Outlines of American Political Economy* (1827) Friedrich List wrote: "American national economy, according to the different conditions of the nations, is quite different from English national economy." I discuss this early period of institutionalism in Hudson (1975):115-32 and 45-54.

11 Calvin Colton. 1848. *Public Economy for the United States*: 18, 46 and 38.

made and regulated. Taking the prices of land or monopoly "tollbooth" rent-extracting rights as "givens" means accepting whatever investors must lay out as a valid cost, including payments for rent-extracting privileges or bank credit created with little inherent production cost. *Rentier* privileges are capitalized without regard to necessary labor cost on which classical economists focused in isolating the "free lunch" element of price *not* reducible to labor.

Housing and land ownership were more widely distributed in the United States than in Europe, largely on credit as banking entered into a symbiosis with real estate and other rent-extracting activities. Mortgage credit often absorbs the entire land rent. Financing charges are built into the acquisition price of property or *rentier* rights, but are not intrinsic to production and have no counterpart in an engineering view of the economy. Wall Street insiders refined the practice of simply issuing bonds to themselves ("watered stock"). These unnecessary "false costs of production," were factored into the cost of operating railroads and industrial trusts.

Such practices prompted Veblen to criticize Clark and also Marshall for ignoring the "pecuniary" financial dimension of life. This was a glaring error of omission in the new mainstream, along with monopolies and large real estate frauds started in colonial times, highlighted by the Yahoo land fraud early in the Republic, and capped by the railroad land grants. As Henry Liu describes how Veblen emphasized the predatory role of high finance:

> Veblen put forth a basic distinction between the productiveness of 'industry' run by skilled engineers, which manufactures real goods of utility, and the parasitism of 'business,' which exists only to make profits for a leisure class which engages in 'conspicuous consumption'. The only economic contribution by the leisure class is 'economic waste', activities that contribute negatively to productivity. By implication, Veblen saw the US economy as being made inefficient and corrupt by men of 'business' who deviously put themselves in an indispensable position in society. [12]

Changing evaluations of Veblen in academia – Dorfman and his critics

"If the eye offend thee, pluck it out" – or at least, distract attention from Veblen's line of analysis that opened the path for thinking about how institutions might be changed. Rather than dealing with Veblen's ideas that offended the post-classical mainstream, his critics ignored those with which they disagreed, and shifted attention to his striking personality. It is an old rhetorical trick of lawyers: character assassination of unfriendly witnesses. As Aldous Huxley quipped in *Brave New World*: "Great is truth, but still greater, from a practical point of view, is silence about truth. By simply not mentioning certain subjects … totalitarian propagandists have influenced opinion much more effectively than they could have by the most eloquent denunciations."

Columbia University professor Joseph Dorfman's long-standard biography of Veblen made him non-threatening by taking his ideas out of their 19th-century political context that focused on land, finance and monopolies with a view to minimize *rentier* charges. Rejecting this intellectual context on ideological grounds, Dorfman wrote an anecdotal soap opera that

---

[12] Henry Liu. 2011. The Rise and Decline of Institutional Economics. *Asia Times on-Line* (April 7). *http://henryckliu.com/page246.html and http://www.atimes.com/atimes/Global_Economy/MD07Dj03.html*

found favor with Columbia's Economics Department's prevailing pro-*rentier* ideology.

The department always had been free trade and pro-British. As the early center for opposition to Henry George's land-tax advocacy – and hence to the analysis of land rent as unearned income – most professors found Veblen's analysis of land speculation anathema. Dorfman's dissertation advisor was Wesley Mitchell. Trained by Veblen, his lectures on *Types of Economic Theory* provide a good fair-minded treatment. But he was on leave out of the United States most of the year when Dorfman was writing his book. [13] The result sanitized Veblen from a perspective typical of his Columbia colleagues, airbrushing out Veblen's focus on *rentiers*. Dorfman did the same thing with his five-volume overview of American economic thought, censoring the protectionist and technology mainstream that dominated U.S. policy and political debates throughout the 19th century. On balance, he was the kind of academic whom Veblen's *Higher Education in America* skewered for being so narrow-minded. [14]

The past decade has seen a reaction against Dorfman's treatment of Veblen. The 4th Conference of the International Thorstein Veblen Association, held at The New School on May 12, 2002, was highlighted by Steven Edgell's paper on "Dorfman's Account of Veblen." Russell and Sylvia Bartley's biographical study of "Veblen's Formal Education at Carleton College 1874-1880" also criticized Dorfman's treatment of Veblen. (Alas, these proceedings were not published.) Their point was that Veblen was in the majority in his own context. Although America is not very Norwegian, Minnesota certainly was. The Bartleys characterize him as a "folk savant," a common phenomenon in Norwegian communities – a brilliant exception to the conformist norm. This role would have provided Veblen with self-confidence to take on the establishment. It certainly helps to be an outsider to recognize dysfunctional social dynamics, economic hypocrisy and egotism – and to see that what most people accept as natural will have to be changed if the economy is to be made more fair, lower-cost and hence more competitive.

Veblen's disparaging view of the business mentality and academia

Veblen criticized academic economists for having fallen subject to "trained incapacity" as a result of being turned into factotums to defend *rentier* interests. Business schools were painting an unrealistic happy-face picture of the economy, teaching financial techniques but leaving out of account the need to reform the economy's practices and institutions.

In a conclusion recalling Veblen's *Higher Education in America*, Herman Kahn describes how peer pressure leads experts to accept explanations that deviate from accepted concepts:

> Educated incapacity often refers to an acquired or learned inability to understand or even perceive a problem, much less a solution. The original phrase, "trained incapacity," comes from the economist Thorstein Veblen, who used it to refer, among other things, to the inability of those with engineering

[13] Dorfman published his study of Veblen before submitting it as a dissertation, which explains why the dissertation did not cite page numbers or other references - not even the title of Veblen's own doctoral dissertation at Yale (which was stolen from the library the following year). Columbia dutifully applauded, awarding Dorfman the Seligman Prize for distinguished scholarship in 1935.

[14] My own impression on meeting Dorfman on a number of occasions was that he was somewhat like how he described Veblen: outsiderish.

or sociology training to understand certain issues which they would have been able to understand if they had not had this training. [15]

Kahn adds that this phenomenon occurs especially "at leading universities in the United States – particularly in the departments of psychology, sociology, and history, and to a degree in the humanities generally. Individuals raised in this milieu often have difficulty with relatively simple degrees of reality testing." The problem is greatest in economics, of course.

Non-industrial character of today's financial crisis

Today's bank privileges and the financial sector's rise to dominance are a survival of these pre-capitalist conquests and royal war debts that took root in Europe's Crusades. From antiquity to the sacking of Byzantium in 1204, the characteristic mode of financial accumulation was to loot the temples and palaces where societies stored their savings, and extract taxes as tribute from conquered populations. Military conquest evolved into the levy of land rent, while creditors used their gains to purchase monopoly privileges.

Industrial capitalism was more productive, although just as cruel in creating an urban labor force by driving cultivators off the land and forcing them to work for wages to live. This exploitation of wage labor at least employed workers, and took a great step forward by accumulating capital as part of the production process. In due course, employers found that increasing labor productivity (so as to create more surplus value) requires raising wages and living standards to provide higher education, better health and diets – and at a point, more leisure. So despite the aim of cutting costs to undersell competitors, technological innovation was accompanied by high-wage labor underselling pauper labor. That is why American manufacturers undersold their British counterparts – not only because of higher labor productivity, but because of the thriving domestic market as labor rose into the middle class.

This was done by a combination of government sponsorship and largely productive credit, including lending for home ownership. Mixed economies were out-competing those lacking strong public sectors to subsidize industry, sponsor rising productivity and prevent landlords, bankers and monopolists from imposing heavy *rentier* charges. By the turn of the 20th century it seemed that the destiny of industrial capitalism was to evolve into socialism. Pensions, health care, roads and basic infrastructure, public education – all were coming to be provided outside of "the market." Industrial capital backed this policy as a means of shifting as many "external" costs as possible onto the public sector.

Writing earlier than Veblen, Marx was more optimistic that the imperatives of industrial capitalism would industrialize banking to fund industrial production. Nobody of his period expected the financial sector to mount a counter-revolution against the Progressive Era's reforms. From Ricardo to Henry George, Marx noted, industrialists had an innate hatred of land rent. Their aim was to obtain the economic surplus for industry, not leave it in the hands of a landed aristocracy. And the interest of banks seemed to lie with industry, not real estate.

---

[15] Herman Kahn. 1979. The Expert and Educated Incapacity. *World Economic Development: 1979 and Beyond.* New York: Westview Press: 482-484.

Along with mineral rights and basic infrastructure, natural monopolies were expected to become part of the public sector, including the bankers' privilege of creating credit and charging interest with no corresponding cost of production. Followers of Saint-Simon hoped that banks would finance capital investment more by equity participation than by interest-bearing debt. The economic program of enlightened industrial capitalism was to tax away rent and develop basic infrastructure, including banking, as a public utility and provide its services at cost or at subsidized rates (*e.g.*, free roads rather than toll roads). This seemed to be the road along which industrial nations were moving in the years leading up to World War I. Economic democracy promised to liberate society from the hereditary land ownership, privatization of natural resources and monopoly privileges surviving from feudal epochs.

But the war deflected the path of Western civilization. Taxes on land, natural resources and the financial sector have been unwound. Labor is exploited fiscally by a regressive income tax (the early U.S. income tax fell only on the well to do at its inception in 1913, not on wage earners), and by sales taxes on consumption such as Europe's Value Added Tax (VAT) as taxes are shifted off property. Property has been democratized – on tax-deductible credit while its price gains are taxed at lower rates than wages and profits, if at all. The 1% have managed to fight back and drive the bottom 99% into debt, headed by mortgage debt and a tax shift off property and financial wealth. Instead of industrial investment and public spending spurring expansion, finance capital's strategy is to find borrowers to purchase rent-extracting tollbooth opportunities.

The end result is austerity as business as well as governments become deeply indebted. Debt pressures are leading governments to privatize public services, enabling a new class of debt-leveraged *rentiers* to make their gains by inflating the cost of living and doing business.

It wasn't supposed to be this way. Bank debts are not the result of prior savings emerging from the dynamic of industrial capitalism. Modern bank credit is created on computer keyboards. Unlike industry employing labor, this electronic credit has almost no cost of production. It is empty "price without value" as defined by the classical economists, and is extractive rather than productive. It is lent against collateral already in place, not to create new means of production.

Aimed at reversing the Progressive Era's reforms, today's neoliberal (that is, anti-classical) counter-reforms have over-layered the industrial exploitation of wage labor, by finance capitalism indebting it via mortgage loans, student loans, auto loans, credit card overdrafts and other bank debt. Labor is exploited as saver as well as debtor, with its pension fund set-asides turned over to financial managers. The pretense is that this turns labor into capitalists-in-miniature. But the dynamic is part of finance capitalism, not industrial capitalism. Instead of investing directly in means of production or giving pension contributors the voice in management that true ownership does, pension savings are lent out to indebt the industrial economy. Hedge funds and corporate raiders borrow to downsize companies, outsource and offshore employment.

The result is a race to the bottom in terms of working conditions and living standards. Instead of making economies more competitive, austerity shrinks markets and leads to loan defaults, foreclosures – and emigration. The resulting crisis is being used as an opportunity to force yet more privatization of the public domain – on tax-subsidized credit. Neither Marx nor Veblen imagined that capitalism would take so self-destructive a path.

From Marx to Veblen

Early (and most non-Marxist) socialism aimed to achieve greater equality mainly by taxing away unearned *rentier* income and keeping natural resources and monopolies in the public domain. The Marxist focus on class conflict between industrial employers and workers relegated criticism of *rentiers* to a secondary position, leaving that fight to more bourgeois reformers. Financial savings were treated as an accumulation of industrial profits, not as the autonomous phenomenon that Marx himself emphasized in Volume 3 of *Capital*.

Headed by Lenin, Marx's followers discussed finance capital mainly in reference to the drives of imperialism. The ruin of Persia and Egypt was notorious, and creditors installed collectors in the customs houses in Europe's former Latin American colonies. The major problem anticipated was war spurred by commercial rivalries as the world was being carved up.

It was left to Veblen to deal with the *rentiers'* increasingly dominant yet corrosive role, extracting their wealth by imposing overhead charges on the rest of society. The campaign for land taxation and even financial reform faded from popular discussion as socialists and other reformers became increasingly Marxist and focused on the industrial exploitation of labor.

Home ownership was rising in the cities, on credit, and commercial investors mounted a campaign to persuade homeowners that cutting property taxes would benefit them as well as absentee owners. But what the tax collector relinquished became available to be pledged as interest to the banks. Mortgage debt soared as property taxes were cut – to a point where most rental value is now capitalized into mortgage loans and paid to the banks.

The Single Taxers slipped off the right wing of the political spectrum as they failed to link their campaign to see that bankers were the major contenders against landlords and the government to end up with the land rent, by capitalizing it into bank loans. They followed Henry George in becoming libertarian anti-government and anti-socialist ideologues – a self-contradictory political stance, because government was the only power strong enough to tax and regulate land and monopolies, and counter the banking lobby. Veblen accordingly poked fun at the Single Taxers as ineffective idealists and out-of-touch sectarians. [16]

Veblen described how the *rentier* classes were on the ascendant rather than being reformed, taxed out of existence or socialized. His *Theory of Business Enterprise* (1904) emphasized the divergence between productive capacity, the book value of business assets and their stock-market price (what today is called the Q ratio of market price to book value). He saw the rising financial overhead as leading toward corporate bankruptcy and liquidation. Industry was becoming financialized, putting financial gains ahead of production. Today's financial managers use profits not to invest but to buy up their company's stock (thus raising the value of their stock options) and pay out as dividends, and even borrow to pay themselves. Hedge funds have become notorious for stripping assets and loading companies down with debt, leaving bankrupt shells in their wake in what George Ackerlof and Paul Romer have characterized as looting.[17]

---

[16] Thorstein Veblen. 1904. *Theory of Business Enterprise*. Ed. A. M. Kelley.: 351-352fn. Thorsetin Veblen. 1919.The Nature of Capital. In *The Place of Science in Civilization*: 337.

After a wave of financial speculation and corporate fraud led the dot.com stock market bubble to burst in 2000, banks nurtured an even larger and more burdensome real estate bubble. Indebting the economy has enabled the financial sector to absorb most of the revenues squeezed out by the insurance and real estate sectors, along with the major monopolies (minerals, fuels and power, radio and television, telephones and transport) and privatized infrastructure sold off from the public domain to become rent-extracting opportunities. On top of the landlords – and now over industry – stand the bankers, lording it over them and using debt leverage to take control of governments as well. Yet neither socialist critiques nor those of mainstream economic futurists have focused on the financial takeover of society and its symbiosis with real estate and monopolies to which Veblen pointed. By the 1960s, theorists of the postindustrial "service economy" were focusing on information technology, not on the financial sector.

In emphasizing how financial "predation" was hijacking the economy's technological potential, Veblen's vision was as materialist and culturally broad as that of Marxists, and as rejecting of the status quo. Technological innovation was reducing costs but breeding monopolies as the Finance, Insurance and Real Estate (FIRE) sectors joined forces to create a financial symbiosis cemented by political insider dealings – and a trivialization of economic theory as it seeks to avoid dealing with society's failure to achieve its technological potential. The fruits of rising productivity were used to finance robber barons who had no better use of their wealth than to reduce great artworks to the status of ownership trophies and achieve leisure class status by funding business schools and colleges to promote a self-congratulatory but deceptive portrayal of their wealth-grabbing behavior.

Yet Veblen was as optimistic as Marx when it came to the prospects for industrial capitalism to uplift society. Whereas Marx expected it to subordinate banking and finance to promote industrial objectives – and for revolution to be led from below, by the working class (or its political party representatives) – Veblen anticipated that a managerial class of industrial engineers might lead the world toward a more rational, socially functional economy. As Ahmet Öncü observes in his remarks to the Istanbul 2012 Veblen conference:

> In his chapter 'A Memorandum on a Practicable Soviet of Technicians' published in *The Engineers and the Price System* [1921], Veblen talks about a possible future scenario. According to Veblen, capitalists will give up, albeit reluctantly, the ownership of industries not by force but by their own choice. Veblen offers this reasoning: 'It should, in effect, cause no surprise to find that they will, in a sense, eliminate themselves, by letting go quite involuntarily after the industrial situation gets quite beyond their control.'

But contrary to Veblen's expectation, industry has been financialized, and planning has been centralized in Wall Street, the City of London, the Paris Bourse and Frankfurt rather than in public hands or those of industrial engineers. Stock and bond markets, and even the mortgage market have been turned into arenas for gambling, with debt leveraging being the new means of appropriating property, using junk bonds as the weapon of choice. Opportunities for rent

---

[17] George Ackerlof and Paul Romer. 1993. Looting: The Economic Underworld of Bankruptcy for Profit. *Brookings Papers on Economic Activity* 2: 1-73. Also published as *NBER Working Paper* No. R1869 (April 1994). This article is thoroughly in Veblen's tradition.

extraction and for capital gains that are taxed at only half the rate of profits, if at all. The upshot of this "economic game," as Veblen put it, is not capital investment in new plant and equipment to produce profits by employing labor, but speculative "capital" gains in asset prices – an exercise in promotion and collusion not unlike his country town example on a more gigantic financial scale.

Industrial engineers have been superseded by financial engineers as economic planners. MIT started as an engineering institution, but ended up with Paul Samuelson and other anti-classical writers teaching that economics was purely abstract and deductive – precisely what Veblen attacked. Virginia Tech founded a College of Business in 1961 and limited the term "rent-seeking activity" to describe public activity (*e.g.*, James Buchanan at the ideological Center for Public Choice), not applying it to private sector *rentiers*.

The financial sector is unwilling to relinquish its hold simply because the economy is shrinking. Its dynamic is now crashing in a wave of debt deflation, imposing economic austerity and unemployment. Debts are going bad, and foreclosure time has arrived. But instead of restructuring the economy to free it for renewed progress, the financial class sees today's crisis as an opportunity for a property grab to vest itself as a new elite to rule the 21st century.

It would be a mistake to view today's finance capitalism as the "final stage" of industrial capitalism. The name of the new game is neofeudalism and austerity, and its preferred mode of exploitation is debt peonage. Like creditors in ancient Rome, today's financial power is seeking to replace democracy with a financial oligarchy. The result is a resurgence of pre-capitalist "primitive accumulation," by debt creation and foreclosure rather than the military conquests of past epochs.

Conclusion

As the heirs to classical political economy and the German historical school, the American institutionalists retained rent theory and its corollary idea of unearned income. More than any other institutionalist, Veblen emphasized the dynamics of banks financing real estate speculation and Wall Street maneuvering to organize monopolies and trusts. Yet despite the popularity of his writings with the reading public, his contribution has remained isolated from the academic mainstream, and he did not leave a "school." The *rentier* strategy has been to make rent extraction invisible, not the center of attention it occupied in classical political economy. One barely sees today a quantification of the degree to which overhead charges for rent, insurance and interest are rising above the cost of production, even as this prices financialized economies out of world markets.

The narrowing of Chicago-style monetarism and neoliberalism has left the economics discipline in much the state that Max Planck applied to physics from Maxwell to Einstein: Progress occurs one funeral at a time. The old conservatives die off, freeing the way for more progressive successors to take the steering wheel. But what makes today's economics differ-ent is that it actually would help to look backward, to the epoch before the financial sector and its allied *rentier* interests hijacked the discipline. The most systematic analysis of this process was that of Veblen nearly a century ago. It remains sufficiently relevant that Marxists and more heterodox critics have incorporated his theorizing into their worldview.

References

Ackerlof, George and Paul Romer. 1993. Looting: The Economic Underworld of Bankruptcy for Profit. *Brookings Papers on Economic Activity* 2: 1-73.

Bartley, Russell and Sylvia. 2000. Stigmatizing Thorstein Veblen: A Study in the Confection of Academic Reputations. *International Journal of Politics, Culture, and Society* 14 (Winter): 363-400.

_____. 2002. The Formal Education of Thorstein Veblen: His Carleton Years, 1874-1880. Paper presented at the *4th Conference of the International Thorstein Veblen Association*. Unpublished.

Coase, Ronald. 1984. The New Institutional Economics. *Journal of Institutional and Theoretical Economics* 140.

Colton, Calvin. 1848. *Public Economy for the United States.* New York.

Dorfman, Joseph. 1946-1959. *The Economic Mind of American Civilization,* 5 vols. New York: Viking Press.

_____. 1934. *Thorstein Veblen and his America.* New York.

Edgell, Steven. 2002. Dorfman's Account of Veblen: An Evaluation of a Problematic Intellectual Legacy. Paper presented at the *4th Conference of the International Thorstein Veblen Association*. Unpublished.

_____. 2001. *Veblen in Perspective: His Life and Thought.* Armonk: M.E. Sharpe.

Hodgson, Geoffrey. 2004. *The Evolution of Institutional Economics.* London: Routledge.

Hudson, Michael. 2011. Simon Patten on Public Infrastructure and Economic Rent Capture. *American Journal of Economics and Sociology* 70 (October): 873-903.

_____. 2010. *America's Protectionist Takeoff: 1815-1914.* New York & London: ISLET.

Kahn, Herman. 1979. The Expert and Educated Incapacity. *World Economic Development: 1979 and Beyond.* New York: Westview Press: 482-484.

Langlois, Richard N. 1989. What Was Wrong With the Old Institutional Economics (and What is Still Wrong With the New)? *Review of Political Economy* 1 (3, November).

List, Friedrich. 1827. *Outlines of American Political Economy.* Philadelphia: Samuel Parker.

Liu, Henry. 2011. The Rise and Decline of Institutional Economics (April 7). *http://henryckliu.com/page246.html.*

Mitchell, Wesley Clair. 1967. *Types of Economic Theory.* New York: A. M. Kelley.

Patten, Simon. 1891. Another View of the Ethics of Land Tenure. *International Journal of Ethics* 1 (April).

_____. 1899. *The Development of English Thought: A Study in the Economic Interpretation of History.* New York: Macmillan.

_____. 1902. *The Theory of Prosperity.* New York: Macmillan Company.

_____. 1912. The Reconstruction of Economic Theory. In *Essays in Economic Theory*, ed. Rexford G. Tugwell. New York: Alfred A Knopf.

Veblen, Thorstein. 1978 (1904). *The Theory of Business Enterprise.* Intro. By Douglas Dowd. New Brunswick, New Jersey: Transaction.

_____. 1964. (1923). *Absentee Ownership and Business Enterprise in Recent Times: The Case of America.* New York: Augustus M. Kelley.

Workmanship, Labor, and Capital

Faruk Eray Düzenli

Introduction

In this paper, I discuss how Marx and Veblen conceptualize and criticize capitalism, and envision non-capitalist alternatives by focusing on the ways they construe (productive) activity/labor. I begin with an analysis of Marx's early, humanist rendition of labor as productive activity, which becomes alienated activity in an economy characterized/dominated by private property. Veblen in a somewhat similar manner considers labor in its qualitative aspects and conceives it as something "irksome," "ignoble," as something to be avoided if possible in predatory societies. Nevertheless, Veblen also refers to the "instinct of workmanship," which remains prevalent, albeit to varying degrees, in all societies—purposefulness, efficiency, and effectiveness that guide human beings in their productive activities. In a capitalist economy — or, to be more precise, in early 20th century capitalism, when *The Engineers and the Price System* was published — engineers, because of the position they occupy in the production process, could be the ones who would ensure "the material welfare of the civilized peoples"; thus, Veblen's (2001: 47) call for, without much optimism or conviction, "a soviet of engineers."

Marx (1973), on the other hand, moves beyond the qualitative aspects of the production process with the *Grundrisse* as he construes labor as the producer of surplus. Deploying this definition, Marx argues that capitalism is an exploitative economic system: those who produce the surplus do not appropriate or distribute it; rather, the right to initially receive and then to distribute the surplus exclusively belongs to those who had nothing to do with its production, capitalists. Marx, however, does not suggest workers should own the surplus or the whole product of their labor, in contrast to what many, including Veblen, think; instead he calls for a non-exploitative economy founded upon a radical equality: "from each according to ability, to each according to needs."

Marx: Labor as (Alienated) Productive Activity

Allow me to begin with one of Marx's many articulations of labor: labor as the productive activity through which human beings objectify, materialize, thus sensuously realize their human essence/species-being. In his early works, for example, in the *Economic and Philosophical Manuscripts of 1844* (Marx 1975a), labor appears as "the activity of alienation, alienation of activity" under a regime of private property. The product of the laborer belongs to someone else, estranged from the laborer; it is someone else's property. The more s/he produces, the lesser s/he has; furthermore, laborers create an alien power that dominates them. Marx contends that this reflects nothing but the estrangement of the laborer from his/her productive activity; labor no longer belongs to his/her essential being but is something that s/he tries to avoid at all costs. This alienation is at the root of private property, even though the relationship between the two becomes mutually constitutive. As a result, s/he is alienated from his/her fellow human beings, not to mention from his/her species-being, as well.

Alienation would be superseded with the (political) emancipation of workers from the rule of private property, which contains within itself the universal human emancipation. Marx construes this supersession of human self-estrangement as individuals' return to their human, social existence, which in turn signifies the end (goal) of history, the founding of genuine communism (Marx 1975a). Labor as such becomes the productive activity, the mediating moment, through which human beings realize their essence ("species-being") and objectify themselves. Through their labor, they produce all that exists by transforming objects furnished by nature; in the process, they reproduce, produce themselves anew.

Labor, construed as such, signifies Marx's first attempt to break away from German idealism and his substitution of matter for mind; yet, this is not to say that Marx has completely freed himself from either Hegel, or a Feuerbachian "contemplative materialism" (Balibar 1995). That is, labor appears as the transcendental, ubiquitous and essential force occupying the center of a Hegelian totality that now traces the stages of coming-into-being not of the Absolute Spirit, but of human beings who realize their self-mediated birth through their own labor. In addition, by superseding all forms of alienation, humanity will become conscious of this coming-into-being, as they sensuously—by means of their senses—perceive their self/essence in objects they create. It is interesting to note that Veblen (1919: 411-414) advances a similar critique of "the socialist economics of Karl Marx and his followers," regarding "the materialistic conception of history;" Veblen suggests despite an inversion of the logical order, still "a creative primacy" is assigned to one element of the totality, to class struggle/conflict, which reflects the Hegelian/Feuerbachian underpinnings of Marx's analysis, rather than a post-Darwinian evolutionary approach.

Similar articulations of labor, for example labor as (a form of) *praxis* or revolutionary, practical activity, can be found in the *Theses on Feuerbach* (1975b); Marx, with Engels (Marx and Engels 1975), further specifies it as "self-activity" in the *German Ideology*. More importantly, such a rendition is arguably epitomized in his *opus magnum, Capital*. There, Marx defines labor that creates use-values as something both independent of, and necessary for the existence of all social formations: "labor...as the creator of use-values, as useful labor, is a condition of human existence which is independent of all forms of society; it is an eternal natural necessity which mediates that metabolism between man and nature, and therefore human life itself" (Marx 1977: 133). Marx further details, rather poetically, labor's ubiquity for human existence—its interminable necessity makes it the eternally essential mediating process between human beings and nature—in his analysis of the labor process in its "simple and abstract elements" (Marx 1977: 283-292). Simply put, in its generality, "man's activity" alters the object (nature) in accordance with the intention he had by means of the instruments of labor (Marx 1977: 283). That is, an individual objectively realizes a preconceived end result, already existing ideally in his mind, by affecting a change in the material he is working on; this object becomes a thing of use as it is "bathed in the fire of labor, appropriated as part of its organism, and infused with vital energy for the performance of the functions appropriate to their concept and to their vocation in the process" (Marx 1977: 283, 287-289; cf. Marx 1973). This "purpose he is conscious of" not only "determines the mode of his activity with the rigidity of a law [to which] he must subordinate his will" but also differentiates man from animals; to the extent that labor is a conscious, and not an instinctive activity, it acquires an "exclusively human characteristic" (Marx 1977: 284). The conscious purpose that drives and determines his activity is in turn shaped by his perceived needs; as the individual adapts and appropriates the nature in a form adequate to his needs, he changes the external, as well as his own, nature, while developing existing potentialities in both and subjecting them to his powers (Marx 1977, 283). It would seem that Marx now equates labor with material production, universalizing and expanding this inevitable and necessary condition of human existence to all societies throughout history. And labor as productive activity seemingly appears as the fundamental quality, the differentiating characteristic, of being human.

Veblen: The Instinct of Workmanship and The Irksomeness of Labor

At first sight, there seems to be certain similarities between Marx's labor as productive activity and Veblen's conception of "instinct of workmanship." According to Veblen, human beings are, and conceive themselves to be, "a centre of unfolding impulsive, teleological activity," seeking "in every act the accomplishment of some concrete, objective, impersonal end" (Veblen 1915: 15). To put it differently, "all instinctive action" of human beings "is teleological" since it is an attempt to accomplish a purpose ascribed by the instinctive proclivity, which controls and directs "intelligent faculty" and "intellectual processes" (Veblen 1918: 31). Here, one can see a certain parallel between Marx and Veblen; not only that they seem to be focusing on the qualitative aspects of productive activity, but that both also ascribe a teleological character to human activity, emphasizing the consciousness, intentionality involved in the labor process (Veblen 1918: 4).

It would seem the instinct of workmanship is similar to labor as the mediating moment between human beings (instincts) and the ends/purposes they have: as Veblen (1918: 31) puts it, "the instinct of workmanship…is somewhat peculiar, in that its functional content is serviceability for the ends of life, whatever these ends may be; whereas these ends to be subserved are, at least in the main, appointed and made worth while by the various other instinctive dispositions." This however does not mean the instinct of workmanship is subsumed under, "auxillary to all the rest" instincts; it, in its own right, is fundamental since "efficient use of the means at hand and adequate management of resources available for the purpose of life is itself an end of endeavor, and accomplishment of this kind is a source of gratification" (Veblen 1918: 31-32).

Veblen (1918: 33) further defines the "instinct of workmanship" as "occup[ying] the interest with practical expedients, ways and means, devices and contrivances of efficiency and economy, proficiency, creative work and technological mastery of facts. "The "instinct of workmanship," as "purposeful," "effective," and "efficient" activity, conduces the "material well-being of the race," "furthers human life on the whole" by ensuring "its biological success" (Veblen 1918: 25); this in turn indicates that human beings have "a taste for effective work, and a distaste for futile effort" (Veblen 1915: 15). They have "a sense of the merit of serviceability or efficiency and of the demerit of futility, waste, or incapacity"; in that sense, the instinct of workmanship is a mediation that ensures the effective, efficient ways and means are deployed to achieve the ends being sought, avoiding wasteful, inefficient, and futile endeavors (Veblen 1915: 15).

Veblen attributes the survival of early humanity in part to the instinct of workmanship; given almost uninhabitable material conditions and limited technological stock and know-how, the subsistence of the group depended on unselfish and impersonal efficiency of all. With improvements in technology came a surplus of goods, which either could be plundered or had to be protected; in addition, emulation attributed importance to visible success, and therefore to the conduct and force of an individual, rather than his/her serviceability to the group, resulting in the emergence of a predatory culture. In a "predatory culture," "workmanship" becomes labor—"irksome," "tainted," "ignoble," "shameful," and "something to be avoided" (Veblen 1898, 1915, 1918); only those who cannot avoid it, essentially the poor, would continue to labor. By implication, those who can avoid labor have the ability to do so because they are wealthy; they have accumulated property, which they consume conspicuously, wastefully.

As individual comparisons are primarily conducted in terms of pecuniary achievement, the instinct of workmanship become somewhat socially reputable again, at least for the working classes, as long as "the work was for the acquisition of wealth" (Veblen 1918, 184). Early on, these craftsmen, eventual first capitalists, were efficient in their pursuit of pecuniary gain: they had technological proficiency, participated in and supervised the production process; thus they contributed to the advancement of industrial arts, furthering the material well-being of humanity. At the same time, they were businessmen; as technological changes made it impossible for most workmen to own their means of production, pecuniary gain once again contaminated workmanship. Businessmen, absentee owners, and eventually, financiers now owned, better yet, usurped the community's technological knowhow, workmanlike skills, therefore workman's productive capacity, which are now subsumed under pecuniary gain.

One possible way to overcome this "barbaric," predatory capitalism which threatens the material well-being and survival of humanity is to appeal to those who have an indispensable role in the material production and who can ensure that that process continues without interruption. Thus, Veblen's (2001) call for a "soviet of engineers" at one point, about which he was not optimistic, to say the least. Engineers who observe the sabotage, wastefulness and confusion of absentee owners realize that these businessmen had nothing to contribute to engineers' work. To quote at length:

> "It became the work of the technologist to determine, on technological grounds, what could be done in the way of productive industry, and to contrive ways and means of doing it... The material welfare of the community is unreservedly bound up with the due working of this industrial system, and therefore with its unreserved control by the engineers, who alone are competent to manage it. To do their work as it should be done these men of the industrial general staff must have a free hand, unhampered by commercial considerations and reservations... there is a growing conviction among them that they together constitute the sufficient and indispensable general staff of the mechanical industries, on whose unhindered team-work depends the due working of the industrial system and therefore also the material welfare of the civilized peoples...the engineers are in a position to make the next move." (Veblen 2001: 38-50)

That is, Veblen (1918: 299; my emphasis) looks at capitalism "from the point of view of technology, and more specifically from that of *workmanship* as it underlies the technological system" and sees underneath the predatory, pecuniary, business interests that prevail in capitalism a group of people for whom the instinct of workmanship (and the parental bent) *might* be more pronounced. This is due to the position they occupy in the production process; their knowledge of the "workings of the industrial system" would ensure that production would continue uninterrupted. In doing so, however, Veblen treats the production process, and the engineers' knowledge of it, as unproblematic, given, and apolitical; in that sense, I would argue he is more of a "materialist" than Marx was.

Marx Again: Labor as The Producer of Surplus

But what about Marx and capitalism? Does private property equal capitalism? Does capitalists' exclusive ownership of the means of production define capitalism? Or alienation what is wrong with capitalism? One would be wrong to suggest that a teleological, creative, productive activity exhausts what labor is for Marx; I emphasize another definition Marx elaborates in the *Grundrisse* for the first time, and which finds its most elaborate articulation in *Capital*—labor as the producer of surplus (Düzenli 2006). That is, labor *can* create more goods and services than what those who produce these goods and services customarily would consume and require to continue laboring (Marx 1977). Marx develops this articulation by discussing the relationship between wage-laborer and capitalist. Both appear in the market as equals, in possession of a property each exclusively owns, and each pursues his/her own self-interest freely, without any coercion; although, Marx is quick to suggest, this freedom, on the part of the worker, is a forced freedom as s/he cannot but have to sell his/her labor-power, that is s/he is freed from the means of production. In addition, what they exchange is at least presumed to be of equal value/worth; thus in principle, no one is being cheated. However, Marx goes on to show that this equal exchange between the worker and the capitalist can only take place if in the end the capitalist ends up with more than what s/he parts with, otherwise there would be no capital, nor a capitalist. As Marx leaves the market and delves into "the hidden abode of production" he finds an antagonistic realm in which buyers (sellers) of labor-power try to get as much (give as little) labor as possible, thus attempting to maximize (minimize) the surplus-labor they appropriate (perform). This is the site of capitalist exploitation, and exploitation is what's wrong with capitalism.

Marx (1977) articulates capitalist exploitation by distinguishing between two values: the value of the commodity that workers sell—labor-power—and the value the use-value of labor-power —living labor— produces during the workday. That is, the laborers reproduce —or more precisely produce an equivalent of— the wages they receive during a portion of the workday, which Marx labels as paid or necessary labor. However, this does not mean that the wage-laborers simply stop laboring as soon as they perform necessary labor; rather, they (are compelled to) continue to work, thus performing uncompensated, surplus labor. That is, since the value laborers create does not depend on the value their labor-power commands in the labor market, but "on the length of time [they are] in action" (Marx 1977: 679), they end up producing surplus-value; this is why Marx emphasizes the difference between the use-value of labor-power and its value as a commodity. This is not to suggest that Marx construes labor's capacity to produce surplus-value as a given, inherent or natural ability; rather, it is a consequence of the continuation of "the process of creating value" beyond the paid portion of the workday (Marx 1977: 302). Only if labor is performed above and beyond what is necessary to sustain the laborers' existence, which Marx assumes to be equal to the value that the workers receive for their commodity, surplus, and surplus performing labor, becomes a possibility: "if the process is not carried beyond the point where the value paid by the capitalist for the labor-power is replaced by an exact equivalent, it is simply a process of creating value; but if it is continued beyond that point, it becomes a process of valorization," a process in which value self-expands and becomes capital (Marx 1977: 302).

Marx refers to another possibility for the production of more surplus: rather than extending the time devoted to the performance of surplus-value, the length of the workday is reduced during which value that is equivalent to the wages workers receive is reproduced (the necessary labor portion of the workday). This will not necessarily deteriorate workers' "quality of life," or lead to a decrease in their real wages; rather, a shorter portion of the workday is devoted to the reproduction of their necessities due to increases in workers' productivity. Thus, the capacity to produce surplus simply results from the extension of the workday and/or the reduction of the portion devoted to the reproduction of the labor-power/work-force.

Capitalism as an Exploitative Economic System [1]

Marx deploys this accounting scheme—dividing the workday into portions in which necessary (paid), and surplus (unpaid) labor is performed—to define capitalist exploitation: capitalists, who do not partake in its production, appropriate the surplus-value wage?laborers' produce for which they are uncompensated.

Construed as such, capitalist exploitation violates "the law of equal exchange": wage-laborers do not receive the equivalent of what they part with, whereas capitalists get "something for nothing." This unequal exchange, in turn, signifies that the "equal rights" of the market in particular, and the capitalist ethics associated with this equality in general, are based on an *exclusion* (Özselçuk and Madra 2005; Madra 2006). In this capitalist economy, all, including the capitalists, exchange something for something else: workers part with their labor-power that can be employed productively—performing surplus labor—or unproductively in return for wages; capitalists exchange their money to hire labor-power in addition to other means of production; and others receive something in return for providing the conditions of existence of the production process. In this sense, all are participating in "the market"; yet, this "all-inclusive" exchange relation however is not replicated in other realms of the economy. More specifically, capitalists are the only ones who do not labor, productively or unproductively, for their share of the surplus-value; that is, they *exclude themselves* from the performance of surplus labor. In addition, they have the *exclusive* right to appropriate the surplus-value, which results in the "unequal exchange" between wage-laborers and capitalists. As such, "equality" in this capitalist framework results in the inequality in—the exclusion of some from—the performance and appropriation of surplus-labor.

---

[1] The following two sections draw heavily from Düzenli (2016).

Exploitation is not limited to capitalism; more generally, exploitation occurs when some, those who produce the surplus, are *excluded* from its appropriation. To put it differently, exploitation takes place when some *exclusively* appropriate the surplus even though they have not participated in its production, or labored for their share in it. In that sense, exploitation is an injustice since it violates "the law of equal exchange": despite the premise of equal exchange—getting the equal of what one gives up—exploitation means that not everyone receives an equivalent of what they part with as they do not have the right to appropriate the surplus. That is, laborers perform unpaid labor—since their contribution to the social output does not only depend on their share in that output, but on how long they perform surplus labor as well—while some get "something for nothing"—the product of laborers' surplus labor are appropriated by those who had no role in its production.

Conclusion: A Non-Exploitative Economy

The question then becomes: how to remedy this injustice? Veblen, in his critique of Marx, contends that Marx's theory of exploitation, derived from his labor theory of value, is based on the liberal utilitarianism and the natural rights tradition of the English; according to Veblen, Marx would inevitably conclude that the whole product is labor's right. In contrast, Marx (1974) calls for a non-exploitative economy premised upon a "radical equality": "from each according to ability, to each according to needs." In doing so, he also refutes one criticism Veblen advances. No one is excluded from participating in this surplus economy as each would contribute to the surplus in accordance with his/her ability, each would receive according to his/her needs, and each would be accorded the ability to appropriate the surplus independent of their participation or responsibility in its production, apropos of "a morality of relatedness and community" (Resnick and Wolff 2001: 265). Since one's access to goods/services does not depend on the provision of something in return, there would no longer be exchange, equal or unequal, in this surplus economy; one simply does not have to do anything to receive something. Each freely and willingly performs surplus given their ability to do so, producing something in return for nothing. One does not appropriate or receive a portion of the surplus because one participates in, or provides the conditions of existence of, its production; rather, each has the ability and freedom to appropriate and receive a portion of the surplus simply because they are not excluded from, but are a part of surplus economy, again apropos of "a morality of relatedness and community." This might not be a "rational economic order" but it is one in which radical equality prevails.

References

Balibar, E. 1995. *The philosophy of Marx*. Trans. By C. Turner. New York: Verso.

Düzenli, F. E. 2006. *Re/presenting labor: Economic discourse, value, and ethics*. PhD diss., University of Notre Dame.

———. 2016. Surplus-producing labor as a capability: A Marxian contribution to Amartya Sen's revival of classical political economy. *Cambridge Journal of Economics* 40 (4): 1019-1035.

Madra, Y. M. 2006. Questions of communism: ethics, ontology, subjectivity. *Rethinking Marxism* 18 (2): 205-224.

Marx, K. 1973. *Grundrisse: Foundations of the critique of political economy*. Trans. By Martin Nicolaus. London: New Left Review.

———. 1974. Critique of the Gotha program. In *The First International and after*. Trans. By D. Fernbach. London: New Left Review.

———. 1975a. The Economic and Philosophical Manuscripts of 1844. In *Early writings*. Trans. By Rodney Livingstone and Gregor Benton. London: New Left Review.

———. 1975b. Theses on Feuerbach. In *Early writings*. Trans. By Rodney Livingstone and Gregor Benton. London: New Left Review.

———. 1977. *Capital: A critique of political economy Vol. 1*. Trans. By B. Fowkes. New York: Vintage Books.

Marx, K., and F. Engels. 1975. *Collected works*, 47 vols. New York: International Publishers.

Özselçuk, C. & Madra Y. M. 2005. Psychoanalysis and Marxism: From capitalist-all to communist non-all. *Psychoanalysis, Culture and Society* 10 (1): 79-97.

Resnick, S. A., & Wolff R. D. 2001. Struggles in the USSR: Communisms attempted and undone. *Re/presenting class: Essays in postmodern Marxism*, eds. J.K. Gibson-Graham, S. A. Resnick, R. D. Wolff. Durham, N.C.: Duke University Press.

Veblen, T. 1898. The instinct of workmanship and the irksomeness of labor. *American Journal of Sociology* 4 (2): 187-201.

———. 1915. *The theory of leisure class*. New York: Macmillan.

———. 1918. *The instinct of workmanship*. New York: B.W. Huebsch.

———. 1919. The socialist economics of Karl Marx I. In *The place of science in modern civilization and other essays*. New York: B.W. Huebsch.

———. 2001. *The engineers and the price system*. Kitchener, Ontario: Batoche Books.

Thorstein Veblen, Business Enterprise and the Financial Crisis

William Waller and Felipe Rezende

Thorstein Veblen, being an evolutionary thinker, only projected his ideas into the short term, what he called the calculable future. This is prudent for an evolutionary thinker. Evolutionary change in social behavior, unlike biological evolution, can be purposeful. Veblen noted that we could engage in collective behavior to change the direction of social change, or we could simply allow blind drift. When we allow blind drift in social evolutionary processes, then like biological evolution, the direction of change is indeterminate and there is no natural order toward which cultures naturally tend. There is no meliorative tendency in blind drift. The characteristic tendency of all evolutionary processes is that the cumulative effects of multitudes of small changes over extremely long periods of time lead to qualitative changes in evolving systems.

Veblen noted that societies have an inherently conservative tendency to preserve archaic traits. The preconceptions of economics and other preevolutionary sciences were that there were meliorative tendencies that led to states of equilibrium that were in harmony with a beneficent nature. This belief has persisted or is resurgent in most modern industrial economies (with the possible exception of the Scandinavian democracies) leading to reactionary political responses to economic problems based on this belief structure, in spite of indisputable evidence that such policies are disastrous for what Veblen referred to as the underlying population or the common man.

At this writing most economies are still reeling from the financial crisis of 2008 and what has come to be called "The Great Recession" in the United States. Indeed, at this time the Eurozone teeters on the brink of collapse and the United States is heading into a second period of decline of this recession. Oddly this second "dip" in the United States economy reflects the same circumstances that caused a nearly identical dip during the Great Depression when fiscal austerity measures were adopted prematurely. Though in the modern case in the United States a conservative political party (Republican) seems willing to cause a second economic collapse simply to remove a president for the other political party (Democrat)—sacrificing the economic well-being of the nation for short term political gain.

These actions give, if not new meaning, at least a stronger element of malevolence to the group Veblen referred to as "the Vested Interest." However, the purpose of this paper is not to recast contemporary economic problems into Veblenian terminology however entertaining and enlightening such an exercise might be. Instead, we will explore how Veblen's system of analysis, supplemented by more recent analytic additions to the body of institutional economics, gives us a clearer understanding of the causes and consequences of the current economic crisis and see what insights this provides in terms of finding solutions to our economic predicaments.

The early chapters of *The Price System and the Engineers* describes the analytic distinction Veblen introduced in *The Theory of Business Enterprise* (hereafter Veblen 1978), that being the distinction between business and industry. Industry is the term Veblen uses to describe the technologically based, socially organized processes of producing and distributing the material and necessary means of life to the community. This behavioral system of production is based on what Veblen calls the Machine Process. To understand Veblen's analysis we need to look at the Machine Process in detail.

The Machine Process

The machine process, described by Veblen, "means something more comprehensive and less external than a mere aggregate of mechanical appliances for the mediation of human labor."(Veblen 1978: 5) Modern industrial economies, while employing machines, must be organized to process materials as they move through the many steps of fabrication that make up modern production processes. For Veblen, "The scope of the process is larger than the machine." (Veblen 1978: 5) The machine process is a concert of industrial operations "taken as a machine process, made up of interlocking detailed processes, rather than as a multiplicity of mechanical appliances each doing its particular work in severalty."(Veblen 1978: 7) It is a process characterized by the "running maintenance of interstitial adjustments between the several sub-processes or branches of industry … and an unremitting requirement of quantitative precision."(Veblen 1978: 8) By which he refers to the coordinating social behaviors that move materials and organize workers to seamlessly coordinate the many necessary processes precisely in terms of both time and quantitative precision of materials in mechanical and human processes. Veblen notes that since "none of the processes in the mechanical industries is self sufficing,"(Veblen 1978: 7) the efficiency of the process is only as strong as its weakest link. Man plays a new role, he becomes a supervisor of machines or an engineer making sure the machines and thus the whole system runs smoothly. It is vital in the machine process that there are no disturbances so as to proceed "with its work in an efficient manner, so as to avoid idleness, waste and hardship."(Veblen 1978: 18)

Veblen is essentially optimistic about the impact of the machine process on culture. He writes:

> The point of immediate interest here is the further bearing of the machine process upon the growth of culture, —the disciplinary effect which this movement for standardization and mechanical equivalence has upon the human material."(Veblen 1978: 306)

> The workman "now does this work as a factor involved in a mechanical process whose movement controls his motions. It remains true, of course, as it always has been true, that he is the intelligent agent concerned in the process, while the machine, furnace roadway, or retort are inanimate structures devised by man and subject to the workman's supervision. But the process comprises him and his intelligent motions, and it is by virtue of his necessarily taking an intelligent part in what is going forward that the mechanical process has its chief effect on him.(Veblen 1978, 307-8)

The effect that the machine process has on the people who work with it is:

"The machine process compels a more or less unremitting attention to phenomena of an impersonal character and to sequences and correlations not dependent for their force upon human predilection nor created by habit and custom. The machine throws out anthropomorphic habits of thought. It compels the adaptation of the workman to his work, rather than the adaptation of the work to the workman. The machine technology rests on knowledge of impersonal, material cause and effect, not on the dexterity, diligence, or personal force of the workman, still less on the habits and propensities of the workman's superiors. Within the range of this machine-guided work, and within the range of modern life so far as the machine process guides it, the course of things is given mechanically, impersonally, and the resultant discipline is a discipline in the handling of impersonal facts for mechanical effect. It inculcates thing in terms of opaque, impersonal cause and effect. To the neglect of those norms of validity that rest on usage and on the conventional standards handed down by usage. (Veblen 1978: 310)

Veblen believes that the machine process will have an increasing impact on the direction of cultural evolution because:

The machine discipline, however, touches wider and wider circles of the population, and touches them in an increasingly intimate and coercive manner. In the nature of the case, therefore, the resistance opposed to this cultural trend given by the machine discipline of the grounds of received conventions weakens with the passage of time. The spread of materialistic, matter-of-fact preconceptions take place as at a cumulatively accelerating rate . . ." (Veblen 1978: 373-374)

But, of course Veblen's optimism was immediately tempered by the knowledge that other cultural factors alien to the machine process might "inhibit its spread and keep its disintegrating influence within bounds." (Veblen 1978: 373) While Veblen noted that working within production facilities governed by the machine processes technical exigencies, the cause and effect reasoning of normally operating industrial production, could create habits of thought and action based upon that same cause and effect reasoning in other social arenas. He was not overoptimistic about the prospect for the public rejecting the conventional wisdom that governed other social behavior based on pre-evolutionary animistic constructs and conceits. In fact, history has shown that Veblen's glimmer of optimism greatly overestimated the possibility of matter of fact thinking overcoming the conventional wisdom.

On the nature of Vested Interests

Before we talk about today's vested interest we need to remember and maybe refine how Veblen used this term. The vested interests are those people who are in control of material resources and their distribution and have the political power to remain so. The term vested is drawn from the term vestment, a French word referring to the clothing worn by Christian clergy. Vestments are ceremonial and official items of clothing that display the clergy's office and the legitimate authority that office represents. The source of the legitimate authority in this case, as in most, is supernatural in character.

Similar to the clergy, those vested interests Veblen refers to also have power and authority that it is similarly legitimized by supernatural sources. Though in the industrial world the supernatural source is often referred to as the natural order, a terminological difference that belies its origins in Christian theology. Specifically, it involves property rights established under natural law. This natural law foundation supports the belief in the inviolability of property rights—because if they are granted as part of natural law, or are possibly divine in origin, then to alter or violate them is a crime, not against a person, but against nature and possibly a divine personage. If property rights are a human discretionary creation, then changing or altering them is simply a matter of social decision-making.

The vested interests that Veblen refers to are those people in modern industrial societies who have rights in property that allow them to control that property for personal interests regardless of the consequences to others or the community as a whole by natural or divine right. They certainly use all the power at their disposal to oppose any suggestion that these rights can be altered through any process of governance. They view the only way to change property rights is by the consent of those whose property relations are being altered.

Given these origins it is clear that the vested interests would absolutely not be moved by arguments based on matter-of-fact knowledge of social processes, since this would call into question the very nature and foundation of their property claims and thereby undermine the legitimacy of those claims. The source of their claims of legitimacy for their control, power, and authority over the material means of life (which is their property) would be completely undermined if the society as a whole adopted the matter-of-fact habits of thought that are the foundation of the machine process and its underlying technological human and mechanical processes.

This is the crux of the threat posed by "the Engineers" in Veblen's essays. This threat has remained unrealized for three reasons, two of which Veblen articulates clearly in *The Engineers and the Price System*. First, most of the persons whose work falls into Veblen's category of engineers have been employed by the vested interest on reasonably favorable terms. This was true in Veblen's time and remained so through much of the twentieth century. John Kenneth Galbraith described this same group of skilled workers that Veblen referred to as the engineers. Galbraith renamed them as technocrats in his book *The New Industrial State* (1967: 60-72). Galbraith saw them as an emergent class that might challenge the control of the vested interests by virtue of their need to coordinate the machine process to avoid recurrent recessions. Both Veblen and Galbraith based their optimism for this class on the fact that the owners of resources in modern industrial economies were so far removed from the technical aspects of production that they had no ability to maintain the system without the engineers. This concern of the vested interest would disappear in part because the process of deindustrialization in the United States that began in the early 1970s changed this need for engineers rather dramatically. A great many highly skilled employees who did the engineering and technical management tasks of these companies have become unemployed as industrial manufacturing has declined in the United States and many of these jobs that remained were, through the process of globalization, removed to foreign production facilities.

Second, as Veblen noted the price system ensures that modern industrial economies operate well below their full capacity in order to sustain prices satisfactory to the needs of the vested interest, who need maximum profits (of course). Any group of people seeking to remove the vested interests must be able to take over the operation of the industrial system immediately. The day after any revolution people want and expect, but more importantly need the power plants to be online, water purification systems to be functioning, transportation systems to be in place, and all the other necessities of life to be in the expected places at the expected times on a secure basis—and as we shall see this includes banks. No group has emerged having both the will and ability to remove the vested interests—though oddly if the vested interests all disappeared tomorrow and no one told us, they would not be missed for they contribute nothing and cost a great deal. We will return to this last point later in this chapter.

The third reason that engineers and technocrats have not and will not be able to even mildly counter the power of the vested interests is that business, especially business of any great size or power, is outsourcing industry as fast as it can. The vested interests that have enormous amounts of power and control do not produce any of the material means of life, instead they outsource, design, and finance production, but they do not engage in production. This is not universally true, but it is becoming so at an alarming rate.

The point to be made is clearly all major business enterprises are engaged in commercial transactions that people voluntarily undertake. Necessarily the people who make purchases from these companies have income to do so. Someone, somewhere is producing goods and service essential to the provisioning of society. Moreover, someone, somewhere is producing something for these major business enterprises to resell, finance, insure, etc. But these goods are not actually produced by the largest and most profitable companies. Increasingly, small companies and foreign producers under contract to these large business enterprises produce the actual goods consumed by ordinary folks. As a result this removes the most powerful and significant business enterprises from any significant encounter with or contamination by the machine process. Surely this means that the cultural incidence of the machine process, if it has any transformative power, is significantly muted in the most advanced industrial economies today.

So the vested interests are those who have property rights over large amounts of the material resources of the community, including the natural resources, land, and industrial appliances—all made productive only with the application of the communities' stocks of shared knowledge and by the human beings with the skills to employ that matter-of-fact knowledge. On their own the vested interests cannot use their property to produce anything, instead, they extort output from those who can produce by threatening to withhold access to that property. Thus property rights allow the vested interests to extort the greater portion of the communities' real incomes. They conduct this extortion rather incompetently through the price system to which we now turn.

The Price System

The price system is the system of interconnected commercial transactions in a modern industrial economy. These commercial transaction are theoretically voluntary but are actually compulsory for all the participants in that no one can survive in a modern industrial economy without participating in these transactions, not workers, not owners, but everyone directly or indirectly. While there have been and continue to be actual market places where transactions occur, when economists, politicians, businessmen, and the public refer to markets they usually are referring to an imaginary space in which all transaction of goods of a particular type take place. The market system is made up of all these imaginary market spaces. Though the markets are imaginary, the transactions are real and interconnected.

This is not the usual way economists or politicians talk about markets, or free markets. Indeed, anytime anyone treats markets as other than the price determining interaction between the forces of supply and demand that allow buyers and sellers to reach equilibrium prices and quantities where the marginal buyer purchases the good at a price exactly equal to their subjective assessment of the value of the good to them and the marginal supplier receives a price sufficient to pay inputs according to their true opportunity costs (equivalent the contribution of value of each input to the value of the final output) and normal profits to the seller because of pervasive and unrelenting price competition among the many buyers and sellers, they are generally ignored as a crank, a heretic, or worst of all, a radical. We have been called all those things. Indeed, we have been told we just don't believe in markets. We want to repeat that: We are somehow flawed in our thinking because we don't believe in markets.

The economists (and others) who make these comments are correct: We don't believe in markets, instead, we study them. They are social institutions—human behavior structured by social norms and individual habits producing certain types of behavior that result in exchanges, including commercial transactions, that distribute goods and services within the community. They are one of a number of institutions used for the exchange of goods and services. When markets work, meaning that goods and services are distributed in such a way that the community's needs on both sides of the transaction are met, then markets are great. When markets don't work, then we alter the structure of the transactions, meaning norms and habits and behaviors, to make the market work, or replace it with an alternative social mechanism. Belief is not the issue. Markets are tools. Sometimes a market is the right tool, sometime not. This pragmatic approach could well be called an engineering understanding of markets.

Now why is it important for some who "believe' in markets that the market should be conceived of as if all the transactions occurred simultaneously and instantaneously in a single location? Why must we have this mythical market in our consciousness rather than conceiving of it merely as the sum of the transactions of a particular good within some approximation of the same time where those transactions are interrelated through the systematic character of our modern industrial economy? Why is the storybook version so important?

This storybook became the condensed version including the description of all of the virtues of competitive markets presented above emerges from the economic theory of markets as carefully defined in contemporary neoclassical microeconomics as is taught to (inflicted upon) all undergraduate economics students in one form or another. It doesn't really tell us anything about how markets actually function. It does tell us that if we have free, competitive, unregulated markets that individuals motivated by only their self-interest will create an outcome that is fair to everyone involved. It is a morality tale dressed up as social science. It tells us that a price system constructed around such markets distributes goods and services based on the value of goods and incomes according to the value that each input contributes to the production of goods. It tells us that prices paid for goods and services are fair and reflect real value. It tells us that we deserve the income we receive and no more.

So how does the real price system work, not the imaginary one of economic theory? The Great Depression of the 1930s occasioned a great deal of economic inquiry into the actual functioning on industrial economies because the mainstream, orthodox economic thinking of the day in the Anglo-American sphere of influence argued that such a phenomena was not possible. Wages would drop to the point where businesses would begin hiring again according to Say's Law therefore the unemployment experienced at that time was, according to the theory, strictly voluntary. This explanation, being absurd in the face of reality, created an opportunity for alternative approaches and theories to be heard. The most famous of these was, of course, the theoretical framework proposed by J.M. Keynes in his famous treatise *The General Theory of Employment, Interest and Money* (1936). But institutionalists in the Veblenian tradition were at work studying the actual workings of the market economy of the United States.

Of particular importance was the research of Gardiner Means (1992) and Walton Hamilton (1938) who both examined the actual price setting practices used in various industries. Gardiner Means, in a famous memo to the United States Congress (1935) which was instantly reprinted under the title "Industrial Prices and Their Relative Inflexibility" (Means 1992), provided compelling empirical analysis that the United States economy's industrial sector was dominated by firms who charged administered prices rather than market prices (as traditionally understood). These administered prices remained inflexible downward in the face of declining demand— rather than lowering prices to sell off an "oversupply" as mainstream theory suggested, firms in these industries simply restricted production until their inventory was sold off. The administered price remained stable and inflexible. [1]

Walton Hamilton and his colleagues did many case studies of major industries in the United States to ascertain how they actually set prices. (Hamilton 1938) [2] In 1975 Means summarized the administered pricing phenomena as follows:

> Because of the great difficulty of setting prices, managements have simplified the pricing process in two major ways. First, they have adopted one or another of a variety of pricing formulas, such as pricing for a target rate of return, full-cost pricing, standard mark-up pricing, index pricing and break-even pricing. Second, they tend to hold prices constant for months at a time, changing them only when changed conditions call for a very substantial price shift, one that is beyond the zone of relative indifference. (Means 1992: 272)

He further noted that steel prices changed so infrequently that when they did change it was front-page news and that automobile prices were generally set for a year at a time. (Means 1992, 272) Certainly the actual price setting methods and frequency of adjustment in these and other industries has changed in the intervening time, but similar studies to find out

---

[1] See especially Means (1992: 32-40) for his empirical analysis.

[2] Hamilton (1938) is a collection of these case studies. There are many more. The field of Industrial Organization within economics was characterized by such empirical work until it was subsumed as a subfield of microeconomic theoretical modeling of both the partial equilibrium variety favored by the Chicago School of economics and game theoretic modeling of strategic behavior of firms by the 1970s. Both approaches have failed to provide the kind of price determining equilibrium conditions sought by these practitioners. The theoretical answer to the question "How are prices set in markets not characterized by pure competition?" remains (as it was in the 1930s): It depends. Alas, neither of these mainstream approaches has going and finding out how prices are set as a part of its methodological tool kit.

the nature of these changes are generally not of interest to economists because mainstream economic theory tells them that they are set by supply and demand, thus no further inquiry is necessary.

But the evidence from the study of actual price setting behavior of firms confirms Veblen's observations that the industrial system under the control of business interests constrains output to maintain prices at the level desired by the vested interests. The mechanisms employed for setting administrative prices do take into account many of the factors incorporated in the mainstream theory as components of the theoretical categories of supply and demand. Input costs of production being a key component of the consideration of firms. Material inputs are sold to firms by the producers of these inputs who themselves are employing some mechanism for setting their prices to maximize their returns. Similarly workers' wages are set by a number of social mechanisms and are costs for firms. There are two other elements of costs that are crucial to understanding Veblen and the contemporary crisis. To understand these additional factors and their importance we must now turn our attention to what is usually referred to as finance.

Finance, Funding and Financialization

Finance

Firms usually need to acquire financing to support their production activity over the period beginning with the purchasing of inputs until the output is sold. To fill this gap the undertakers [3] of production must purchase the inputs and pay the workers using their own money, and/or they must secure loans for this purpose. Repaying the principle and interest on these loans is a cost to the firm. Established firms often avoid this kind of borrowing by using retained earnings from a previous production period to fund the current production period. Veblen, in *The Engineers and the Price System,* calls this corporate finance and contrasts it with the finance undertaken by investment banks. To help keep our analysis clear we will refer to this necessary borrowing to facilitate the time between the beginning incursion of costs prior to production and the receipts resulting from the sale of the output, as corporate finance following Veblen. For contrast and to avoid confusion we will refer to the activities of investment banks as funding. Note that obligations to provide returns to owners of the enterprise, be they investors, partners, or stockholders, occur after the sale of output and thus are not a cost of production—though certainly the undertakers must be both cognizant of and ultimately meet these obligations and expectations of these agents.

---

[3] We follow Veblen's use of the term "undertaker" for the person in charge of a business enterprise because it describes the actions of that agent. We avoid the use of the word "entrepreneur" because its use in the business and popular press is more of a designation of a cultural hero and is applied to any successful businessperson no matter how derivative or mundane their business activity may be. Joseph Schumpeter coined the term to describe someone involve in the activity of producing new products and/or introducing new productive processes or business processed. While a source of development in Schumpeter's analysis entrepreneurs altered the economy by borrowing at higher rates of interest which resulted in depriving pre-existing, successful businesses of the funding necessary to remain in business.

The activity of providing finance for business enterprises is an essential activity of commercial banks. They do this by accepting the IOUs (promises to pay) of borrowers (such as firms and consumers). The bank issue their own IOUs (to the borrower) that are more liquid (easier to convert to cash) and are more acceptable (easier to exchange) than borrower's IOU. The interest income generated by earning assets (banks' loans to borrowers) has to be higher than the interest rate paid on liabilities (deposits and borrowed reserves) plus administrative costs to presumably generate profits for the bank. It turns out these conditions are not so easy to meet.

Usually, the liabilities of borrowers and lenders are denominated in the states' unit of account. They represent a promise to pay or to deliver the state currency at some future date. This means that borrowers and lenders are short the state currency. [4]

In addition, commercial banks serve an important public purpose by providing checkable deposits to consumers, both individuals and businesses. These consumers deposit money in an account; they use checks as a means of payment for their purchases and to meet their financial obligations. Of course in order for this to work two things are necessary. First, reserves must be lent to banks on demand to minimize funding liquidity risk. [5] Since the creation of the Federal Reserve System in 1913 it has served as lender of last resort to insure that this does happens. Thus, permanent access to the discount window (the Federal Reserve's reserve lending facility for banks) allows banks to meet their funding needs and maintain the stability of the payment system. Second, prior to 1980 the United States had regulations in place that insured that no interest was paid on demand deposits insuring a reasonable spread on commercial bank loans thereby insuring a profit for commercial banks. Federal deposit insurance insured the depositors against any losses (up to the insurance limit) if the bank made poor loans. And the Federal Reserve Banks served as lenders of last resort to insure that there were no runs on banks. Bank examiners were called in to check the books of banks with suspect loan or underwriting policies. Frankly, almost anyone could run a profitable bank. But in the late 1970s deregulation became a political priority for conservatives and the regulations put in place in the 1930s that stabilized commercial banking were systematically removed. Indeed, it may very well be the case that deregulation made it impossible to run a profitable commercial bank providing loans and checking services to individuals and businesses.

Funding

Investment banks, on the other hand, are in the business of underwriting and issuing securities, including both stocks and bonds of various types, on behalf of clients who typically need long term funding for their projects. Historically this necessity arose because the projects

---

[4] We are introducing some financial terms that may be unfamiliar and we will try to define them as we proceed. The term "short in the state currency" means that the lender has a liability to depositors or lenders of reserves to pay them back in the state currency. The plan of the bank is that the asset they have purchased, namely the loan obligation of the entity to which they made a loan, will be worth more than the value of the state currency that they have to return. Similarly the borrower must repay the lender in state currency in the future. Their plan is that the assets they purchased with the loan will be worth more than the state currency they need to repay the lender.

[5] The "banks liquidity risk" is the need of the bank to rapidly get state currency to meet current liabilities.

proposed were too large and possibly too risky like railroads in the private sector. Banks prefer short-term lending. A bank attempting to provide long-term funding would unacceptably increase the maturity mismatch on the banks balance sheets. These loans would mature over a long period of time tying up the bank's funds, but the bank would have many short-term obligations it could not meet if their funds were all invested in such long-term assets. Borrowing to cover such short-term obligations would make providing the long-term loans too costly and probably unprofitable. An investment bank can access the capital markets allowing it to transform the maturity of short-term obligations, such as short-term borrowing, into long-term funding via equity and/or the bond market (selling securities). The model used was to form large partnerships to underwrite securities to the public to raise the necessary funds similar to the way Lloyd's of London offers insurance. Investment banks were originally partnerships and often, even usually, a large issue of bonds would be underwritten by a number of investment banks simultaneously. Investment banking was basically a fee driven broker activity, which, until the megamerger period of firm consolidation in the 1980s, required no great acumen of any sort.

In the United States, after the Great Depression the Banking and Glass-Steagall Acts of 1933 (along with other banking regulations) kept the activities of investment banks and commercial banks separated. There had been a history of, shall we say, inventive banking practices in the United States that contributed to the impression that bankers were possibly of low moral character and often engage in practices that were in direct conflict with their customers' interests. Post-Great Depression investment banks could not legally hold customer deposits (though they often do) so they did not (in theory) compete with commercial banks on that account. Similarly commercial banks were prohibited from issuing and dealing in securities. All such banking restrictions were removed by the passage of the Gramm-Leach-Bliley Act of 1999, though many firms were already acting simultaneously as commercial banks, investment banks, securities firms and insurances companies by that time. This help set the stage for both the ensuing period of financialization and the collapse of the system in 2008.

Veblen explored the process of how investment banks constructed securities and their role in normal business practice in *The Theory of Business Enterprise*.

Veblen notes that business principles are based on western European conceptions of private property. (Veblen 1978: 82) The businessperson employs his/her property for the purpose of pecuniary gain. This gain is measured by business accounting principles. (Veblen 1978: 84-85) All of this seems commonsense and straightforward. But the question quickly arises what is the value of the firm as a going concern? This is a firm's so-called capitalization. Now the straightforward answer is that it is the net present value of the future income stream generated by the continued operation of the enterprise into the future that constitutes the firms actual value. What the income will be in the future can, of course be estimated, projected, or guessed at, with varying degrees of inaccuracy. Indeed, it is this uncertainty that would lead to J.M. Keynes basing his analysis of the operation of the macroeconomy of modern industrial economies on this very uncertainty.

Alternately we could value a business enterprise on the basis of the sum of the market values of the firm's assets including its tangible and intangible assets. The nineteenth century norm was to use this definition where the intangible assets were valued at some minimal amount. However, since these intangible assets have become the foundation of the value of common stock in the modern era they have taken on greater significance and, of course, are of greater value.

Two firms with identical material assets would be of equal productivity and consequently could be considered (as they would have in the 19th century) of equal value. Intangible assets are those non-material assets owned by one firm, but not other firms with equivalent tangible assets, that make the firm with the intangible assets more valuable than the others lacking those intangible assets—where more valuable means more profitable. The fact that the intangible assets are not material does not mean they are insignificant; indeed it is quite the opposite. Intangible assets include: goodwill, copyrights, patents, first mover advantages, acquired monopoly power, name recognition, reputation, business alliances, contracts, and connections with similarly situated firms. It is all the unquantifiable, immeasurable, intangible social relations that produce nothing, but give one firm an advantage over its equally productive, but not similarly situated, firms. The value of intangible assets adds nothing to the community; they provide a differential access to income for their owners. There is no objective way to value these advantages, no independent measure, so it is valued by the guesswork of the owners of the common stock. The premium that stockholders pay for the common stock of a firm with intangible assets over the price of the stocks of a similarly productive firm without those assets is the value of the intangible assets. While the historical profitability of such a firm may be the basis upon which stockholder pay such a premium, however, the price they pay is not unaffected by salesmanship of those purveyors of securities who sold them the common stock. Moreover, all carry the usual disclaimer required by securities that past performance is not an indicator of future profitability. So the value of common stock is based on the value of intangible assets of the firm as guessed at by the purchasers of that common stock at any particular moment. Of course, mainstream economists embrace the "efficient markets thesis" which claims that efficient stock exchanges will result in the accurate valuation of stocks in light of extant events and circumstances, excepting of course when they don't (for example during bubbles, booms, periods of "irrational exuberance" and just preceding the phenomena known as periodic "adjustments" which collectively account for just about all of the time when common stock is not considered undervalued). The point of this description is that the value of intangible assets can disappear in an instant.

Now in order for the owner of a business to capture this premium at any point in time he/she must sell common stock to others at that premium or undertake the risk of waiting for the future income streams to materialize, which are radically uncertain. Thus the owner of such an enterprise will hire an investment bank to sell the shares of common stock to capture a portion of the premium in the here and now. The investment bank sells the shares for what the market will bear. The premium thus realized goes to the owner of the enterprise (who will have kept sufficient shares to remain in control of the enterprise) and the investment bank on a prearranged basis. However, note that the new stockholders will expect that future income stream to materialize on the most favorable of terms to be paid to them as dividends, consequently the firm must now add those favorable terms to the necessary cost of producing its output, thereby adding a significant increment to be added to the price at which the firm will sell this output.

A similar process occurs with preferred stock and bonds. These securities are issued ostensibly to purchase material assets that serve as the collateral for these obligations. In both cases the cost of issuance of the securities, the cost of selling them, and the interests and other administrative costs of servicing these securities become a part of the cost structure of the firm that has to be paid from the revenue received from the sale of output, thereby necessarily increasing the price for which the firm must sell its output. Since this new price is higher than the old price, the firm is unlikely to increase output; instead it is likely to further restrict output even more to enable the firm to charge the new, higher price, thereby further sabotaging the industrial system and providing even less of the necessary means of life at a new, higher price to the common folk who produce the output in the first place.

Veblen describes all this in detail in *The Theory of Business Enterprise* (1978, Chapters 4-6). The key point of this analysis is that funding (as in issuing securities) is unrelated to corporate finance (meaning funding the process of production).

The function of funding through securities is to allow property owners to capture the value of their property in the form of money. The consequences of funding are to add to the price of output—it is a tax on the production available to the community. It diverts additional income from workers and consumers to owners of property thereby increasing income inequality. It leads to a diminution in the productivity of the modern industrial system. When we contemplate, in this era of modern finance, the huge amount of financial wealth that is created by taxing such a small amount of production (in the United States) our awe of the incredible actual and potential productivity of modern industrial economies is reawakened.

No matter the amount obligations incurred by firms through financial "management", the revenue of the firm still depends on the sale of its output. Indeed, here emulation served an important role in Veblen's analysis of consumption as a motive for people to consume goods and services for reasons other than meeting the material means of life. Emulation serves to motivate conspicuous consumption creating additional incentive for people to consume goods and even waste them to maintain or enhance their social status. (Veblen 1934) J.K. Galbraith introduced the concept of the "revised sequence" where firms in modern industrial economies developed the products first, then created the market for those goods by persuading the consumer to buy the product they wished to sell at the price they wished to sell it. Galbraith's "revised sequence" turns the notion of consumer sovereignty and consumer choice as put forth in neoclassical microeconomics completely on its head. (Galbraith 1967: 211-218) The point is that the firm in question must now sell whatever it produces at a price that supports its "capitalization", meaning the financial burdens of finances, therefore they will engage in all manner of promotion, advertising, marketing, packaging and salesmanship to encourage, persuade and cajole consumers to buy their product at their price. But all these efforts cost money as well. So these additional sales costs must be added into the cost of doing business and is a further tax on the productivity of the industrial economy. Another cost that adds nothing to the well being of the community and only benefits the owners of property at the expense of the common good. Again we marvel at the ability of the modern industrial economies' productivity to carry this enormous burden and still produce as much as it does. Imagine if the economy was relieved of these unnecessary burdens.

Financialization

The system of funding and finance described above are really mundane activities. While the finance contributes to the sabotage of the industrial system, it is historically clear that our economies can support the activities of funding production, financing large investments in material assets, and the chicanery of common stock sales. When we look for the causes of economic and financial crisis while these processes are implicated they are rarely causal. The Great Recession begun in 2008 had four other components: financialization, speculation, failure to regulate and fraud.

The United States has had a number of historic periods where banking was unregulated. These periods demonstrated that human ingenuity is almost boundless in creating ways for one person to cheat another out of the means of life both financial and material. Until the 1970s the 'financial architecture' of the United States could be seen as a two-stage process. Commercial banks (traditional depository institutions) provided financing for consumer and industrial loans while investment Banks facilitated funding through underwriting stock shares and other long-term securities. This latter process allows wealth owners to indirectly fund capital projects and thus capital accumulation. In this pre-1970s financial system, financing took place through the banking system while funding occurred in capital markets. (Kregel 2007)

Much of the change in the United States' system was a result of the movement to deregulate the banking system begun in earnest in the late 1970s. But the genesis of this actually begins with the beginning of modern banking regulation. Banking and Insurance activities in the post-Depression era were tightly regulated. As with everything in the United States, it began as a combination of federal and state regulation with national banks being regulated by the Federal Reserve and state banks and insurance companies being regulated by the states. The securities industry was regulated separately by the Securities and Exchange Commission (SEC) at the Federal level. Each level of regulations defined the kind of institutions over which it had regulatory authority, usually by a list of activities engaged in that defined the institution.

This regulatory regime created the opportunity for the emergence of financial institutions that did not meet the definitions of the regulated firms because these new firms did not engage in one or more of the activities that were used by regulators to define an institution and provided the legal basis for the authority of the regulator to regulate the firm. For example, a firm could make consumer and industrial loans but if it did not accept deposits, it was not a commercial bank and thus avoided regulation. These firms, sometime referred to as non-bank banks, and other firms constructed along similar lines in other financial service sectors gave rise to a parallel system of "shadow banking" outside the reach of regulators. While many types of unregulated financial firms have been part of the United States financial system for a long time after the beginning of serious deregulation shadow banking began to grow in size and importance. [6]

The securitization of home mortgages has its origins in regulatory changes of this era. Savings and Loan institutions (mutual savings banks) traditionally made home mortgages. However, deregulation in the late seventies allowed them to engage in many different types of lending. This deregulation along with a significant amount of fraud made possible by regulatory forbearance led to a collapse of these institutions. The savings and loan crisis contributed to the development of the securitization of home mortgages as an alternative to this diminished source of home financing. Securitization allowed institutional investors through capital markets, to supply funds to finance housing in the United States.

Financial Crises

Veblen certainly understood the operations of a credit economy and financial crises. In *The Theory of Business Enterprise* he argued that the recognition that securities were overvalued relative to the actual earning capacity of the underlying assets could lead to a collapse in securities' prices. If this occurred after the run up in securities' prices during a speculative boom, then that recognition of the mismatch between the nominal value of the security and its earning capacity could result in system wide economic dislocations. Access to credit provided a differential advantage to firms not only to increase their earning capacity, but also to augment their business capital. Firms that could not charge a price sufficient to cover their financial obligations would cease production and cause large scale unemployment of resources and workers. The corrective to this problem was a decrease in costs of inputs or improved efficiency thus allowing a price to be charged that supported the capitalization of such firms leading to the re-employment of the resources, or combinations and business coalitions or other ways of "regulating" prices to restore the flow of income to the owners of securities (Veblen 1973: 237-243).

Investor's changing expectations about future streams of income and revaluations of the prospective earnings of their assets are a destabilizing force as in Veblen's analysis. In any credit economy, the vendibility of corporate capital fuels speculative prosperity and increases the reliance on borrowed funds. However, when debt issuers are unable to meet, or rollover, their liability commitments the debt issuers must sell their assets to meet their current need for state currency to meet their liabilities. These distress sales cause further declines in asset prices that deepen the deflationary spiral. The subsequent crash in asset values results in massive defaults, bankruptcies, and liquidation of many enterprises before a recovery commences.

---

[6] The so-called shadow banking system emerged during the 1920s as nonbanking financial institutions and even nonfinancial corporations lent money to investors. For instance, margin accounts and broker loans sharply increased as investors were buying stocks on margin. J. K. Galbraith noted that brokers loans increased rapidly and that corporations and individuals were supplying more than half of the volume of these loans. (Galbraith 1955: 67). "By early 1929, loans from these non-banking sources were approximately equal to those from the banks" (Galbraith 1955: 31). Investment trusts also played an important role in fueling the speculative boom.

The key components of Veblen's analysis that remain salient to the modern situation is that the cause of a crisis are speculative activity increasing the nominal value of securities; current prices become unable to compensate investors for these inflated nominal values; a decrease in real economic activity until prices for the material means of life are sufficient to cover the cost of the revalued capitalization of firms; and the real losses to the community from this purely financial conundrum. If you consider Veblen's identification of the cause of a depression, the policy of bailing out the banks and investors rather than homeowners and citizens makes perfect sense as long as the goal is to restore the speculators among the vested interests.

Economic crises and speculative booms and bubbles have increased in size and significance since Veblen presented his analysis. This increase was so great that by 1929 crises had ceased being national issues and became international, (and eventually global) issues. In response to this growth the institutionalists' theory of the financial system has developed significantly. Specifically, economists referred to as Post Keynesians, and most especially Hyman Minsky, have given us a better understanding of our modern financial system.[7]

Minsky's analysis is very complex. Minsky's most well known analysis is what he referred to as "The financial instability hypothesis." Minsky shows that well-functioning modern economies have within their normal operations and conventional ethos the seeds of instability. As an economy experiences healthy functioning, firms are engaged in what Minsky calls hedge finance; where the cash receipts of the enterprise or activity exceed cash payments in every period (Minsky 2008: 79). Continued success encourages and enables individuals to begin new enterprises and activities where cash payments exceed cash receipts, this Minsky calls speculative financing. This is, of course, riskier since it depends on sufficient growth in the value of the enterprise or activity such that cash receipts begin and continue to exceed cash payments (Minsky 2008: 48). Minsky notes the importance of speculative finance, but also its contribution to systemic instability:

> In an economy characterized by privately owned capital assets, uncertainty, and profit –maximizing behavior by business, good times induce balancesheet adventuring. The process by which speculative finance increases, as a proportion of the total financing of business, leads to higher asset prices and increased investment. This leads to an improvement in employment, output, and business profits, which in turn proves to businessmen and bankers that experimenting with speculative finance was correct. Such deviation –amplifying reactions are characteristic of unstable system– and thus of our economy. (Minsky 2008: 48)

To handle the increased risk Minsky notes: "Any prudent unit engaging in speculative finance will have alternative financing facilities available, including some backup financing in case some primary channel either becomes too expensive or is no longer available" (Minsky 2008, 48).

As an economy with significant speculative finance as part of its financial structure grows, and as speculative finance continues to be successful the opportunity for another kind of finance enters the picture. Ponzi finance is an extension of speculative finance in that current receipts are insufficient to cover current cash payments. In Ponzi financing additional debt is

---

[7] The development of Institutional Economics and Post-Keynesian economics into Post-Keynesian Institutionalism is explored in Whalen (2012).

incurred to pay current interest payments that has the effect of turning current accrued interest into principle increasing cash payments in the next period. Ponzi finance is the basis for financial fraud though it is not always intentionally fraudulent (Minsky 2008: 231). But an increase in Ponzi financing for any reason increases the fragility of the financial system.

Minsky argues that the normal progression of an economy is to get increasingly unstable the longer an economic expansion or boom continues. The economy begins with primarily hedge financing, but continuing expansion demonstrates the success of speculative financing. This causes speculative finance to increase as a proportion of the overall financial structure creating a more fragile structure. The continued growth and success of speculative financing lead some individuals and enterprises to undertake even riskier investment opportunities leading to an increase in Ponzi financing which further increases the overall fragility of the financial system. This may continue to become or be fueled by an investment bubble for some time. Eventually this fragile financial structure is disturbed by the slowing of prices, a rise in interest rates, a series of insolvencies, or any other of a number of endogenous forces that trigger a rush to liquidity by investors and the financial structure collapses (Minsky 2008: 234).

Expanding on Minsky's Analysis

Minsky also emphasizes the evolution of financial structures in market economies, which he referred to "as stages in the development of capitalist finance" (Minsky 1992: 107). As Minsky put it,

> The independence of operating corporations from the money and financial markets that characterized managerial capitalism was thus a transitory stage. The emergence of return and capital-gains-oriented block of managed money resulted in financial markets once again being a major influence in determining the performance of the economy. However, unlike the earlier epoch of finance capitalism, the emphasis was not upon the capital development of the economy but rather upon the quick turn of the speculator, upon trading profits. (Minsky 1993:111)

In finance capitalism, pecuniary gains derive primarily from the production of goods and services by businesspersons based upon their assessment of future income streams. If the outcome of this future profit expectation is below what is necessary to induce him/her to produce today then production comes to a halt. For this reason, the existence of profit opportunities and the 'vendibility of output' are important variables in his/her production decision.

Veblen noticed, as did Marx, that credit increased a firm's earning capacity. External borrowing (i.e. debt issuance) allows the firm to expand its balance sheet and boost its return on equity. To increase shareholder value, money managers can use a combination of increasing their exposure to riskier assets and activities to increase return on assets and increase the leverage [8] ratio. Debt issuance increases the speed of asset acquisition thus potentially creating asset price inflation. Positive feedbacks from increases in asset prices widen the difference between how much the company owns and how much it owes encouraging firm's managers to increase debt issuance.

---

[8] Leverage is the term used in American finance to refer to using equity as collateral to borrow funds, then using the borrowed funds to purchase additional financial or productive assets. This magnifies the potential gains to the original equity, but it also magnifies the potential losses.

Debt issuance increases the amount of financial assets on the balance sheet of financial institutions that in turn create liabilities for borrowers that use the borrowed funds to increase financial or productive asset holdings. The emergence of the financial industry as the motor force driving modern capitalist economy leads us back to Veblen's argument that the business persons and vested interests primary concern is with the increase in the wealth of its shareholders, not production of the necessary means of life.

Indeed, during the past 30 years debt issuance in the capitalist world reached record levels and several studies point out that this trend will continue over the next decades. It represents a new stage of capitalism in which trading financial assets become the primary source of income. Veblen, in his *Theory of Business Enterprise*, had already anticipated the shift towards finance and away from production. When finance capitalism becomes the dominant force, it augments asset price inflation that can lead to widespread insolvency, a decline in industrial production and employment. Minsky's stage approach is similar to Veblen's approach. Firms (financial and non-financial) increasingly rely on financial instruments to boost their returns.

There is also another consequence of the accumulation of capital and financial wealth generated by this debt issuance. It generates pools of funds that institutional investors manage. This stage is Minsky's money manager capitalism stage.

> Money managers who actively manage portfolios trade their assets as they pursue higher total returns…As the portfolio being managed grew and as active management replaced a passive buy-and-hold strategy for managed money (as the short view replaced the long view) demand for the services for the position-takers emerged. Organisations which would buy securities for their own portfolio, with the object of selling the position to some other portfolio manager or to break the purchase into smaller units, began to make large profits from trading securities. For the large funds the market never was a broker market, it always was a dealer market. (Minsky 1993:112)

Money managers seek investment alternatives (mainly financial) to generate short-term returns. It creates additional demand for financial assets and this behavior accentuates asset price inflation and deflation.

> As managed money grew in relative importance, more and more of the market for financial instruments was characterized by position-taking by financial intermediaries. These positions were bank-financed. The main financial houses became highly-leveraged dealers in securities, beholden to banks for continued refinancing. A peculiar regime emerged in which the main business in the financial markets became far removed from the financing of the capital development of the country. Furthermore, the main purpose of those who controlled corporations was no longer making profits from production and trade but rather to assure that the liabilities of the corporations were fully priced in the financial market." (Minsky 1993:112)

Minsky observed that changes in financial markets affected not only financial structures and relationships between firms, households, banks, financial institutions, and the nature of financing but it also changed economic behavior toward a "dealer market".

> In the present stage of development the financiers are not acting as the ephors of the economy, editing the financing that takes place so that the capital development of the economy is promoted. Today's managers of money are but little concerned with the development of the capital asset of an economy. Today's narrowly-focused financiers do not conform to Schumpeter's vision of bankers as the ephors of capitalism who assure that finance serves progress. Today's financial structure

is more akin to Keynes' characterization of the financial arrangements of advanced capitalism as a casino.

The Schumpeter-Keynes vision of the economy as evolving under the stimulus of perceived profit possibilities remains valid. However, we must recognize that evolution is not necessarily a progressive process: the financing evolution of the past decade may well have been retrograde. (Minsky 1993:113)

Moving away from the machine process towards financialization (and the dominance of financial engineers seeking the maximization of short-term total returns by trading financial securities using other people's money), or what Minksy called the rise of money manager capitalism, changed the vested interests into creditors having claims on capital assets and claims on financial assets. At this stage, the struggle between borrowers and lenders become apparent as the generation of cash flows might be insufficient to meet debt obligations. Rising defaults and delinquencies impose losses on debt holders who use all the power at their disposal to unevenly distribute losses between borrowers and lenders (Kregel 2011; Hudson 2012).

The recent meltdown in the global financial markets and the 'Great Recession' that followed have challenged economists worldwide to explain its roots and to formulate policies that address its consequences. The crisis that began in late summer 2007 emerged as a liquidity problem for lenders that triggered the sale of assets at 'fire sale' prices. This in turn created a major disruption in credit markets resulting in a massive solvency problem in the global financial system that led to rescue plans designed to support a shaky banking systems and various financial institutions. While many mainstream economists attempted to explain the crisis based on failures in the market mechanism and financial frictions, Kregel (2008) emphasized that the 2007-2008 global financial meltdown "had "little to do with the mortgage market (or subprime mortgages per se), but rather with the basic structure of a financial system that overestimates creditworthiness and underprices risk" (Kregel 2008: 24).

The U.S. financial crisis revealed a major weakness of the financial system in which risks were never assessed properly. [9] He argued that, "[t]his is basically due to the fact that those who bear the risk are no longer responsible for evaluating the creditworthiness of borrowers" (Kregel 2008: 21). According to him the "originate and distribute" model [10] is fundamentally flawed because "[u]nder this system, the banker has no interest in credit evaluation, since the interest and principal on the loans originated will be repaid to the final buyers of the collateralized assets" (Kregel 2008, 11). The development of this system also created a widespread illusion of security by employing "risk management models" thereby persuading market participants to price risky mortgage-backed securities as if they were as safe as U.S. government securities.

In addition to loose lending standards, William K. Black has stressed that 'control fraud' produced an "epidemic" of mortgage fraud in the U.S. that we will discuss in detail later. The invention of credit derivative instruments, such as credit default swaps which are derivative

---

[9] Wray (2009) argues that the global financial crisis of 2007-08 was the result of a long historical transformation of the United States economy and it represented the second major collapse of finance capitalism.

[10] This is discussed in detail later in this paper in the section entitled: **Three recent factors that increased system instability**. It is the second factor discussed in that section.

financial products that allows the buyer to speculate on a third party's default, were widely used by investors seeking to short (bet against) a wide range of assets such as risky subprime mortgages and asset-backed securities. What is worse, the same firms selling the asset-backed securities created and sold credit default swaps to investors to bet against those asset-backed securities without disclosing these actions to the buyers of the asset-backed securities (Wray 2012; Lewis 2010).

Three recent factors that increased system instability.

The current crisis had the normal characteristics of increasing instability as the economy grew as described by Minsky. But there are three additional factors that contributed to recent events and the unique characteristics of this crisis.

The first factor is the growth in demand for high quality securities. Many financial institutions, pension funds, and particularly insurance companies, desire or in the latter case are required to hold high-grade securities as reserves. The declining deficits and then surpluses (1998-2001) of the Clinton administration slowed the growth of treasury bonds that were the preferred security. Additionally, financial institutions had to compete with foreign governments and foreign financial institutions that also sought to purchase United States Government bonds. This created excess demand for high-grade, non-government securities. The reason that United States Government securities are highly desired is that they are sovereign debt. They are bonds that the interest and principle are paid in United States currency. Consequently (excepting the insanity of the current Republican members of the United States House of Representatives) there is no possibility of United States government (involuntarily) defaulting on these debt obligations. The executive branch could simply instruct the Treasury to print money to pay its obligations (with or without Congressional approval). Such a policy might eventually become inflationary—but that is hardly a serious concern in the current economic situation.

This excess demand for investment grade securities occasioned the desire to create exotic instruments like securitized debt obligations whether based on home mortgages, credit card debt, or student loans. These new instruments theoretically created a technical means of creating very safe securities by dividing large bundles of this debt into tranches. The best tranches would be very secure, low interest bearing, investment grade securities, other tranches would be riskier, higher interest bearing securities that could be sold to other sorts of investors seeking higher returns.

Securitization allowed the sellers of these securities to tap new sources of income and wealth to be funneled into the financial system. Large fees were paid to originators of the underlying loans and large fees were paid to the firms that bundled this debt and issued these securities. Ratings agencies were complicit in this exercise in that they rated the top tranches of these new securities as investment grade securities. These securities were traded over the counter so that buyers and holders of these securities could, in theory, sell them and obtain liquid assets. This system created the necessary securities that institutions demanded, earned profits for loan originators, investment banks, and other financial firms involved in creating and selling these securities.

This expansion of the securities market and the tapping of new ways of funding debt was not necessarily a bad thing. But it created a huge number of incentives to the participants not to be adequately concerned about the quality of the underlying debt obligations or of the quality of the securities constructed upon that debt.

We mentioned earlier that these new securities were sold over the counter. This means that their valuations in these secondary markets fluctuated through time creating new opportunities for speculation. Many of the financial institutions involved in creating, underwriting and selling these new securities began to hold them as investments and engaged in the secondary trading of these securities on their own account. Again there is nothing intrinsically wrong with these practices. Just as the machine process has impacts on culture and work, the emergence of the captains of finance, or money managers, produced a shift toward generating pecuniary gains by trading financial instruments using external funds. The generation of pecuniary gains through industrial production processes was replaced with active buy and sell strategies by money managers to generate short-term profits.

The second new factor in the current crisis is really the long-term devolution of regulation of the financial services industry. There are a number of interacting processes that led to this devolution. Until the Great Depression reforms American banking could best be described as having a history of chicanery, fraud, mismanagement, and failure. It was so bad that during the Depression bank robbers had higher social standing than the bankers they robbed. The Federal Reserve System and the New Deal banking reforms fundamentally altered this history creating a very safe and stable, but regulated banking system.

There has been a concerted effort by the vested interests assisted by conservative members of the economics profession from the 1950s to the present day to discredit this regulatory regime as hampering economic growth. Government regulation of any sort was seen as a burden on business and a source of economic inefficiency. So they began an intellectual campaign to convince the public and policy makers that the removal of all government regulation was the answer to our economic problems. [11] This movement was a complete failure up until the energy crisis and the deindustrialization and dismantling of the United States' manufacturing industries in the 1970s.

The process of deregulation was given a significant push in the late 1970s when federal financial service industry regulators failed to prohibit thrifts that were not commercial banks from offering deposits subject to check. This privilege had been reserved for commercial banks and was the source of the low cost funds they used for making consumer and business loans. It was the source of and the guarantee of their profitability. Other thrift institutions began to create accounts that had negotiable orders of withdrawal (NOW accounts) thereby allowing these thrifts to create a new means of exchange. Moreover, these thrifts offered interest on these checkable deposits. Naturally deposits left commercial banks and moved to these other thrifts creating a disintermediation crisis. The creation of money market mutual

[11] The neoliberal collective described by Rob Van Horn and Philip Mirowski (2009) was successful through its influence on the academy and through think tanks in changing the policy discourse in the US. Naomi Klein (2008) has ably demonstrated the significance of this ideological movement and its impact on international events in her book *The Shock Doctrine*.

funds in the 1970s also created additional competition for traditional banks as an alternative source to bank deposits and as a provider of liquidity to firms issuing commercial paper (unsecured promissory notes) as an alternative to bank loans (Rezende 2011). Rather than regulators quickly stepping in to prohibit this practice and again restrict checkable, no interest deposits and all other emergent means of payment instruments to commercial banks thereby restoring the viability and stability of commercial banks they allowed the crisis to persist. This created the opportunity anti-regulatory advocates had needed to push their agenda. The Carter administration signed into law the 1980 *Depositary Institutions Deregulation and Monetary Reform Act* that propelled forward the efforts to eliminate the Depression era Banking Act of 1933. These efforts continue today in efforts to stop even the symbolic attempts at reregulation of financial services proposed since the crisis of 2008. The history of banking in the United States was characterized by stability and no crises until the 1970s. From the 1970s to today it has been one financial crisis after the other.

The above historical summary illustrates the general pattern beginning in 1970 when deregulation, promoted on the basis of both the imagined increase in efficiency it would bring and the belief in the efficient markets hypothesis—that financial market would self-regulate because financial and capital markets accurately and continuously re-assessed the value of financial instruments. Financial institutions, managed by rational and competent professionals, acting on behalf of the owners of these institutions, would self-regulate and thus avoid excessively risky behavior. Additionally, audits by reputable and independent auditing firms and ratings by reputable and independent ratings agencies would provide transparency thus insuring against fraudulent behavior. Veblen, who repeatedly described instances of the use of force and fraud by vested interests for personal gain and against the public welfare as revealed in *Reports of the Industrial Commission*, would be unable to contain himself in the face of such fatuous, ahistorical, justifications for the removal of a well-functioning regulatory regime. He would have identified these justifications as enabling myths in service to the fraud committed by those involved.

The other part of the pattern is the election and appointment of government officials who shared the ideological fantasy of the vested interests described above, so that when they attained positions within the regulatory structure that would have allowed them to reign in the excesses and dangerous new practices of the financial firms they regulated, they did not use the authority they had to regulate this behavior. This was taken as further proof that the regulation did not and could not work, fueling the push towards further deregulation.

Put together the cycle of failure to regulate and the ideological fervor of conservative policymakers to deregulate, all with public support, created an environment that was profoundly unstable because the very stabilizing tools went unused or had been removed over the last thirty years. The irrational exuberance, noted by Alan Greenspan as head of the Federal Reserve, rather than sounding an alarm, became a call for further deregulation or legislation prohibiting the regulation of these new practices. The levels of reserves held by firms taking on these new debt obligations were reduced, restrictions on the amount firms could leverage their reserves were reduced, and regulators and executives at the institutions dealing in these new securities admitted they did not understand the new financial instruments.

The final factor contributing to the current crisis is pervasive fraud at every level of the financial system. Systematic and pervasive frauds in the financial services are not new phenomena as we mentioned earlier. Indeed, William Black carefully documented the fraud involved in the Savings and Loan Crisis of the 1980s. The fraud Black documented was the systematic looting of Savings and Loan institutions by their own owners and management, in what he coined "control fraud" (Black 2005).

The fraud leading up to the financial collapse in the United States in 2008 was equally pervasive. The first element of fraud certainly has to be the irresponsible behavior of regulators betraying the public's trust by failing to enforce existing regulations. Of course most of the individuals in charge of regulation efforts are political appointees who are drawn from the executive ranks of the very banks they regulate and are ideologically opposed to regulation in the first place. It is not hard to see why they might be lax, so to speak, in their regulatory efforts. Other regulators are drawn from those in the economics profession who are also ideologically opposed to regulations and not infrequently (before and after their tenure as regulators) draw large fees from the same financial firms that they are regulating as consultants, members of the financial firms' boards, or as employees. But little more need be said except in a democracy you don't always get the public servants you want, but you probably get the ones you deserve.

The second element of fraud that was crucial to the financial crisis had to do with the origination of the loans that were bundled and securitized, especially home mortgages. The traditional lending process for home mortgages was an integrated process involving a commercial bank or thrift issuing a mortgage to a borrower that the bank would hold to maturity. This single institution would internally undertake to determine the creditworthiness of the borrower and the servicing of the mortgage. This was a face-to-face transaction between lenders and borrowers who had a prior and on-going relationship. This process devolved. In the new system a broker or banker originated the loans. The loan originator is paid a fee for creating the loan by the lender and a fee from the applicant. The fee from the lender depends on the nature of the loan product the originator presents to the potential borrower. The broker may or may not offer the potential borrower multiple possibilities or reveal the fees the broker will receive for different loan options. This means that the borrower is not necessarily offered the lowest cost options for their mortgage, indeed, they are most likely to be offered the options that generated the highest fees for the loan originator—who will never have to deal with the borrower again. The loan is turned over to an underwriter for a fee; the underwriter checks to see if the borrower has provided accurate information and assess if the borrower can pay back the loan. An underwriter who does not favorably assess the potential borrower can be replaced. Appraisers are hired for a fee to determine if the property is worth what the seller and buyer claim it is so that the property is adequate collateral for the mortgage. Appraisers working for a fee also have an incentive to deliver appraisals that allow the mortgage process to continue to move forward. The loan is sold to a mortgage company that bundles the loans for securitization. Another company is hired to service the mortgage. This new division of labor in the mortgage creation process means that everyone is working for a fee dependent on the mortgage being made.

None of the firms involved in this new devolved process are actually going to hold the mortgage; so they have no incentive to insure that the mortgage is sound; but instead, to move it along, get it approved, make the deal, and pass it on to the next stage of the process. Consequently, it is just as lucrative for all of these fee-based service providers to make a bad mortgage as a good one. As the housing boom continued the ongoing appreciation in the value of housing meant that most of these loans could be rolled over based on that higher valuation and on better terms by even the weakest borrowers; but when the appreciation of real estate values stopped those with undesirable loans either had to refinance or liquidate. Most could not meet the new more stringent loan requirements or their property was not worth what they had claimed. This led to record foreclosures. But this also meant record defaults on mortgages that meant the securities based on these debt obligations were similarly likely to be in default.

But the companies involved in creating these debt obligations were not the victims of unscrupulous loan origination fraud. These firms offered the loan products to the mortgage brokers and bankers who sold them to lenders in order to provide them with the mortgages to securitize. Kregel (2008) argues that the underlying structure of the United States financial system favors the creation of Ponzi financing schemes. The financing of subprime mortgages and the origination and sale of risky loans, made possible by the originate to distribute model, created inherently fragile Ponzi structures that were guaranteed to fail. This financing system also allowed the rapid growth of control frauds while minimizing the risks of detection and prosecution (Black 2005: 23). We have great reservation about the underlying theoretical soundness of securitization itself; it is based on assumptions about the underlying probability distribution of loan defaults that needs careful empirical examination, but that is a systemic problem and not one of fraud (and beyond the scope of this paper). However, knowing of the underlying flawed process of obtaining these loans, the companies constructing and selling these securities portrayed them as having the same level of risk of default as home mortgages conventionally had during the pre-bubble era (an empirical necessity of the modeling process itself). Moreover, the rising real estate prices associated with the bubble allowed them to portray these mortgages as less risky to their customers. There has been considerable public discloser that the brokers selling these debt instruments considered them junk. The fraudulent nature of the ratings of these securities as investment grade bonds by the prominent ratings agencies has been the subject of Congressional hearings, is also amply documented, and public knowledge. The creation and offering of credit default swaps— essentially insurance for fee against losses as a result of default on these securitized debt obligations—by the same companies selling and holding these same securities as investments and reserves attest to the fundamental dishonesty of those involved in this market. Selling insurance against default on a security while at the same time selling the security to your clients as a good investment is self-dealing and dishonest in a profound way. Selling securities that you are purchasing insurance against default in case you get stuck with them is rational if you know the securities might not be as riskless as you have portrayed them. But selling credit default swaps against securities to other customers -thereby betting they will fail-while holding those same securities as reserves indicates either heretofore unknown levels of stupidity, ignorance, or criminal negligence of fiduciary responsibilities on the part of the executives, officers, advisors and board members of these financial institutions.

Possible Solutions

Veblen rarely wrote about policy matters. Additionally, as we mentioned at the beginning, he limited his efforts at prognostication to what he called the calculable future. This was consistent with his evolutionary methodology. There are many possible policies that might improve our current economic situation. Our discussion will be divided into two parts. The first part will be specific policies and technical adjustments to the financial system designed to address specific problems emerging from the analyses of past and current financial crises. The second part will focus on the broad strokes of institutional adjustments—changes the operating norms and analytic frameworks necessary in order to address the larger systemic conditions that sabotage efforts at change. Our discussion will be limited to policies, institutions, and behaviors with reference to the United States economy, except where otherwise noted.

Specific Policies and Technical Adjustments

Currently, the United States regulatory structure and supervisory system is inadequate to minimize the growth of financial fragility and the transmission of instability within the system. To understand the problems with its current structure it is necessary to redefine banking. As our analysis suggests the nature banking involves the transformation of illiquid IOUs (the liability of borrowers), into liquid instruments used to buy real and financial assets. The creation of debt is essentially a swap of liabilities: the borrower issues its liabilities (for example a loan obligation) and the lender issues its own liability to the borrower that is acceptable in several transactions. This transformation has two primary components: (1) proper credit assessment and underwriting standards and (2) the creation of liquidity. The nature of banking is liquidity creation and the securitization process is banks creating liquidity.

The banking reforms implemented in the 1930s identified the causes of financial instability in the US banking system and based on those findings formulated regulatory reforms to prevent (and also prohibit certain practices) the growth of fragility inside the banking sector. Today we need a similar policy response. First, a serious reform of the financial system has to identify all liquidity creators, their corresponding liquidity creation instruments, and the instruments used as a means of payment, and regulate all liquidity creators in the same manner as traditional banks. Any banking (in the sense described above) institution has to have access to the central bank discount window (or any other permanent lending facility created by the central bank) to minimize funding liquidity risk. While monetary authorities discouraged the use of the discount window to better control the supply of available funds to financial institutions to lend and fight inflation, history has shown that such a view is flawed and is one of the factors that contributed to the transformation of the U.S financial system towards fragility (Rezende 2011).

Traditional depository and shadow banking institutions (hereafter banking institutions) rapidly increased in size in spite of Federal Reserve's contractionary policies. Banking institutions simply created new monetary instruments to expand their balance sheets and access to credit demonstrating that contractionary monetary policy was profoundly limited and ultimately ineffective. This activity resulted in Debt and credit creation in the US exploding to more than 200% of U.S. GDP in 2011 from 100% in the 1980s.

Second, the adoption of minimum underwriting standards to assess loan repayment ability has to be at the core of the banking business. Third, the development of early warning systems based on the identification of the erosion of margins of safety, access to backstop lending facilities and the need of asset liquidation to meet financial needs, and that is able to capture borrower's debt service ability, is necessary. A step in this direction is the work of Tymoigne who developed, based on Minsky's approach, a financial fragility index to capture the growth of financial fragility in the housing sector for different countries (Tymoigne 2012).

Fourth, cash-flow waterfalls from securitized products have to be prohibited to avoid the transmission of fragility. While mainstream economics believe that financial deepening promotes economic growth, it unleashes powerful destabilizing monetary forces that must be contained. Finally, it becomes important to develop a career path for regulators so that they can effectively independently supervise the financial services industry. The regulatory approach has to shift towards a different paradigm, one that recognizes that the worst loans are made during good times and that financial fragility develops during economic expansions. Thus, regulators' independence from pressures stemming from politicians and lobby groups has to be preserved to allow them to enforce regulatory norms during good times.

Addressing Reregulation through Institutional Adjustment

Financial services, regardless of the type of firm offering those services, must be reregulated. If a particular activity of any firm includes taking deposits, making loans, providing a means of exchange, issuing or underwriting securities of any sort, the sale and trading of securities of any sort, currency exchange, selling annuities, or insurance—any financial service—it must be regulated. Innovation is both expected and desired in financial services as it is in all other industries so regulators must have the authority to bring any new product or activity under their authority.

Finance creates credit, credit is money and money is debt the government has a monopoly on the issue of money, and hence any firm engaged in financial services is necessarily doing so at the sufferance of the Federal government so this does not preclude such a policy. Private liquidity creators operationally represent outsourcing of the government's issuance of money powers in the financial sector. Private liquidity creators issue liabilities denominated in the state currency, or promises to pay cash at some future date. When those institutions become too big to fail, then expectation of government intervention to rescue these firms increases the moral hazard created by the system.

Since the products and practices of the financial services industry will evolve as the society as a whole evolves the regulatory structure must evolve in response. This means new regulatory regimes need to be conceptualized in a co-evolutionary framework which we have discussed elsewhere (Rezende and Waller 2012). The reconceptualized regulatory regime must have the flexibility and the real time information to respond to changes in the behavior of firms and financial market instability in a timely fashion.

Regulators must be held accountable for both their actions and inaction. Regardless of the ideological climate, individuals who accept the responsibility to serve as a regulator must be committed and compelled to enforce existing regulations. Their discretion should be limited. And supervision and management of regulatory agencies should not be in the hands of individuals who themselves have been recruited from the management of the regulated firms. The revolving door must be eliminated. Put simply, bankers can't regulate bankers. The executives of the financial service firms have demonstrated that they cannot self-regulate. Leaving the stability of our economies and financial systems to the vagaries of the markets is also foolish because markets do not, on their own, reward, select, or create stability, indeed, quite the contrary.

Once a new regulatory regime is in place, the penalties for violation must be severe, indeed, draconian. Individuals violating these regulations should receive long prison sentences, confiscation of all ill-gotten gains plus significant fines, and a life-long ban from further participation in the financial service industry in any capacity. Financial service firms that violate regulations should be forced to give up all ill-gotten gains, face crippling fines, and their operations be put in regulator's hands until all executives and employees involved in the violations are removed from their jobs. When all injured parties are financially restored and fines paid, then these firms might be allowed to resume private operation. However, the possibility of receivership leading to liquidation of the firm should remain an option, especially for repeat offenders.

Institutional Adjustments for Dealing with Failed Firms

Financial firms should never be bailed out. They should be resolved. Their assets should be used to compensate those who have been harmed by their activities—but most especially *not their investors*. Reserves should be required sufficient to insure relative stability based on historical, non-investment-bubble levels, though this will obviously be a matter for much study and discussion. The amount of leverage financial firms will be allowed should be regulated to a modest amount since all such leverage is a tax on the industrial system of production, adding nothing but income to the propertied classes, paid for through higher prices by consumers.

Breaking-up large financial services firms into smaller units or liquidating them completely should be the remedy for resolving large firms in difficulty and insolvency. We should never again allow financial service firms to grow large enough to compromise the stability of the financial system. Those that remain should be encouraged to down size or split into several smaller firms. If they should become unstable or insolvent they should also be put in federal receivership and liquidated. [12]

---

[12] Minsky suggest similar resolution processes for very large firms. See Minsky (2008: 368-369).

Finance has to be reoriented to allow the expansion of the capital stock of the economy rather than the funding of financial assets. Bank credit and capital markets funding play an crucial role in financing the working capital needs of firms and long-term investment projects. The expansion of credit growth to acquire financial assets has to be contained to minimize the impact of the resulting asset price inflation (it increases the cost of borrowing for firms for productive reasons).

Additional Suggested Institutional Adjustments

The United States government should issue bonds to meet the needs of financial service firms to hold in reserve or as safe investments. Sovereign debt should be used to stabilize the financial sector. Moreover, the government should use the its monetary powers to employ their citizens and create an employment buffer stock. This raises real questions as to the viability of the Eurozone. Countries adopting the Euro have given up their ability to issue sovereign debt in their own currency to meet their needs to stabilize their financial and real sectors. Their economies are at the mercy of the politics of their currency union partners. This eliminates their most powerful tool for stabilizing their financial sector and guaranteeing full employment.

In the United States consumer and business banking must be re-stabilized. The profitability of institutions offering checkable, insured deposits and making consumer and business loans always needed a guarantee of its profitability. While turning back the clock is not possible, the government can recover its monopoly on providing a means of payment and restrict checkable deposits, debit cards, negotiated orders of withdrawal and other such means of payment to specific types of banks and other thrifts at regulated interest rates.

All securities should be traded in well-supervised exchanges rather than unregulated over the counter markets. This is especially true with new and emerging financial instruments. Often exotic financial instruments and products trade in a very shallow secondary market consisting of relatively few buyers and sellers. This creates the possibility that decisions by a few of the participants in these markets could create extremely variable price fluctuations that are not based on any change in the underlying debts. A well-regulated market with real time access to this information could insure that such decisions and their consequences were limited to revaluations and not cause panics.

Both Veblen (1978: 203-205) and Minsky noted that bankruptcy resolves firms' financial difficulties. Indeed, Minsky (2008: 234, footnote 10) noted that bankruptcy could transform both Ponzi and speculative financing into nice, safe hedge financing. But both noted that this process is extremely socially disruptive, sometimes for the economy as a whole and always for the common folks. Unwinding and resolving the Savings and Loan crisis of the 1980s in the United States was expensive for taxpayers and adversely affected the economy. We do not really have a regular economic institution for containing the damage of failing firms and preventing their failure from causing additional firms' bankruptcies and creating overall economic instability.

Bailouts have restored the wealth of vested interests and restored system stability at the expense of the real sector of the economy. Often the victims of the firms (whose misbehavior or poor decision-making resulted in the bailout) end up paying for the restoration of their victimizer while receiving no assistance themselves. This is what happened to mortgage holders in the recent financial crisis. So bailouts as a policy, reward the miscreants, at the expense of the victims. As such they do not serve as a deterrent to future bad behavior.

Liquidation of insolvent firms is an appropriate way of redistributing the remaining assets among a firm's creditors. Alas, one firm's failure may very well precipitate additional failures among its creditors magnifying the effect of the single firm's failure. However, if firms facing liquidation were given over to a conservator to resolve its debts and with an agency to make low cost loans for uncompensated balances to debtor firms so that they too were not sent into bankruptcy some damage could be avoided. Of course if the initial firm's bankruptcy, were not a function of bad decision-making, but instead structural problems in the economy, more systemic policy options would have to be considered. Workers employed at failed firms are often the overlooked creditors of failed firms. If the government served as employer of last resort to stabilize employment as it serves as lender of last resort to stabilize finance for the vested interest, then some modicum of social justice might emerge.

The Unlikelihood of Genuine Change

Veblen noted that the engineers of his day were the only class able to operate the modern industrial economy in order to preserve the common peoples' quality of life in the event of a revolution removing the dead hand of propertied interests' sabotage of the industrial system. But Veblen noted that the engineering class was divided, many of its members sharing ideological predispositions and identifying their interest with those of the propertied class that employed them. Thus while able to replace their masters—they were not, in the calculable future, inclined to lead or participate in such a transformative social movement.

We are in a similar situation today. The people today with the knowledge, skills and experience to operate our modern industrial economies remain (for the most part) the faithful retainers of the propertied class. Financial engineering is now at the center of the income generation process for both financial and nonfinancial firms. Moreover, our current day engineers often aspire to become members of that propertied class (and on rare occasion succeed just often enough to contribute to the continued belief in the possibility of upward mobility for members of the property-less classes). Additionally, the reactionary, market ideology driven political ethos of the citizenry of many modern industrial economies precludes the likelihood that the policies recommended above will even enter policy discussions much less have a serious chance of being adopted. The many restrictions and regulations on capital and financial markets we have suggested are ideologically unacceptable in the current political climate. And the simple fact that these policies would limit the ability of the vested interests to continue the process of diverting income to themselves by adding the costs of finance to the prices of the material means of life paid by the common people, means those vested interests will resist them with all of the considerable resources at their disposal.

As in Veblen's time, pragmatic solutions to our economic problems exist. There are many people trained in the techniques of operating our industrial economies and in proposing public policy solutions aimed at solving our current problems. But obsolete, enabling myths of idealized and perfect markets, inculcated in the public consciousness, supported by vested interests, and reinforced by ideologically bound practitioners within the economic profession, ensure that no real transformation or reform of the price system in general and the financial system in particular is possible. Indeed, this confluence of myth, public opinion and the political power of the propertied vested interests insure that even minor progress of reform is probably beyond our reach in the calculable future. Nevertheless, we can still choose to press for transformation and reform or to throw our fate to blind drift.

References

Black, William K. 2005. "Control frauds" as financial super-predators: How "pathogens" make financial markets inefficient. *The Journal of Socio-Economics* 34 (6): 734-755.

Galbraith, John Kenneth.1955. *The Great Crash 1929*. Boston: Houghton Mifflin.

_____. 1967. *The New Industrial State*. Boston: Houghton Mifflin.

Hamilton, Walton. 1938. *Price and Price Policies*. New York: McGraw-Hill.

Hudson, M. 2012. The Road to Debt Deflations, Debt Peonage, and Neofeudalism. *Levy Institute Working Paper* No. 708. Annandale-on-Hudson, New York: Levy Institute.

Klein, Naomi. 2008. *The Shock Doctrine*. New York: Picador.

Kregel, Jan. 2007. The Natural Instability of Financial Markets. *Levy Institute Working Paper* No. 708. Annandale-on-Hudson, New York: Levy Institute.

_____. 2008. Using Minsky's Cushions of Safety to Analyze the Crisis in the U.S. subprime Mortgage Market. *International Journal of Political Economy* 37 (1): 3-23.

_____. 2011. Debtors' Crisis or Creditors' Crisis? Who Pays for the European Sovereign and Subprime Mortgage Losses? *Levy Economics Institute Public Policy Brief* No. 121. Annandale-on-Hudson, New York: Levy Institute.

Lewis, Michael. 2010. *The big short : inside the doomsday machine*. New York: W.W. Norton & Co.

Means, Gardiner. 1992. Industrial Prices and Their Relative Inflexibility. In *The Heterodox Economics of Gardiner C. Means: A Collection*, eds. F. Lee and W. Samuels. Armonk, New York: M.E. Sharpe Inc.

_____. 1992. How to Control Inflation in the United States. In *The Heterodox Economics of Gardiner C. Means: A Collection*, eds. F. Lee and W. Samuels. Armonk, New York: M.E. Sharpe Inc.

Minsky, Hyman P. 1992. Schumpeter and Finance. In Market and Institutions in Economic Development: Essays in Honour of Paolo Sylos Labini, eds. A.R. Salvatore Biasco and Michel Salvati. New York: St. Martin's Press.

_____. 2008. (1986). *Stabilizing an Unstable Economy*. New York: McGraw-Hill.

Rezende, F. C. d. 2011. The Structure and the Evolution of the U.S. Financial System, 1945-1986. *International Journal of Political Economy* 40 (2): 21-44.

Rezende, F. C. d. and William Waller. 2012. An Evolutionary Approach to Regulation: The Case of Financial Services. Presented at the *Annual Meeting of the Western Social Science Association and the Association for Institutional Economics*. Houston, TX. Unpublished.

Tymoigne, E. 2012. Measuring Macroprudential Risk Through Financial Fragility: A Minskyan Approach. *Levy Economics Institute, Working Paper* No. 716. Annandale-on-Hudson: Levy Institute.

Van Horn, Rob and Philip Mirowski. 2009. The Rise of the Chicago School of Economics and the Birth of Neoliberalism. In *The Road from Mont Pelerin: The Making of the Neoliberal Thought Collective*, eds. Philip Mirowski and Dieter Plehwe. Cambridge: Harvard University Press.

Veblen, Thorstein B. 1934 (1899). *The Theory of the Leisure Class.* New York: Modern Library.

_____. 1978. (1904). *The Theory of Business Enterprise.* New Brunswick: NJ: Transactions Press.

_____. 1921. *The Engineers and the Price System.* New York: B.W. Huebsch.

Waller, William. 2007. Veblen's missing theory of markets and exchange, or can you have an economic theory without a theory of market exchange? In *Thorstein Veblen and the Revival of Free Market Capitalism,* eds. J. Knoedler, R. Prasch and D. Champlin. Northampton, MA: Edward Elgar.

Whalen, Charles. 2012. Post-Keynesian Institutionalism after the Great Recession. *Levy Economics Institute Working Paper* No. 724. Annandale-on-Hudson, NY: Levy Institute.

Veblen's Theory of Business Cycles [1]

Gülenay Baş Dinar

Introduction

Veblen examined the features of modern capitalism in his seminal works *The Theory of Business Enterprise* (1904) and *Absentee Ownership* (1923). He reasons the most distinctive characteristic of 19th century capitalism is that production becomes a monetary phenomenon. By this he means businessmen direct their efforts to financial rather than industrial activities.

According to Veblen, businessmen engage in financial instead of production activities. He claims the behavior of businessmen actually inhibit the efficient functioning of industry. In the interests of business enterprise, it is necessary production be reduced or slowed in order to ensure more profit. As a result, the profit motive of businessmen overshadows the means of industrial production. Veblen conceptualizes business enterprise (financial activities) as a conservative element that hinders institutional development and classifies businessmen's activities as a static institution. In this regard, Veblen expresses that these institutions are in conflict with dynamic institutions directed at material production.

Veblen's ideas form the foundation for his business cycles theory. He characterizes the attitudes of businessmen and financiers in a modern financial economy as a mere continuation of predatory instincts located in the primitive stage of human development. In this regard, Veblen emphasizes the conflict between industrial activities that are beneficial to society and predatory activities (based on exploitation) that are harmful to both the community and industrial development. The version of this conflict — exercised in modern capitalist conditions — represents the conflict between financial and industrial activities. As becomes evident across the course of this essay, Veblen draws attention to the dichotomy between financial and industrial activities and focuses on the effects of this dichotomy on the economy. In particular, he concentrates on how domination of financial over industrial activities is cause for instabilities and fluctuations in the economy. Veblen asserts that fluctuations in the economy do not originate in the industrial sector, but are born out of the activities that business enterprises execute in order to accrue profit. In this sense, Veblen indicates that crises in the modern economy are not a result of the industrial economy but rather of the monetary economy (Veblen1920/1904: 180).

This essay studies Veblen's rationale regarding fluctuations in the economy under conditions of modern capitalism, taking as a basis, the conflict he defined between industrial and business (financial) activities. To this purpose, the study comprises three parts. First, Veblen's opinions about modern capitalism are analyzed; in the second part, his ideas on economic instabilities are explained and the essay concludes with a discussion on how Veblen's notions about instabilities in the economy may be utilized to understand the current financial crisis.

---

1 I would like to thank Ahmet Öncü, Anita Oğurlu and Cem Somel for their valuable comments and suggestions.

The Basic Elements of Modern Capitalism in Veblen's Analysis

Veblen argues capitalism enters a new stage beginning in the second half of the 19th century. He describes the era as one based on a credit economy that is distinctly different from the previous period because capital markets drive the economy rather than former commodity markets. In *The Theory of Business Enterprise* and *Absentee Ownership*, Veblen analyzes the features of modern capitalism in detail with an aim to locate and define the institutional reasons for instabilities. In this context, the most significant feature of modern capitalism in the 19th century is that production becomes a monetary process where businessmen engage in financial rather than industrial activities. The main features of modern capitalism are realized through a change in the conceptual understanding of capital that shifts to the diffusion of credit use.

Veblen describes the *machine process* as activities for improving industrial production to benefit the general welfare of the community carried out by employees, laborers, engineers, and technicians. In contrast, he defines *pecuniary employment* or *business enterprise* that is not directly related to material production, as activities of property owners, entrepreneurs and businessmen to gain financial profit. Veblen emphasizes that industrial activities have dynamic features while non-industrial activities have conservative features. Industrial production processes and use of machines are a source of progressive institutional change whereas financial business or business enterprise is as an obstacle to benefit institutional change. Thus, a conflict arises between these two institutions in modern capitalism.

In addition, Veblen points out that the traditional role of an entrepreneur becomes differentiated as a result of the machine process itself (industrial business) toward business enterprise (financial business), a condition that arises in modern capitalism. In *The Engineers and The Price System* Veblen defines entrepreneur as "a technical term to designate the man who takes care of the financial end of things". In this respect, an entrepreneur has diverse functions as a *businessman, corporation financier* and *financial manager* (Veblen 1954/1921: 29).

Over time, the entrepreneur lost his function as a progressive force for dynamic technological development—the role he once occupied in the early 19th century. By the end of the 19th century, for Veblen, the entrepreneur has evolved into an entity whose sole aim is to accumulate wealth from financial rather than industrial activities. The thrust of his argument is that the entrepreneur becomes a *corporation financier* from the second half of the 19th century onward. Entrepreneurs deal with controlling industry in line with their profits instead of improving the productive capacity of industry, as was once their main function (Veblen 1954/1921: 30-31; 1964/1923: 82-83).

Veblen defines the innovative entrepreneur of yesteryear—one who performs production activities with an aim to increase profit by decreasing production costs through technological development—as a *captain of industry*. He suggests the number of such entrepreneurs decreased by the late 19th century, when business activities came to dominate industry. A new type of entrepreneur emerges whose chief aim is to accrue profits through financial activities (Veblen 1954/1921: 33). With the emergence of this entrepreneurial type, his status as an entrepreneur and main actor in capitalist development alters with his abandonment of industrial activities.

The entrepreneur no longer continues to be the main force for social change through technological development. Instead, the entrepreneur becomes a static individual focusing on financial profit rather than being dynamic and open to development, hence he hinders institutional change (Gürkan 2007: 269-270).

Consequently, the relation between financial capital and industrial processes becomes modified through the creation and implementation of credit economy conditions that alters the concept of capital accordingly. For this reason, Veblen divides capital into two—industrial capital and financial capital—suggesting that the value of these types of capital is determined separately. The magnitude of financial capital changes independently from changes in the magnitude of industrial capital. In this context, financial capital changes as a result of assessments driven by actors in capital markets altering and directing the value of capital. Hence, the value of financial capital is mostly determined by 'folk psychology'. [2] By contrast, the value of industrial capital is related with tangible processes (Veblen 1920/1904: 148-149).

Determining the value of financial capital mostly based on folk psychology causes instability in the value of financial capital. Moreover, under the conditions of a modern credit economy, corporate managers also have the power to change the value of financial capital in the market through various maneuvers. [3] Corporation managers engage in business coalitions and organizations in order to increase their profit. The purpose of their activities is to control the buying and selling of assets. As a result, an illusory false perception is created in the market that works to benefit the manager, but also inevitably causes instability and volatility in the value of financial capital.

One of the main characteristics of the modern credit economy is the diffusion of credit use skewed in line with internal activities of corporations. Credit use may occur in various ways ranging from purchases and sales of contracts and loans from commercial banks to exporting securities. Credit plays a central role in the finance era of capitalism because credit increases the turnover rate of capital and forms the most important basis of sustaining financial profits in this respect. For Veblen, it is not possible for a capitalist market economy to expand without credit. Thus, one of the main characteristics of financial capitalism is credit use. Credit use ensures entrepreneurs grow their existing capital, realize production in more efficient ways and craft more competitive methods by way of sales activities. Also, businessmen make new investments with credit. In Veblen's analysis, credit is the main element of expansionist trends emerging in the economy. Increase in credit use becomes the reason for an increase in business activities. Veblen thinks that in most cases both exist simultaneously (1920/1904: 190).

---

[2] The concept folk psychology has an important place in philosophy and cognitive sciences after the 1950s. It is used to refer to a particular set of cognitive capacities that include the prediction and explanation of behavior. Philosophers sometimes use folk psychology synonymously with 'commonsense psychology' (Ravenscroft 2010). Veblen used it to explain "variations of confidence on the part of investors [...] current belief as to the probable policy or tactics of the business men in control [...] forecasts as to the seasons and the tactics of the guild of politicians, and on the indeterminable, largely instinctive, shifting movements of public sentiment and apprehension" (1920/1904: 149).

[3] Veblen called the corporate managers "masters of financial intrigue" who are "highly skilled in the higgling of the market" (Veblen 2005/1919: 89).

The essential factor behind credit expansion is a raised expectation of profits that increases accordingly the value of the corporations' capital assets. Increase in the value of capital assets of the corporation stimulates the use of more credit. And the use of more credit results in an increase in business activities. Credit use raises capitalized values, which in turn facilitates the use of more credit and increases the difference between values of industrial and business capital (Wray 2007: 618). Credit is not only the central facilitator of a speculative expansionist period emerging in the economy for Veblen, but also one of the main reasons for the start of a deflationary period. Here, the significant point in his analysis is how credit-loans, stock prices and capital cause fluctuations in the economy during periods of prosperity, crisis and depression (Raines and Leathers 2008: 63).

Veblen's Theory of Business Cycles

The reason capitalism is internally prone to crises stems, in Veblen's view, from the fact that businessmen and financers do not produce goods to meet the needs of consumers but on the contrary focus on financial activities to secure greater profits. He criticizes explicators of the traditional economy for merely explaining the reasons for economic crises within the frame of industrial activity. In contrast, Veblen proposes the main reason for fluctuations in a modern economy should investigate the speculative activities of business enterprise that seek to gain more profit.

Veblen's theory provides concrete reasons for fluctuations in economic activity. Importantly, he points out two significant features. First, he examines the role of altering prices; current and expected profits; and tangible and intangible capital assets and how they provoke fluctuations. Second, he explains the emergence of prosperity and depression periods on the basis of psychology (Veblen 1920/1904: 185-186). Both of the above play a crucial role in Veblen's theory of business cycles.

Fluctuations in the economy basically stem from financial activities, but Veblen keenly points out that instability in the financial sector inevitably spreads to the industrial system to negatively affect the entire economy since financiers already control activity in the industrial sector. Furthermore, expansionist and prosperity periods are followed by depression periods or rather the circumstances they bring about act as precursors to a depression. But, according to Veblen, every depression is not a forerunner of an expansion period (1920/1904: 183). The main factor causing business cycles in the economy is the change in prices. Veblen makes a crucial point here because the factors defining the expansionist and deflationary periods are related to prices. In Veblen's own words, "since business has become the central and controlling interest, the question of welfare has become a question of price" (1920/1904: 177).

Veblen asserts it is possible to divide business cycles into three phases namely, expansion, deflation and chronic depression. The following sections address his analysis on how the conditions of expansion and prosperity periods cause economic depressions.

The Expansion Period

Veblen suggests an expansionist period, which he describes as periods of speculative advance, 'eras of prosperity' or 'brisk times' starts with the rise of prices (1920/1904: 180, 198). Price rises primarily occur as a result of demand generated in one or several industries. An increase in demand in certain industries generates, overall, an atmosphere of optimism. Owing to a psychology of optimism, setting higher prices becomes a kind of habit to increase putative profits in economic activities (Veblen 1920/1904: 198).

By increasing prices businessmen maximize their profits. Success depends on the realization of profits. In other words, the businessman should sell the produced goods in such a way to gain higher sales profits than the capital required for production. To this end, the businessman acts to maximize the difference between the starting capital and sales revenue. Higher prices also increase the production of goods by firms and thus putative aggregate sales revenues enable more profit. Firms hoping to benefit from an artificial rise in prices expand their industrial activity by either enhancing their production capacity or making new investments. Increased prices combined with optimistic expectations for the future, actually work to increase the capital asset prices of corporations (Veblen 1920/1904: 247).

In Veblen's analysis, the rise of asset prices initiates an expansion period in the economy. In the expansionist period, asset prices rise for two reasons. First, as mentioned above, a rise in prices tends to stimulate optimistic expectations in the economy due to increasing demand in one or more sector(s) and second, the conscious manipulation of capital asset prices by corporation managers increases profit based on the difference between current earning capacity and expected earning capacity.

Within the conditions of a credit economy, Veblen claims capital is tangible and intangible. The value of intangible capital, what he defines as 'goodwill' is determined based on the perception and expectations of public opinion in the market whereas tangible capital mostly reflects the putative earning capacity of the corporation. Moreover, the current earning capacity of the industrial capital value of the corporation may differ from the putative earning capacity because the value of these two types of capital is determined by different factors.

It is in the best interests of a corporation manager to create a difference between the current earning capacity and putative earning capacity of the firm because in case the putative earning capacity is higher than the current earning capacity, the corporation manager has the possibility to increase profits by selling the capital assets of the corporation. Thus, corporation managers offer capital asset prices higher than the actual prices in order to earn more profit and increase asset prices. Since outsiders generally have limited or incorrect information about the corporation, corporation managers, called "insiders" by Veblen, can easily achieve their goals. Consequently, corporation managers' activities that involve manipulating asset prices by showing them higher than their real value is cause for an atmosphere of artificial or illusory optimism in the economy.

An optimistic atmosphere in the economy makes credit use attractive for investors. The firms, whose profit expectations rise due to increased prices, either export bonds or use credit from banks, in addition to their internal sources, in order to fuel investments. As a result of the increase in actual and putative profit expectations and manipulation of asset prices by corporation managers, high asset prices function as collateral for credit. Aggregate spending power in the community expands and for Veblen this spells an increase in demand and increase in the use of credit. Increased demand causes an increase in prices and thus inflationist trends in the economy. Increased prices, owing to inflation, encourage the use of new credit that, in turn, triggers speculative expansion (Veblen 1920/1904: 198).

Due in part to the abovementioned speculative trend, an increase in social welfare hinges on the psychology of businessmen (Veblen 1920/1904: 195). Speculative expectations that profits will forever increase, becomes widespread across the entire economy. Debt in the business sector rises as corporate managers acquire more debt and export more securities thus causing dependency on the increase in capitalization of corporation assets (Veblen 1920/1904: 99-100).

Credit plays a central role in the emergence of this cycle. For Veblen, an expansion period is not possible without the increased use of credit. Credit has an enlarging effect on the economy not only by ensuring future purchase-sales contracts but also through the practice of borrowing. Profits accrued in the expansionist period—owing to increased prices and credit use—actually lowers costs incurred by businessmen. In fact, their costs remain lower than those needed to accrue profits by enhancing production. Obviously credit use becomes more attractive to businessmen because it ensures an increase in investment and the signing of lucrative business contracts (Veblen 1920/1904: 95). The most significant feature of an expansionist period is that it encourages an increase in optimistic expectations for the future and hence increases capital asset prices of the corporation (Veblen 1920/1904: 197-198). In Veblen's evaluation, high asset prices are the most significant source of prosperity during this period since they increase expected profitability rates and credit use. Therefore, Veblen's main focus in *The Theory of Business Enterprise* is not the rise in prices of consumer goods but rather the rise in asset prices because the rise of consumer goods prices are directly related with demand. But asset prices are related to capital that is also directly related to profits (Veblen 1920/1904: 194). Rising asset prices disclose that prosperity is a psychologically driven phenomenon fostered by optimistic expectations of businessmen about future profits, hence investments increase speculatively.

At this point, the realization of profits poses an important problem. A gain in future profits must be higher than outstanding debts such that investments financed through borrowing—due to optimistic expectations—remain profitable. It is vital prices be kept high. Another significant issue in terms of profit realization is the turnover rate of the capital of businessmen. The faster the turnover is, the higher their profits. In this respect, businessmen take efforts to shorten the turnover rate in production. There are two basic approaches to shorten the capital turnover rate. The first is to accelerate production through technological development. The second is to increase the price level by adopting more competitive methods vis-à-vis sales strategies such as advertising, which is an easier and more preferable method for businessmen (Veblen 1920/1904: 93-94).

Although the latter always seems to be a better and more preferable method for businessmen, they also employ advances in production technologies to enhance their competitiveness. However, the efforts of capitalists to this end also constitute one reason for the system to enter a chronic depression. A decrease in costs due to technological developments also brings about a fall in prices and thus profitability levels. But a fall in prices and profitability levels can be quelled by creating demand in the way of wasteful consumption, war and military expenditures. In this manner, the prosperity period can be temporarily prolonged. But according to Veblen, the economy is eventually bound to enter a chronic depression period expressed by low profit rates and underproduction.

The Deflation Period

In Veblen's analysis, prices are the main factor not only for inciting a period of prosperity but also for starting a deflationary period. The latter eliminates the advantageous difference between the current earning capacity and putative earning capacity in the prosperity period, resulting in a decrease in profit expectations and investment in the economy.

In Veblen's mind, the main reason for an economy to enter deflation is the disappearance of the differential advantage in the expansion period between the putative earning capacity and current earning capacity. In this case, the expected profitability levels cannot be realized through increased investments brought about by high prices in the expansion period. The rise in prices once driven by demand in a period of prosperity weakens and eliminates the opportunity for firms to secure more investments and generate high profits. Inevitably, the economy spirals in to a depression.

A deflationary period in the economy may generally be signaled by the bankruptcy of a firm or a considerable decrease in demand for the goods it produces. In such a case, it is recognized that the current earning capacity of the corporation is lower than its expected earning capacity. In other words, its asset prices are artificially high. Creditors identify the value of the assets (accepted as collateral against credit) as higher than the real value causing the firm to face a liquidation crisis. Creditors may demand their credit back or ask for additional collateral against their loans. In corollary, a fall in prices impedes firms from fulfilling their commitments. When credit institutions decide a firm has a liquidity problem, the firm is unable to fulfill its liabilities through refunding. And when a firm cannot fulfill its liabilities—owing to credit used to enhance financial activities with the anticipation of high profit expectations in the expansionist period— creditors are inclined to sell some of the firms' assets to generate collateral that eventually spells a change of ownership for the firm (Veblen 1920/1904: 192).

One significant feature of a depression period is the low rate of interest. Based on the former capitalization process, in case of a bankruptcy or transfer of a firms' excessive liabilities, new investments are made at lower interest rates, therefore enabling an advantageous difference between the current and putative earning capacity. An entrepreneur likely perceives this a reasonable advantage. Thus a change in ownership and new capitalization in an economic crisis is realized on the basis of low interest rates. Production from new investments can be sold at lower prices, which causes a fall in prices and acute difficulties for firms with liabilities based on previous capitalization (Veblen 1920/1904: 218).

The expected profitability rate of new investments at the beginning of a depression, according to Veblen, is relatively high due to low interest rates. While technological innovations in the industrial process initiate the production of capital goods through more effective methods, there is still a fall in the price of capital goods that strengthens the advantageous position of new investors in the market. Thus, new firms and new owners of old firms entering industry in a depression period obtain capital goods at lower prices. One of the main reasons for the depression is that old capital has to compete with new capital. Lower market prices set by new investments decrease the profitability level of old investors. Production also decreases because old investors recognize it is not feasibly profitable to produce at such low prices (Veblen 1920/1904: 230).

Veblen offers that despite a number of contracts that support demand in industries, the psychological effects of amassing wealth incite a "habit of buoyancy" and "speculative recklessness" permitting speculative prosperity to continue indefinitely (1920/1904: 196). As in an expansionist period, asset prices also play a central role at the start of a depression because credit institutions realize the value of the assets accepted as collateral for loans are higher than the real value. Creditors panic because of insufficient collateral and demand their payment of credit or request additional securities for credit. Widespread anxiety in the economy prompts the depression to deepen and spiral into a prolonged crisis (Veblen 1920/1904: 202).

The main factor characterizing this crisis period is the decrease in loans or a reluctance to lend thanks, in part, to the fall in asset prices due to low future profitability expectations. Falling asset prices cause a 'credit crunch' [4] and eventually a crisis (depression). Therefore, in Veblen's analysis, asset prices are the main corruptive power that derails the economy and creates an atmosphere of panic inciting investors to make rash, sudden decisions that reek havoc in the economy.

As we have seen, in Veblen's analysis there are two main elements that trigger a depression in the economy. First, precipitous asset prices brought on by a 'credit crunch' and second, a significant decrease in profitability levels of old investors due to competitive price levels created by new investors and a decrease in the production costs of capital goods. Veblen put it this way: "An industrial crisis is a period of liquidation, cancelment of credits, high discount rates, falling prices and "forced sales" and shrinkage of values" (1920/1904: 191).

The Chronic Depression Period

A period of prosperity cannot be sustained indefinitely and sooner or later will devolve into a chronic depression. Veblen termed this period a 'protracted depression.' For him, one of the central reasons the economy enters a chronic depression is that businessmen still seek more financial profit and, as a result, trigger the use of credit and a speculative increase in investments. Within this context, as long as the element determining the value of the capital is its earning capacity, entrepreneurs will forever attempt to create a difference between current earning capacity and putative earning capacity which will drive the economy into an inevitable depression. Hence, for Veblen, a chronic depression stems from the business activities of entrepreneurs. Succinctly, a chronic depression is directly related to the earning instinct of businessmen (Veblen 1920/1904: 213).

---

4 'Credit crunch' is not a Veblenian term. First appearing in 1906 - incidentally the year there was a stock market decline - it is likely a conceptual term used by U.S. media to dissuade populist anxiety over banks not giving credit. It temporarily stands in for the recognized economic terms recession and depression. Mainstream media used the term 'credit crunch' in the 1970s and from mid-2007 onward (Kehoe and Gee 2009: 260, 273).

The most significant result of a depression period is that the price level no longer ensures the realization of profits desired by businessmen and for this reason production decreases when they concede it unprofitable to produce. Costs of a depression to the community are high. Consumer goods needed to sustain a community decrease as unemployment rises (Raines and Leathers 2008: 68).

Veblen argues it in correct to assume the economy faces overproduction or under consumption in a chronic depression. As he put it: "The supply of consumable goods is, practically, never greater than the community's capacity for consuming them" (1920/1904: 215). On the contrary, there is a state of underproduction in times of depression. Even in a depression, a large productive capacity exists, with an abundance of competitive producers but with too much industrial apparatus to supply the market at profitable prices. Owing to immense production capacities, too many efficient producers, and a surplus of costs, these harrowing elements deter the possibility to maintain prices at a reasonable level (Veblen 1920/1904: 217). In short, full employment is not profitable in an age of mass production where costs are reduced through new technologies because these technologies initiate a fall in prices and hence, putative profits in the economy. To eliminate the situation—unwanted by investors—monopolies become alternatives and production is taken below its potential level by taking measures to eliminate competition in the market (Dillard 1980: 266).

Veblen considers chronic depression in the economy as a normal situation under financial capitalism and views periods of prosperity, emerging at times, as temporary exceptional incidents derailing the economy from chronic inflation (Veblen 1920/1904: 253, 184). Based on his observation of the U.S. economy in the last decade of the 19th to the beginning of the 20th century, Veblen stated, "during this recent period, and with increasing persistency, chronic depression has been the rule rather than the exception in business" (1920/1904: 251). The normal situation in modern financial capitalism is that of chronic depression or what he termed "dull times". Dullness *is* the essence of the process. Buoyancy or "brisk times" is "a temporary and exceptional situation granted by God or created by people" (Veblen 1920/1904: 183).

Of considerable importance in Veblen's analysis, is the role of technological development in capital goods production. The price of capital goods in competitive markets falls as the production cost of industrial equipment constantly decreases triggering the precipitous price of goods produced with new equipment, and with it, a permanent shrinkage in profits. Due to the unbridled speculative activity by an outsider the earning capacity of old investors precipitously decreases with constancy. Hence, over time, the circumstances ensuring profitability of new investments will change and this will result in a new period of crisis.

Conclusion

The great financial crisis that unsettled the world in the late 20th and early 21st centuries proves neoclassical economics and its variants fail to explain the crisis. This unfortunate circumstance is coupled with the generally accepted idea the current crisis should be managed with more heterodox economic models. This study addressed explanations Veblen offered on macroeconomic instability.

That Veblen grounds his investigation on the dichotomy between industrial and financial activities is striking. One of the main topics of debate over the current financial crisis is that financial activities dominate industrial activities, hindering development. Veblen highlights precisely this phenomenon in his assessment of the unstable structure of capitalism. Respectively, Veblen includes money in his analysis as a variable affecting the level of economic activity and continues his analysis within the framework of a monetary production economy. He emphasizes the unstable structure of capitalism by examining instabilities embedded in capitalism based on the tension between financial and industrial activities. Additionally, he stresses a change in future profit expectations are the main destructive power that foment crises and depressions in the economy.

To explain the current financial crisis, three aspects underscore Veblen's economic analysis. First, a focus on *asset price bubbles* in his *business cycle* theory. Second, the role of *insiders* and *outsiders* on financial instability — incidentally the central thrust of Veblen's analysis — is an important topic in current debates. Third, the decrease in costs as a result of technological change. Veblen's analysis is useful to understand the current financial crisis as he addresses some of the most crucial factors emerging as financial instabilities in today's economies.

The issue of *asset price bubbles* forms the basis of Veblen's *business cycle* theory. The rise of asset prices has a central place in driving an economy into an expansionist period. Asset prices do not only drive the economy into an expansion period but also are the main reason for entering into a deflationary period. Asset prices are the corruptive power that derails the economy by creating an atmosphere of panic inciting investors to make sudden, rash decisions that generate turmoil. Today's crises are mainly characterized by the excessive inflation of asset prices. Keeping this factor in mind, a more realistic explanation of the financial crises should be welcome in the discussion.

Expressed earlier, of central importance in Veblen's economic analysis is the role of 'insiders' and 'outsiders' on financial instability, incidentally, one of the most vibrant topics of discussion in behavioral finance today. For Veblen, the most distinctive feature of 'corporation finance'— which cumulatively developed across the 19th century — is that corporations are under the direction of 'corporation managers' with limited stocks. Managers defined as 'insiders' in behavioral finance terms, use all the information at hand about the corporation to manipulate the value of corporate capital assets through misrepresentation. Veblen explains their role as creating a difference between the current earning capacity and putative earning capacity. Corporation capital managers tend to earn profit from this difference.

Corporation managers (*insiders*) show the value of corporation capital assets, or current earning capacity, different than the actual value and thus direct other investors' (*outsiders*) investment behavior. The ability to manipulate perception in capital markets becomes the foundation or even prerequisite for management. Through these activities they cause an excessive increase in investments and indebtedness and initiate the start of a cycle chartered toward financial crisis.

These activities, Veblen asserts, are rejected by the efficient markets hypothesis on the basis all investors have the same information. Yet, as Veblen's analysis has shown, these activities actually comprise the operations of modern capitalism. In this respect, Veblen has laid bare the activities of corporate managers' manipulation of the market through the distortion of financial information at hand, as one of the most important factors in explaining economic instability. Today, the use of information about a corporation by 'insiders' to manipulate capital markets is a common phenomenon (2001 Enron Scandal).[6] Veblen's analysis can be considered a most useful model to evaluate the role of multinational corporations in fomenting crises in economies in the modern era (Ganley 2004: 403).

Another central factor in Veblen's analysis is that decreased costs caused by technological changes are included in the process. As emphasized earlier, rapid technological advancement is cause for certain production processes and product innovations in the economy and consequentially a fall in product prices and profitability levels accordingly, triggering a chronic depression in the economy. Decreased costs instigated by technological development results in important institutional changes such as increased mergers and monopolization tendencies, and the gross misuse of human and natural resources by conspicuous waste consumption.

Veblen addresses three elements prevailing in modern capitalism. His analysis presents a useful framework to explain business cycles and financial instabilities caused by such business cycles and how they frequently reoccur in the economy. Moreover Veblen's theory may provide economists and scholars alike, a more comprehensive and better-informed reasoning against the neoclassical argument that insists market economies are equipped with self-regulating and stabilizing mechanisms.

References

Allen, L. 2003. *Keseden Bankaya Tezgahtan Borsaya: Küresel Finans Sisteminin Öyküsü.* Trans. By M. Tekçe. Istanbul: Kitap Yayınevi.

Dillard, D. 1980. A Monetary Theory of Production: Keynes and Institutionalists. *Journal of Economic Issues* 14 (2): 255-273.

Ganley, W.G. 2004. The Theory of Business Enterprise and Veblen's Neglected Theory of Corporation Finance. *Journal of Economic Issues* 38 (2): 397-403.

Gürkan, C. 2007. Veblen, Schumpeter ve Teknoloji. *Kurumsal İktisat,* ed. E. Özveren. Istanbul: İmge Kitabevi.

Kehoe, A. and M. Gee. 2009. Weaving Web Data into a Diachronic Corpus Patchwork. In *Corpus Linguistics: Refinements and Reassessments,* eds. A. Renouf and A. Kehoe. Amsterdam, New York: Rodopi B. V.

Raines, J. P. and C.G. Leathers. 2008. *Debt, Innovations, and Deflation: The Theories of Veblen, Fisher, Schumpeter, and Minsky.* Cheltenham, UK: Edward Elgar.

Ravenscroft, Ian. 2010. Folk Psychology as a Theory. *The Stanford Encyclopedia of Philosophy,* ed. E. N. Zalta. *http://plato.stanford.edu/archives/fall2010/entries/folkpsych-theory.*

Veblen, Thorstein. 1920. (1904). *The Theory of Business Enterprise.* New York: Charles Scribner's Sons.

———. 1954. (1921). *The Engineers and the Price System.* New York: Viking Press.

———. 1964. (1923). *Absentee Ownership and Business Enterprise in Recent Times: The Case of America.* New York: Augustus M. Kelley.

———. 2005. (1919). *The Vested Interests and the Common Man.* New York: Cosimo Inc.

Wray, L. R. 2007. Veblen's Theory of Business Enterprise and Keynes's Monetary Theory of Production. *Journal of Economic Issues* 41 (2): 17-624.

———. 2011. Minsky's Money Manager Capitalism and The Global Financial Crisis. *Working Paper,* no. 661. The Levy Economics Institute of Bard College.

Business Ideology and Engineers as Vanishing Mediators: A Reflection on Veblen's Theory of Engineers

Ahmet Öncü [1]

The common intellectual theme of the investors from Graham-and-Doddsville is this: they search for discrepancies between the value of a business and the price of small pieces of that business in the market. Essentially, they exploit those discrepancies without the efficient market theorist's concern as to whether the stocks are bought on Monday or Thursday, or whether it is January or July, etc. Our Graham & Dodd investors, needless to say, do not discuss beta, the capital asset pricing model, or covariance in returns among securities. These are not subjects of any interest to them. In fact, most of them have difficulty defining those terms. The investors simply focus on two variables: price and value.

Warren E. Buffet, 1984 (in Miles 2004: 226)

Introduction

Veblen (1857-1929), an "intellectual wayfaring man and a disturber of intellectual peace," became a mythical figure in American academic circles at the beginning of the twentieth century (Kazin 2004/1942: 82). He was educated at Yale University, one of the elite colleges of the country, and later led a nomadic academic career, moving from one college to another (Chicago, Stanford, Missouri, the New School). In the words of Kazin (2004/1942: 89), "Veblen was an alien to the end, and the torment of his alienation is forever to be felt in his prose." As Lerner (1975:42) remarks, Veblen's estrangement from his time and social environment ensued from "the conflict between his essential belief in men and the desolate wasteland he saw all about." Nevertheless, he was not a naïve humanist with unwarranted hopes for the future of "civilization." Neither an anthropologist nor a historian, he had an insightful view of "man" as an evolutionary being taken hostage by "imbecile institutions" (Veblen 1975/1914: 312). He thought of the pecuniary class involved in "invidious comparison" dominant in his society as an "imbecile institution." "So far as concerns the present question," Veblen (1994/1899: 20) wrote in *The Theory of the Leisure Class*, "the end sought by accumulation is to rank high in comparison with the rest of community in point of pecuniary strength." This is a futile end, the "insurgent scholar" contemplated, because "in the nature of the case, the desire for wealth can scarcely be satiated in any individual instance, and evidently a satiation of the average or general desire for wealth is out of the question" (Veblen 1994/1899: 21). For him, his fellow Americans had repressed their "instinctive insight for survival" and been living in "chronic dissatisfaction" with their present lot. Certainly, he wasn't the type of intellectual that most Americans wanted to hear.

---

1 This paper was originally published with the title "Wither Business Ideology: Revisiting Veblen's Theory of Engineers as Revolutionary Actors" in *Review of Radical Political Economics* (Volume 41, No. 2, Spring 2009, 196-215, DOI: 10.1177/0486613409331431).

In spite of this, on the basis of his enigmatic writing, Veblen became the focus of attention for the American intelligentsia of his own times. Even so, throughout the large parts of the twentieth century, he remained mostly a neglected theorist both in America and elsewhere. With the rise of a theoretical interest in institutions in the last decade, he has acquired widespread recognition, and his works have come to be seen as rich and stimulating sources by economists, political scientists and sociologists. Thus, a significant contemporary literature on Veblen has begun to emerge (Dugger 1995; Hodgson 1995a, 1995b; Loader and Tilman 1995; Dugger and Walter 1996, Kabel 1996; Nitzan 1998; Rutherford 1998; Knoedler and Mayhew 1999; Mouhammed 1999; and Fusfeld 2001).

All serious social theorists are primarily theorists of their own societies. Veblen is undoubtedly one of the principal theorists of American social formation. He is the forerunner of those who view American capitalism as stock market capitalism. For him, "acquisition-minded" managers of industrial enterprises aim to maximize "the value of their common stock" or "the putative earnings" of corporations that "absentee owners" sell and buy "in small pieces" in the "market" (Ganley 2004:398). In that sense, business managers or "captains of industry" are only secondarily concerned with "production" and sale of "products." At the present time, this specific aspect of Veblen's theoretical *corpus* makes him particularly significant on the global scale because the world economy integrated as a web of national stock markets has come to be dominated by an American-like capitalism. Today, Veblen has a lot to offer for making sense of the social and economic anguish resulting from this particular form of economic organization.

In the post-1980s, market-driven neoliberal economic policies that have unequivocally served business interests rendered the legitimation of nation state ever more problematic (Barrow 2005). Nonetheless, from the North to the South, from the West to the East, a majority of governments with diverse political inclinations have kept backing these policies favoring absentee owners at the expense of endangering their legitimation, and stayed unmoved despite social and political opposition to market fundamentalism. Thus, it is possible to suggest that a resilient ideology, or in the Veblenian parlance a resilient "point of view," must have been at work in legitimating otherwise disagreeable economic policies in the midst of political discontent. This paper rests on the assertion that the point of view rendering socially and economically detrimental economic policies tolerable over the world is business ideology. It is at this juncture that Veblen gains a renewed significance for both Americans and non-Americans, viz., the people of a "business civilization," because, as the editor of the 1958 edition of *The Theory of Business Enterprise* put deliberately on the cover, he is "America's most brilliant and influential critic of modern business and the values of a business civilization."

In what follows, I argue that in Veblen's critique of business civilization his conceptualization of modern technology occupies a central place (Veblen 1990/1919). For him, modern technology is not only a very distinctive point of view but also associated with an idiosyncratic habit of mind that contradicts the institution of private property. While the former disposes the individual to cooperation and solidarity for the livelihood of community, the latter renders the economic process "a struggle between men for the possession of goods" (Veblen 1994/1899: 16). Modern technology differentiates modern industry from earlier forms of industrial organizations by enforcing "the recognition of casual sequence in the practical contact of mankind with their environment" (Veblen 1994/1899: 237), and making it reliant on "exoteric knowledge" of "industrial processes and of natural phenomena which [are] habitually turned to account for the material purposes of life" (Veblen 1994/1899: 225). In this sense, modern technology as the point of view of modern industry is the externalized form of the disposition of "instinct of workmanship" that "conduces directly to the material well-being of the race" (Veblen 1975/1914: 312). Thus, it is the modern form of consciousness of other-respecting or other-regarding.

"Under the regime of individual ownership," however, "the self-regarding antithesis between man and man reaches fuller consciousness" (Veblen 1994/1899: 22). For Veblen, business is the highest stage of the consciousness of self-regarding. In almost all of his writings on business civilization, he draws attention to the clash between the consciousness of self-regarding and the consciousness of other-regarding by criticising the institutions of business and private property: leisure class versus drudgery class, pecuniary interest versus material interest, business versus industry, individual wealth versus social welfare, businessmen versus engineers and, last but not least, business as a point of view or ideology versus modern science or technology are the different polarities of the same underlying contradiction between the two disparate consciousness of modern life. This contradiction is a direct result of the emergence of the institution of private property.

Reading Veblen in the manner of "reading Marx" as suggested by Louis Althusser (1969, 1970) requires moving beyond Veblen's individual concepts in isolation and locating their specific meanings in the theoretical framework in which he uses them. In his major works, Veblen, to quote what Althusser (1969: 302) says in regard to Marx's *Capital*, "deals with something 'abstract' (something that cannot be touched with one's hands)"; they are therefore not books which deal with "concrete history or empirical economics, as the 'historians' and 'economists' imagine it ought to do." They are works of theory. Because of this, reading any significant text of Veblen in isolation requires having understood his *problematique* in the first place. By *problematique,* Althusser "refers not to a single problem but to an entire theoretical apparatus deployed around the solution of a problem" (Wight 1999: 137). Thus, only by clarifying Veblen's *problematique* we can move beyond an empirical, generalizing reading of his particular texts and grasp how he had struggled to develop wittingly and unwittingly a gamut of theoretical concepts and relations to solve the fundamental riddle of both business civilization and a large part of human history. But before moving on to this discussion, a brief clarification of the concept of ideology as it is used in this paper together with the meaning attached to the expression "business ideology" is in order.

In the Marxist tradition, ideology is considered to be a misrepresentation of reality. The notion of misrepresentation has been interpreted in two different manners. First, it has been thought to be referring to an untrue representation of reality that veils contradictions in the interest of the dominant class. Second, it has been assumed to be a partial representation of reality that emanates from the deceiving nature of everyday life phenomena. In other words, ideology has been considered both a conscious distortion of reality by the dominant class and a flawed yet spontaneous appropriation of the meanings of lived experiences. It was Althusser

(1971) who moved beyond this *impasse* by transcending the notion of ideology as distortion of reality. For him, ideology is a means of sense making that constitutes social life as experienced by individuals. As Eagleton (1991: 18) puts it, Althusser leads us to conceive ideology as the "particular organization of signifying practices which goes to constitute human beings as social subjects, and which produces the lived relations by which such subjects are connected to dominant relations . . . in society."

Drawing from Althuser's conceptualization but also deviating somewhat from it, Zizek (1989) suggests that subjects are inconsequential to the operation of ideology, as ideology, rather than being a veil obliterating "reality," is a material force embedded in everyday life activities of subjects. In his view, "man" always lives in "truth" but "truth only exists 'symbolically' – i.e. as story, as signifier – and that 'man,' being the subject of that story, literally falls outside its scope" (De Kesel 2004: 307). With his own words, "the mask is not simply hiding the real state of things; the ideological distortion is written into its very essence" (Zizek 1989:28). In other words, to act in a particular manner is to put on a "mask" with its associative frame of mind and scheme of seeing, interpreting and understanding, and hence, to leave reality behind for a "virtual world" (De Kesel 2004: 301). Thus, acts require "lies" about reality (i.e. thing in itself) if they are ever to be taken.

Using Veblenian terminology, Zizek seems to suggest that ideology is a "point of view" that helps subjects to interact within and through a "make-believe" world. Veblen (1919:2) in turn gives us the following definition for his "point of view" that can now be related to Zizek's conceptualization of ideology:

> What is spoken of as a point of view is always a composite affair; some sort of a rounded and balanced system of principles and standards, which are taken for granted, at least provisionally, and which serve as a basis of reference and legitimation in all questions of deliberate opinion.

Certainly, it is the commonly taken for granted points of view that can constitute a shared make-believe world, and may not only naturalize relations of domination and subordination between people but also help them carry on "wisely" with their daily activities.

For a point of view to serve as *the* basis of reference and legitimation in a given collectivity, it must be protected from other points of view so that it is made to seem as if it is the only way of describing reality that subjects want to freely hold on to. For Zizek (2002: 113-127), this can be achieved by "enunciating" a certain revered thing such as God, Nation or State, evoking the point of view in question. This in turn may impose on its addressees a "symbolic engagement" or "commitment" and urge them into obeying the authority of the point of view. Borrowing from Lacan, he refers to such words utilized to symbolize some "sublime objects" as "Master Signifiers." Although nobody knows what Master Signifiers exactly mean or stand for, they appear to have a kind of "hypnotic force" relying only on their "own act of enunciation." In other words, Master Signifiers are words with an influential "symbolic efficiency" in terms of preventing subjects from a critical reflection on the point of view that conditions their very own actions. Once a word gains the quality of being a Master Signifier, subjects who do not know the exact meaning of it but still feel obliged to act in accordance with the "injunctions" associated with it develop a tendency to believe in the knowledge of those who occupy authority positions. This also explains how a particular point of view turns into a hegemonic system of principles and standards used in deliberations. Faced with certain troubles subjects thus believe in the knowledge of "authorities" and have faith in their diagnoses and solution strategies. Nevertheless, no hegemonic point of view can fully explain "reality" because there always remains something "lacking" on the part of subjects.

In the remainder of the paper by the expression business ideology I refer to that particular point of view which has been rendered hegemonic globally by turning the term Business into a Master Signifier. Although nobody –even those who teach at business schools- knows what this symbolically efficient signifier exactly means, when individuals come into contact with it are driven into an undeniable yet freely experienced submissive aura and act according to the principles and standards of the end of maximizing putative earnings of absentee owners. In this symbolic order businessman emerges as the possessor of true vision and gains the veneration of masses, and thereby their trust in his "sagacity." In a manner similar to Veblen's views, I suggest that this particular ideology legitimates the management of industrial enterprises on the basis of profitability rather than on the basis of efficiency. Thus, contrary to some widespread postmodern convictions, the time for modern science and technology to be the paramount point of view in making sense of social problems and individual troubles is yet to come.

The paper has three main parts. The first part offers an account of Veblen's *problematique*. The aim of this part is to emphasize that each major work of Veblen is a theoretical step taken further towards the solution of the problem already posed in *The Theory of the Leisure Class*: the continuity of the habit of invidious comparison that renders humans self-centric agents. The second part presents a reading of *The Engineers and the Price System* congruent with his *problematique*. On the basis of this particular interpretation of *The Engineers and the Price System,* the third part, for a conclusion, offers some reflections for questioning the legitimacy of business ideology from the technological point of view. Here, I argue that Veblen's theory of "engineers" is grounded in his *problematique*; and that his depiction of engineers as potential revolutionary actors cannot be seen as an ephemeral desire of an "estranged" intellectual disgusted with business civilization. To substantiate the latter I argue that Veblen's conceptualization of engineers is reminiscent of treating them as "vanishing mediators" between the old industrial order driven by profitability and "the incoming industrial order" driven by efficiency.

Veblenian *problematique*

Although Veblen wrote many books, his first work, written at the very beginning of the twentieth century, *The Theory of the Leisure Class* (1899) was the one that aroused most interest among social scientists and has come to be identified with his name (Diggins 1999). [2] According to Heilbroner's (1953) account, when the book was first published, many thought of it as a satire on the lifestyle of the "aristocratic class" and the defects of the rich in America. In effect, the book describes the lifestyle of America's rich in a contemptuous manner, heaping

---

[2] For reviews of Diggins' work on Veblen, see Hamilton (2000) and Sent (2001)

example upon example, each more striking than the other, and thus may be considered more as a compilation of empirical observations than a theoretical study. The background to this rich narrative, however, also possesses a hinterland of inquiry important in its theoretical and political ramifications (Ritzer 2000; Fine 1994).

From the first sentence of the preface to *the Theory of the Leisure Class* we read that Veblen presents *a theory* of "the place and value of the leisure class as an economic factor in modern life" (Veblen 1994/1899: v). Because Veblen focuses on both the objective and the subjective positions of the leisure class in his analysis, his theory offers a structural as well as a cultural theory of classes in modern life. While the structural theory helps specify the objective relations between classes in connection to the "place" of the leisure class in the economic organization of society, the cultural theory allows having a sociological conceptualization of classes in connection to the "value" of the leisure class in the ideational construction of society. In other words, the structural theory leads to dividing the society into two objective classes, i.e., the pecuniary class, which is the leisure class *proper*, and the industrious class. The cultural theory allows conceiving the society as constitutive of a multitude of social strata ordered hierarchically according to their cultural formations in regard to values, beliefs, ideologies and life styles.

Veblen develops both class theories in a historical manner. Yet the method by which he introduces history into each of these frameworks differs. The structural class theory traces the historical process in connection to the economic organization of life and analyzes the contradiction between classes in terms of the objective interests of these classes. From the historical record he derives a generalization for all times and spaces of human civilization after a certain stage: "Wherever the institution of private property is found, even in a slightly developed form, the economic process bears the character of a struggle between men for the possession of goods" (Veblen 1994/1899: 16). As mentioned earlier, the consequence of this particular struggle is the reproduction of the two clashing structural class locations: the owners and the non-owners of wealth.

The contradiction between the two classes derives from their dissimilar practices or *activities* in their capacities as social agents. The owners of wealth are concerned with "exploit," which "is the conversion to [agent's] own *ends* of energies previously directed to some other *end* by another agent" (Veblen 1994/1899: 8; emphases added). The non-owners of wealth are involved in "drudgery" or "industry," which is "the effort that goes to create a new thing, with a new purpose [i.e. end] given it by the fashioning hand of its maker out of passive ("brute") material . . ." (Veblen 1994/1899: 8). Thus, the contradiction between the two classes is not only about the acquisition and accumulation of the products of society by one of the classes at the expense of the other but also about the different kinds of ends that each class seeks in their relations with others and the material world. In other words, Veblen focuses on the contradictory moral values of the two classes as much, if not more, as the contradictory material interests of them. According to him, although the forms of "exploit" and "industry" have changed in the historical evolution of societies, the fundamental contradiction between the two classes in terms of their disparate ends has remained intact. In this sense, the structural element that combines different forms of association in different eras of human civilization into a single common human history and does not change across different times and spaces is the clash of dissimilar orientations of the two contradictory classes to social relations. To see this, we need to look at how Veblen conceives human beings.

For Veblen, "man" is first and foremost an "agent." This is to say that "he" is a self-conscious being, who selects for himself "teleological" activities:

> He is an agent seeking in every act the accomplishment of some concrete, objective, impersonal end. By force of his being such an agent he is possessed of a taste for effective work, and distaste for futile effort. . . . This aptitude or propensity may be called the instinct of workmanship. (Veblen 1994/1899: 9)

Veblen expands on these statements later in *the Instinct of Workmanship and the State of the Industrial Arts* (1914), where he elaborates on the roots of institutions. In this text, he states that the sense of workmanship, very much similar to the "parental bent" (i.e. the parental concern that "has a much wider bearing than simply the welfare of one's own children"), is a disposition that helps protect and improve the "material well-being of the race." Because of this particular feature of their agency, "people . . . have by force of instinctive insight saved themselves alive out of" desperately precarious institutional situations (Veblen 1975/1914:312). In other words, human beings by heeding their "instinctive insights for survival" have proved to be capable of resisting the social institutions that have inhibited those activities whose ends have been serving others, i.e. community. This explains why, in Veblen's (1975/1915: 318) view, human beings in their genetic coding always bear the "intelligence" of beings of other-regarding, which ensures the conditions of their collective survival. Yet "history records more frequent and more spectacular instances of the triumph of imbecile institutions" over this intrinsic intelligence of people (Veblen 1975/1914: 312). At the root of all those imbecile institutions lies the disposition to "invidious comparison":

> Wherever the circumstances or traditions of life lead to an habitual comparison of one person with another in point of efficiency, the instinct of workmanship works out in an emulative or invidious comparison of persons. (Veblen 1994/1899: 16)

With invidious comparison becoming dominant in community – which is a major shift in signifying practices, i.e. ideology- the "activity" of "men" takes on the character of "exploit." This is because under such circumstances "tangible evidences of prowess – trophies – find a place in men's habit of thought as an essential feature of the paraphernalia of life" (Veblen 1994/1899: 10). Now, in the activity of "men" not the production but the acquisition of goods becomes the end. Thus, for the "man," other people become merely a means for his end of accumulating "trophies." He becomes truly a self-interested and self-regarding creature, who turns his back on to his instinctive insight for collective survival and the sense of other-regarding. This leads to perceiving work as an "irksome" activity and the seizure of the products of labor of others as a pleasant or rather an "honorable" pursuit (Veblen 1994/1899: 11).

Seeing the habit of invidious comparison as the underlying source of the solidity of the institution of private property in human history, in his subsequent books, Veblen proceeds to discern a type of activity that can nourish a habit of mind that is critical of private property.

He thinks that with the spread of such a habit of mind and its becoming dominant in human association, people may break up with invidious comparison. Beginning from his second major work, *The Theory of Business Enterprise*, and continuing with *The Vested Interests and the Common Man*, he keeps building up his theoretical apparatus to show that "modern life" provides a contingency for bringing invidious comparison to a close because of "the peculiar character of its intellectual outlook; particularly the scope and method of modern science and technology" (Veblen 1919: 7). Yet, parallel to the sophistication of this idea that is already being touched upon in his first major work, Veblen unwaveringly refines his *theory* of business in order to better expose how and why this institution remains legitimate in modern life and keeps hindering the possibility of putting an end to invidious comparison, even though its "norms of thought" belong to the previous epochs of civilization.

In this context, Veblen's cultural class theory of modern life in *The Theory of the Leisure Class* gains a new significance because this particular theory focuses on the discontinuities in history by treating industrial society as a distinct historical form of social organization. In modern industrial societies, although wealth (i.e. pecuniary strength) and leisure are still fundamental in class distinctions, in comparison with previous forms of social organization, the structure of social stratification is characterized more by consumption patterns and propensities (i.e. lifestyles) than leisure. Here wealth still allows one to have leisure, which in turn implies the absence of the compulsion to work. Leisure by creating a sphere of "conspicuous consumption" makes possible the display of wealth. Yet, more importantly, by providing a certain ideal conception of life at the aesthetic and ethical levels, conspicuous consumption (more than leisure itself) creates a field of attraction that prepares the ground for the existence of a range of social strata. The upper strata, which are entitled to have not only more but also a variety of "paraphernalia" to consume, are also the symbols of good life. This is because in these societies the diversity and the level of consumption operate as the prime determinants of social stratification. It is as if a multitude of social strata on a continuum are constructed culturally and ordered hierarchically in terms of the dimensions of how much and how many different things can be consumed in excess of the necessities of life.

Discerning the distinctiveness of the modern form of social stratification provides the Veblenian *problematique* with a significant theoretical input for at least two reasons. First, it helps grasp the reason as to why the lower strata buttress the ideology of the pecuniary class that legitimates the supremacy of business in society. Second and perhaps more important, it allows specification of the cultural condition that may facilitate the possibility of suppressing invidious comparison and hence the pecuniary class.

To establish this, we need to have a closer look at Veblen's cultural class theory of modern society and how this relates to his structural class analysis applicable to other forms of society within which the institution of private property also exists. At this point, Ritzer's (2000) reflection on Veblen's cultural class theory of modern life provides us with an engaging elucidation: "the influence of the leisure class [i.e. the pecuniary class] is not direct, except on the class immediately below it in the hierarchy . . . each class tends to emulate [the lifestyle] of the one in the stratum immediately above" (Ritzer 2000. 335). Given this peculiar feature of modern life, the ideological legitimacy of the pecuniary class can be secured only if everyday practices or "actions" of the social stratum just below it continue to emulate the lifestyle of the pecuniary class and thereby the values, beliefs and ideas embedded in that lifestyle. A crack in the "top down" simulation of the pecuniary class in the upper echelons will not only lead to the emergence of a new and possibly a different lifestyle but also put a break to the adoption of the values, beliefs and ideas of the pecuniary class by the lower strata through their copying of the altered lifestyle of the stratum just above them. For sure, Veblen thought intensely about a historical rupture of this kind that could contingently be triggered by contradictions implicated in the structures of modern industrial order. In the end by juxtaposing "industrial experts" (i.e. "engineers" as "the stratum just below" the pecuniary class) to the pecuniary class he sought to illustrate a contingency for the negation of invidious comparison, which may wither the business ideology and its reckless and futile end of accumulation of personal wealth. The next section takes up this side of Veblen's construction of his "theoretical apparatus."

The structural paradox of business and engineers as agents of industry

Before moving any further it must be stated that the following discussion has less to do with engineering as a "profession" than modern technology or engineering as a point of view or more correctly as an activity that nurtures a distinctive habit of mind. Obviously, any one who has been educated and/or trained in accordance with the logic of modern science can adopt the engineering or the technological point of view, although a practicing engineer may have a better chance to come to terms with it. Having said this, I also have to acknowledge that there are several interpretations of Veblen's views on modern technology and engineers, which may refute my reading of *The Engineers and the Price System* here. Most of the readers of this highly controversial text criticize him for "technological determinism" and thus "technocratic elitism" (Bell 1963; Dobriansky 1957; Riesman 1953; Stabile 1986; 1987; Rutherford 1992). Yet there are also ample reasons to suppose that these readings cannot say the final word on "the debate over Veblen and engineers" (Tilman 1996: 177; Davis 1980; Lauer 1991; Öncü 2003a and 2003b).

In his book *The Engineers and the Price System* (1983/1921), Veblen tries to identify the fundamental contradiction of business civilization in the tension between the industrious class and the pecuniary class (i.e. between the two contradictory objective classes) by using the term sabotage. In Veblen's view, sabotage appears to be "the conscientious withdrawal of efficiency" by the pecuniary class, whom he refers to as "business men" and sees them as the social class that owns and controls the "country's industrial output" (Veblen 1983/1921:8-9). Veblen uses the term "conscientious withdrawal of efficiency" rather contemptuously to explain the tactics of businessmen in the face of "overproduction." For him, "overproduction means production in excess of what the market will carry off at a sufficiently profitable price." Thus, in order to restore a profitable price the excess output should be eliminated in one way or another. This seems to be the *core activity* of businessmen.

[Thus] the requirements of profitable business will not tolerate [overproduction]. So the rate and volume of output must be adjusted to the needs of the market, not the working capacity of the available resources, equipment, and man power, nor to the community's need of consumable goods. (Veblen 1983/1921: 9)

At a later stage in his discussion, Veblen makes a statement that sounds somewhat uneasy regarding the control exercised on the industrial system by businessmen.

Their only salvation is a conscientious withdrawal of efficiency. All this lies in the nature of the case. It is the working of the price system, whose creatures and agents these business men are. (Veblen 1983/1921: 14)

In other words, Veblen perceives businessmen as "agents" whose activities take "profitable price" as their end, just like the "Graham & Dodd investors" (Buffet 1984, in Miles 2004: 226). In another statement, Veblen writes: "Price is of the essence of the case, whereas livelihood is not" (Veblen 1983/1921: 17).

The "essence of the case" leaves businessmen face to face with a challenging task. On one hand, they are driven towards controlling the rate of output as a function of profitability; on the other, as the leaders of society, they are required to organize industrial production in such a way that the provision of the means of subsistence to the population is ensured. In this sense, the institution of business comprises a paradox that places businessmen in a contradictory social location in itself. Because of the requirement of a profitable price, businessmen have to act in terms of their self-interest. However, this may pre-empt their social responsibility stemming from their leadership position in society and industry (Veblen 1983/1921: 17). This can be conceived as the structural paradox of business. In the words of Veblen:

Those wise business men who are charged with administrating the salutary modicum of sabotage . . . [are] faced with a dubious choice between a distasteful curtailment . . . and an unmanageable onset of popular discontent that may be in prospect . . . . (Veblen 1983/1921: 16)

According to Veblen (1983/1921:34), in the history of American capitalism businessmen turned their attention away from profits that could be made directly on the basis of production and commerce to concentrate on profits to be made through the mediation of financial operations in the securities market. In fact, Veblen, who died just before the New Deal, wrote most of his controversial texts during one of the most severe overproduction crises of the capitalist world system. In the context of overproduction, for the businessman who is nothing but an absentee owner or a representative of absentee owners, the financial return on production gains more importance than production itself and thus the financial criterion predominates in his decisions, while productive activities and the technical staff responsible for these functions lose their relative importance.

The question to be answered at this point is why the large segments of common people, who subsist on the basis of production, consent to the control established over the management of industry through financial power by businessmen who nonetheless remain indifferent to production, the mainstay of material life. Veblen's explanation unequivocally draws attention to what we have earlier referred to as the business ideology, the legitimation of which is secured by the top down emulation of the lifestyle and its associative practices of the pecuniary class. His view on this point in the American context sounds very assured indeed:

By settled habit, the American population are quite unable to see their way to entrust any appreciable responsibility to any other than business men . . . This sentimental deference of the American people to the sagacity of its business men is massive, profound and alert. So much so that it will take harsh and protracted experience to remove it, or to divert it sufficiently for the purpose of any revolutionary overturn. (Veblen 1921:69)

In addition to the dominance of business ideology in society, Veblen explains the reason for "the sentimental deference" of the industrious class to the pecuniary class, i.e. the "authorities," by the fact that, despite the sabotage of businessmen, American society as a whole has been able to regularly increase its prosperity. [3] Ironically, the death of Veblen in 1929 was to coincide with the beginning of the Great Depression, which revealed the results of sabotage in dragging society into actual poverty. In fact, one can read between the lines in *The Engineers and the Price System* what may be considered to be a farsighted prediction of this crisis that was to erupt ten years later. According to Veblen (1983/1921:41), in any overproduction context, business corporations have two basic policy options in order to protect profits: they can either reduce supply or raise production by reducing production cost. Of the two options, it is evident that the first has no bearing on production processes, that is to say that it amounts to overcoming the problem through pricing operations without a major modification in the given technical design of production. The second, on the other hand, obviously enters into the sphere of responsibility of production management and calls for the technical staff to improve the design and organization of production. However, the subordination of industrial enterprises to financial interests results in the decisions being taken in line with the first option. This links the use of technology to the decisions of financial management in line with the priorities of businessmen and creates a pressure on production staff to comply with these decisions. As a result, under conditions of overproduction, the option of controlling prices through a reduction of the volume of output in the face of falling prices is preferred to the search for a better application of technical possibilities leading to a reduction in production costs, the aim being to meet the expectations of businessmen largely and practically divorced from production. For this reason, the moment of economic downturn is the point when the undermining or sabotaging of material life is clear for all to see and doubts regarding the legitimacy of business ideology peak. To see this, we need to look at briefly how Veblen explains the failure in the modern industrial order "under the restraining hand of safe and sane business men" and the position of engineers therein.

The modern industrial order as a form of industrial organization is an interdependent system of production of goods and services. Each unit in this system is connected to the rest in a dynamic process of input and output linkages. In the terminology of mainstream organization theory, each unit is an open system that must interact with other units in the industry to accomplish its individual objectives; it both receives resources from and sends resources to the other units. Thus, as an open system, each unit must control and coordinate its internal

---

[3] In *Vested Interests*, Veblen (1919:56) provides two main reasons for this: "(a) the exceptionally great natural resources of the country, and (b) the continued growth and spread of population." The reader may refer to the text for the details of this highly interesting observation.

activities subject to conditions current in the industrial system. Veblen considers this unique nature of the modern industrial enterprise as of utmost significance in specifying the position of engineers in the production of the material welfare of the common people:

> [Modern industrial order] runs on as an inclusive organization of many and diverse interlocking mechanical processes, interdependent and balanced among themselves in such a way that the due working of any part of it is conditioned on the due working of all the rest. (Veblen 1983/1921: 52-53)

According to Veblen, each production unit can work optimally if the industrial system as a whole works optimally. In other words, optimum use of productive capacity in individual organizations presupposes optimum use of productive capacity within the industrial system as a whole. Veblen argues that such a condition can be arrived at if "industrial experts, production engineers . . . [i.e. the industrious class] work together on a common understanding" (Veblen 1983/1921: 53). More particularly, he says, "on condition that they must not work at cross purposes."

Although the existence of a common understanding does not necessarily preclude the existence of cross purposes, it can be argued that the former may help work out the negative tendencies stemming from the consequences of the latter. Thus, the first condition for an improvement in the use of available resources and capacities within the industrial system as a whole is the industrious class coming together around a common point of view - i.e. a certain shared habit of mind providing not only a basis for technical appraisal of the interdependencies among the units of industry but also a sense of identification that may constitute them as autonomous "agents" of industry.

As we have already seen, subjectivity of this kind –lacking in the current situation- can emerge if those individuals who occupy the tasks of production planning and management as well as production supervision and execution stop acting as deferential employees of "sagacious" businessmen (whose sole aim is to "maximize the value of their common stock"), and begin to act as "industrial experts" responsible for improving the efficiency of industrial system as a whole. By transforming the "end" of their acts in this manner, they may articulate a new meaning for their "expertise" outside the scope of the business point of view. [4] Once such a "being" come into existence, agents of industry may generate a set of objectives defined as ends to which each individual organization should strive to make its particular contribution. Since the generation of ends involves the participation of all individual organizations and their representatives, there is no need for any outside institution such as "businesslike management" to control production decisions. In the terminology of game theory, this is not a zero-sum game. It is simply an industrial organization model based on a strategy of cooperation among interdependent units "interlocked in an inclusive network." The key assumption of this model is that it includes only the agents of industry whose subjectivity takes the habit of mind associated with the point of view of modern technology as its basis. It excludes those who control industry as, for example, absentee owners (i.e. "investors") and "simply focus on two variables: price and value" (Buffet 1984, in Miles 2004: 226). When the latter group is introduced to interactions, it may turn into a zero-sum game.

---

[4] There is more on this point in the concluding part.

Thus, the following quote from Veblen must be read in the light of the cooperative industrial organization model suggested:

> And for the due working of this inclusive going concern it is essential that . . . technological specialists who by training, insight, and *interest* make up the general staff of industry must have a free hand in the disposal of its available resources, in materials, equipment, and man power . . . Any degree of obstruction, diversion, or withholding of any of the available *industrial forces*, with a view to the special gain of . . . any investor, unavoidably brings on a dislocation of the system, which involves a disproportionate lowering of its working efficiency and therefore a disproportionate loss to the whole, and therefore a net loss to all its parts. (Veblen 1983/1921: 54; emphases added)

At this point, Veblen returns to the concept of sabotage as the main impediment to the due working of the modern industrial system. We must remember that for Veblen, modern technology goes beyond the technical design of production processes and constitutes a particular point of view. As such, it encloses the interaction among the agents of industry in terms of causally explainable statements on industrial processes and natural phenomena, which are geared toward improving the efficiency of the use of available resources. However, this interaction may involve complex and multifaceted issues given the breadth and the depth of the industrial order, and can be strategically manipulated by businessmen with reference to the requirements of profitability – supported, of course, by the legitimacy of business ideology in society. If this happens, the focus of interaction moves away from efficiency considerations to the conditions of business success. Thus, sabotage, it can now be suggested, is the effective reorientation of interaction among the industrious class by the pecuniary class through the act of providing them with deliberate opinions on complex technical issues in order to stop any kind of critical reflection from the technological point of view and thus a concomitant increase in the wealth of businessmen at the expense of a reduction in the welfare of the industrious class. Sabotage is the ages old exploit that is naturalized and normalized by the taken for granted point of view of profitability, viz. the business point of view or business ideology.

In the case of overproduction businessmen speak to the industrious class from an apocalyptic position as if they are the messengers of the Divine Providence. For example, one may hear from an exceptionally "sane" and "safe" investor that "the business environment, although very promising, is unfortunately not right for growth!" Thus, with reference to the Master Signifier Business, the high priests of business civilization summon all individuals to ascetic modesty and simplicity, i.e. unemployment and misery. In other words, they deny all prospects other than "slowing down the traffic." In doing so, they incarcerate themselves into what Zizek (2001) calls "totalitarian logic," which rests on the denial of the provisional quality of truth claims by rendering them absolute principles. "Here, the lie underlying truth . . . is disavowed: truth is claimed to have fully real ground" (De Kesel 2004: 305). However, by framing the truth that is valid only in the symbolic order of business civilization as if it is real (i.e. thing in itself), they also deny the "avowed aim of business", that is, the production of essential goods for common people. It is not difficult to see that the structural paradox of business is resolved here by refusing the leadership responsibility associated with being a businessman.

So it happens that the industrial system is deliberately handicapped with dissension, misdirection, and unemployment of material resources, equipment, and man power, at every turn where . . . the captains of finance can touch its mechanisms, and all the civilised peoples are suffering privation together because their general staff of industrial experts are in this way required to take orders and submit to sabotage at the hands of . . . the vested interests. (Veblen 1983/1921: 54-55)

Veblen surmises that the more this arises, the more obvious becomes the difference between the avowed purpose of business and its tangible performance. On the basis of this particular observation, he draws one of his significant conclusions about the subjectivity of businessmen, which he conceives as an objective condition in any society driven by business principles: "Tangible performance in the way of productive industry is precisely what the business men do not know how to propose" (Veblen 1921: 68). And he goes on to make an assured, or what he would have said, a "matter of fact" prediction: "but it is also that on which the possible success of any projected plan of [revolutionary] overturn *will always* rest."

At this point, a brief reflection on Veblen's treatment of vested interests is in order. Such a digression may provide a better understanding as to why Veblen views the general staff of industry as potential actors who are qualified for coming up with "a plan of revolutionary overturn" in order to abolish the businesslike management of industrial enterprises.

"For they know not what they do"

Veblen's (1958/1904: 67-86) conceptualization of late capitalism as a system of economic organization takes into account the historical shift from the money economy to the credit economy. In the credit economy, "the basis of capitalization has gradually shifted, until the basis is now no longer given by the cost of material equipment owned, but by the earning-capacity of the corporation as a going concern" (Veblen 1958/1904: 70). In other words, with the shift, the nature of business capital has drastically changed. Because of this, Veblen, "at least under the new order of business enterprise," conceives capital as the capacity of making claim to a prospective income over the initial cost laid out on any investment, be this a productive or financial activity.

> From this arises one of the singularities of the current situation in business and its control of industry; viz., that the total face value [of the assets] . . . always and greatly exceeds the total market value of [those assets] to which the securities give title of ownership and to which alone in the last resort they do give title. (Veblen 1990/1919: 60)

Veblen defines the difference between the total face value and the total market value of the assets as "the margin of free earning capacity." Thus, the higher the margin is, the higher is the free, i.e. unearned income accruing to the investor holding the ownership title. In this sense, the owners of productive assets always want to increase the margin in order to increase their unearned income.

> In case the free income, which is gained in this way, promises to continue, it presently becomes a vested right. It may then be formally capitalised as an immaterial asset having recognized earning-capacity equal to this prospective income. That is to say, the outcome is a capitalised claim to get something for nothing; which constitutes a vested interest. (Veblen 1990/1919: 60)

In other words, a vested right may arise from the legal ownership of productive assets. The vested right in its turn may give rise to "immaterial assets" which can be bought and sold for realizing the gains from the capitalized claim or the vested interest.

The New Dictionary of Cultural Literacy (2002) defines vested interest as a "deep personal (possibly financial) interest in some political or economical proposal. The plural, vested interests, often refers to powerful, wealthy property holders." Vested interests are, to be sure, what Veblen refers to as absentee owners in *The Engineers and the Price System* and elsewhere. They demand from their captains of industry (i.e. executives of corporations) to oversee their vested interests congruent with "three main lines of businesslike management: (a) Limitation of supply, with a view to profitable sales; (b) Obstruction of traffic, with a view to profitable sales; and (c) Meretricious publicity, with a view to profitable sales" (Veblen 1990/1919: 57). In other words, absentee owners are the agents who bear the major responsibility for the management of industrial organizations as going business concerns. Because they have personal interests in promoting their capitalized claims (i.e. the "small pieces of businesses" that they own), the end of gaining free income not only governs their daily activities but also constitutes their only truth, i.e. the "story" of their life. They lack an ontological basis for being concerned with "tangible performance in the way of productive industry." Thus, as the leaders of industrial order, they cannot even notice what they are doing, i.e. "the conscientious withdrawal of efficiency", -to use an expression introduced to social theory by Zizek - "for they know not what they do." [5] Paradoxically, the ontological lack of absentee owners (i.e. the act of improving the efficiency of industrial order as a whole) is the ground on which know-how of industrial experts can be inscribed.

Conclusion: "Engineers" as "Vanishing Mediators"

This brings us to one of the most controversial parts of *The Engineers and the Price System*, its concluding part: "A Memorandum on a Practicable Soviet of Technicians." Here, Veblen takes up the question of "revolutionary overturn" under the leadership of "engineers," which may "unsettle the established order" for replacing it with a new industrial system "designed to correct the shortcomings of the old." The text begins with an earnest reminder that there is no reason for being fearful about or hopeful for such a transformation under existing circumstances, because, as he notes, "engineers" "still are consistently loyal, with something more than a hired man's loyalty, to the established order of commercial profit and absentee ownership" (Veblen 1921:63). Yet he also maintains that this *transition* will eventually be inescapable in that the vested interests "will, in a sense, eliminate themselves, by letting go quite involuntarily after the industrial situation gets beyond their control" (Veblen 1921:64). With reference to the prevailing economic conditions, he states that the absentee owners have already "sufficiently shown their unfitness to take care of the country's material welfare" (Veblen 1921:64). This corroborates the fact that they are losing the "ground on which they

---

[5] This expression originates from the Bible. They are "Jesus' words from the cross, asking forgiveness for those who put him to death. More widely, of course, the plea was for all humanity. From the Bible, *Luke 23*:
23:33 And when they were come to the place, which is called Calvary, there they crucified him, and the malefactors, one on the right hand, and the other on the left.
23:34 Then said Jesus, Father, forgive them; for they know not what they do. And they parted his raiment, and cast lots." (http://www.phrases.org.uk/meanings/142050.html)

can set up a colourable claim to their vested interests" (Veblen, 1921:64). This in turn leads him to believe that he is not dealing with a "purely speculative novelty" here in presenting a case for "a discontinuance of the existing system of absentee ownership."

It must be emphasized that *eradication* of the disposition to "invidious comparison" and all that goes with it (such as emulation of the pecuniary class by the industrious class) is the underlying theme of the *Memorandum*. Nevertheless, what appears on the surface of the text is as important as this deeper meaning of it. A close reading of the *Memorandum* reveals that there are at least two particular lines of argument running through the text. The first of these is about the organizational features of "the incoming industrial order" and in what ways it will be different from the old one. This involves first and foremost the specification of the composition and structure of "the directorate" that will take charge of the new order during the transition and the principles and standards that these directors must use in deliberations in regard to planning and coordinating the activities of the productive industry. The second line of argument is about the emergence of a revolutionary subject in the form of a "Soviet of Technicians." Needless to say, this part of the *Memorandum* is more exigent than the first line of argument given that "engineers" as members of American society are not "in the habit of taking a greatly different view of their own case. They still feel themselves, in the nature of things, to fall into place as employees of . . . businessmen." That is to say, they also act within and through the make-believe world constructed by the business ideology. Thus, before concluding this paper, I briefly take up these two separate yet interrelated issues of the *Memorandum* to argue, as I have promised in the beginning, that Veblen's proposal for a revolutionary overturn under the leadership of "engineers" is a part of his *problematique* and theoretically grounded rather than being passing wishful thinking of an "enigmatic intellectual" in a certain historical and empirical milieu.

As to the first issue, we have already seen why the new industrial order needs to be devised as a cooperative system, i.e. a system resting on the condition that discrete units of industry "must not work at cross purposes." We have also seen that this calls for a common shared view among technicians, uniting them on the basis of a common cause. In the *Memorandum* Veblen finally embarks on an explicit exposition of this common point of view to argue that the industrious class must conceive their knowledge of "the state of the industrial arts" (i.e. their know-how of technology *as such*) as a collective capacity that determine social welfare on the basis of given resources and skills. They also need to see using technology *as such* unrestrained by any other condition except for the constraints of industrial infrastructure as the sole limitation of raising efficiency, and thereby the material life of "underlying population" to the highest level possible. This means that, in order to attain the efficient use of productive capacities of society, the industrious class has to perceive technology not only as the sum of production techniques but also, what I suggest, as a particular point of view of social and political deliberation.

Technology as a point of view of social and political deliberation implies the need to examine, given the fact that production activities are also subject to social institutions such as absentee ownership, whether social welfare is curtailed by institutions beyond the technological constraint and to come up with an explanation of this "inconvenience." Hence, the industrious class assuming various different productive roles in the industrial order, as an inevitable consequence of their class position, comes directly face to face with the material conflict between absentee owners and almost all other social strata. Thus, during the transition to the incoming industrial order, it is a must for the leadership of this class, i.e. "the directorate," to "investigate and set out in a convincing way what are the various kinds and lines of waste that are necessarily involved in the businesslike control of industry; what are the abiding causes of these wasteful and obstructive practices; and what economies of management and production will become practicable on the elimination of the present businesslike control of industry" (Veblen 1921:69).

It is apparent that doing all this to begin a new industrial order requires taking on a "revolutionary posture" on the part of "engineers." Here finally comes up the disquieting riddle: where will this revolutionary subjectivity originate? In other words, how will "engineers" stop to emulate their "sagacious" bosses and turn themselves into a revolutionary force? Veblen's answer is an unambiguous one. For him, this kind of an ideational transformation can only originate from an "Act" - if I put it in a Zizekian way: "So soon . . . as the engineers . . . decide to disallow absentee ownership out of hand, that move will have been made" (Veblen 1921:76).

Zizek uses the word Act (with capital "A") to differentiate it from every day acts that are taken in conformity with the inscriptions of the current symbolic order. Unlike acts, an Act is an action that may contest the current symbolic order at that particular point where this order denies or represses a contingency (Zizek, 2000). As we have seen previously, within the make-believe world of business ideology businessmen deny the possibility of questioning "the conscientious withdrawal of efficiency" that they do because, for them, nobody can question the profitability goal of business enterprise. Thus they incarcerate themselves into a totalitarian logic. In this context, then, *the* Act is the denial of this denial. The Act, in other words, is to question why we cannot question "the conscientious withdrawal of efficiency." It should also be emphasized that this very Act is a "jump beyond the symbolic order," beyond the virtual world of business and into contingency through revealing the totalitarian logic of businessmen. Here, we come to the most critical passage of the *Memorandum*, in which Veblen suggests a particular Act to "engineers" so that they can take on a revolutionary posture:

> The obvious and simple means of doing it is a conscientious withdrawal of efficiency; that is to say the general strike, to include so much of the country's staff of technicians as will suffice to incapacitate the industrial system at large by their withdrawal, for such time as maybe required to enforce their argument. (Veblen 1921: 76)

In his reflection on Max Weber's account of the transition from feudalism to modern capitalism, Fredric Jameson (1988: 3-34) argues that "protestant ethic" acts as a dialectic category in transcending the limitations of the feudal order before the emergence of capitalist society, and vanishes once the transition is completed. He uses the term "vanishing mediator" to refer to this category. For Balibar (2003: 334), the vanishing mediator introduced by Jameson is a transitory category that brings into being the conditions of a new social order by "rearranging the elements inherited from the very institution that has to be overcome." Zizek (2000: 142) in connection with Jameson suggests conceiving the "vanishing mediator" as a "paradoxical agent," and explains its historical role with an illuminating example:

> In political theory, the exemplary case of a "vanishing mediator" is provided by the Hegelian notion of the historical hero who resolves the deadlock of the passage from the natural state of violence to the civil state of peace guaranteed by legitimate power. This passage cannot take place directly, in a continuous line, since there is no common ground, no intersection, between the state of natural violence and the state of civil peace; what is therefore needed is a paradoxical agent who, by means of violence itself, overcomes violence, i.e., the paradox of an act which retroactively establishes the conditions of its own legitimacy and thereby obliterates its violent character, transforming itself into a solemn founding act.

Thus, to conclude this paper, I suggest the following: For Veblen, engineers conceived as a theoretical category constituted a manifest "paradoxical agent" who could supersede the business civilization to move towards a cooperative industrial civilization. As industrial experts, they represented a stratum within the industrious class, who, because of their training, insight and interest, could lead the movement against the totalitarianism of businessmen revealed by their persistent sabotaging of social welfare through withdrawing the efficiency of industrial enterprises for higher profits. As a direct result of the latter engineers were declined fulfillment of their very potentials to improve the efficiency of the industrial order as a whole. They could have discerned the withdrawal of efficiency for private gain as the fundamental condition of the failure in the industrial order, a condition that could not have been even contemplated by businessmen. Therefore, engineers could have taken on the character of *the* paradoxical agent who could discover the paradox of modern business civilization, i.e. the structural paradox of business. Although the concept was not available to Veblen, his conceptualization of engineers as revolutionary actors was very much reminiscent of seeing them as "vanishing mediators" who could "resolve the deadlock of the passage" from the industrial order based on profitability to an industrial order based on efficiency. His suggestion for the "solemn founding act" of the new industrial order revealed this unmistakably. He thought that engineers by means of a "conscientious withdrawal of efficiency" itself, could overcome "*the* conscientious withdrawal of efficiency," i.e. the "violence" of businessmen - a story which was beyond the scope of the story of absentee owners. Thus, in order to be able to tell the untold story of "man," engineers could jump beyond the story of their "sagacious" bosses and into *de te fabula narrator.*

References

Althusser, L. 1969. How to Read Marx's Capital. *Marxism Today*. October, 302-305.

————. and Ballibar, E. 1970. *Reading Capital*. London: New Left Books.

————. 1971. *Lenin and Philosophy*. London. New Left Books.

Balibar, E. 2003. Europe: Vanishing Mediator. *Constellations* 10 (3): 312-338.

Barrow, C. W. 2005. The Return of the State: Globalization, State Theory, and the New Imperialism. *New Political Science* 27 (2): 123-145.

Bell, D. 1963. Veblen and New Class. *American Scholar* 32 (Autumn): 616-638

Buffet, W. E. 2004. (1984). The Superinvestors of Graham-and-Doddsville. In Robert P. Miles. *Warren Buffet Wealth*. New Jersey: John Wiley & Sons Inc.

Davis, A. K. 1980. *Thorstein Veblen's Social Theory*. New York: Arno Press.

De Kesel, M. 2004. Act Without Denial: Slavoj Zizek on Totalitarianism, Revolution and Political Act. *Studies in East European Thought* 56: 299-334.

Diggins, J. P. 1999. *Thorstein Veblen: theorist of the leisure class*. Princeton N.J.: Princeton University Press.

Dobriansky, L. E. 1957. *Veblenism: A New Critique*. Washington, DC: Public Affairs Press.

Dugger, W.M. 1995. Veblenian institutionalism: The changing concepts of inquiry. *Journal of Economic Issues* 29 (4): 1013-1027.

————. and W. Walter. 1996. Radical institutionalism: From technological to democratic instrumentalism. *Review of Social Economy* 2: 169-189.

Eagleton, T. 1991. *Ideology: An Introduction*. New York: Verso.

Fine, G.A. 1994. The social construction of style: Veblen, Thorstein the theory of the leisure class as contested text. *Sociological Quarterly* 35 (3): 457-472.

Fusfeld, D.R. 2001. Marx, Veblen, and contemporary institutional political economy: Principles and unstable dynamics of capitalism(by O' Hara, P.A.). *Journal of Economic Issues* 35 (4): 1033-1035.

Ganley, W. T. 2004. The Theory of Business Enterprise and Veblen's Neglected Theory of Corporation Finance. *Journal of Economic Issue* 2: 397-403.

Hamilton, D. 2000. Thorstein Veblen: theorist of the leisure class (by Diggins, J.P.). *Journal of Economic Issues* 34 (4): 981-983.

Heilbroner, R. 1953. *The Worldly Philosophers*. New York: Simao&Schuster.

Hodgson, G.M. 1995a. The political economy of utopia. *Review of Social Economy* 53 (2): 195-213.

————. 1995b. Varieties of capitalism from the perspectives of Veblen and Marx. *Journal of Economic Issues* 29(2): 575-584.

Jameson, F. 1988. The Vanishing Mediator; or, Max Weber as Storyteller. In *The Ideologies of Theory*. Vol. 2, ed. Fredric Jameson. Minneapolis: University of Minnesota Press.

Kabel, H. 1996. Money, alienation, and the leisure class: Henry James, Edith Wharton, Thorstein Veblen. *Zeitschrift Fur Anglistik Und Amerikanistik* 44 (4): 346-357.

Kazin, A. 2004. (1942). An Insurgent Scholar: Thorstein Veblen. In *Alfred Kazin's America*, ed. Ted Solotaroff. New York: Perennial.

Knoedler, J. and A. Mayhew. 1999. Thorstein Veblen and the engineers: A reinterpretation. *History of Political Economy* 31(2): 255-272.

Lauer, R. H. 1991. *Perspectives on Social Change*. Boston: Allyn and Bacon.

Lerner, Max. 1975. *The Portable Veblen*. New York: The Viking Press.

Loader, C. and R. Tilman. 1995. Veblen, Thorstein anlaysis of German intellectualism: institutionalism as a forecasting method. *American Journal of Economics and Sociology* 54(3): 339-355.

Miles, R. P. 2004. *Warren Buffet Wealth*. New Jersey: John Wiley & Sons Inc

Mouhammed, A.H. 1999. Veblen and Keynes: On the economic theory of the capitalist economy. *Journal of Institutional and Theoretical Economics* 155 (4): 594-609.

Nitzan, J. 1998. Differential accumulation: towards a new political economy of capital. *Review of International Political Economy* 5 (2): 169-216.

Öncü, A. 2003a. Political identity as structure and agency: an institutional analysis of the organization of engineers in Turkey. *International Review of Sociology* 13 (2): 303–320.

———. 2003b. *A Sociological Inquiry into the History of the Union of Turkish Chambers of Engineers and Architects: Engineers and the State*. New York: Edwin Mellen Press.

Riesman, D. 1953. *Thorstein Veblen: A Critical Interpretation*. New York: Charles Scribner's Sons.

Ritzer, G.. 2000. *Classical Sociological Theory*. New York: McGraw-Hill.

Rutherford, M. 1992. Veblen and Engineers. *International Review of Sociology* new series 3: 125-150.

———. 1998. Veblen's evolutionary programme: a promise unfulfilled. *Cambridge Journal of Economics* 22 (4): 463-477.

Stabile, D. R. 1986. Veblen and Political Economy of the Engineers. *American Journal of Economics and Sociology* 45: 41-52.

———. 1987. Veblen and the Political Economy of Technocracy: The Critic Developed a Collectivist Ideology. *American Journal of Economics and Sociology* 46 (January): 35-48.

Sent, E.M. 2001. Thorstein Veblen: Theorist of the leisure class (by Diggins JP). *Journal of the History of the Behavioral Sciences* 37 (2): 189-190.

Tilman, R. 1996. *The Intellectual Legacy of Thorstein Veblen: Unresolved Issues.* Wesport: Greenwood Publishing.

Veblen, T. 1994. (1899). *The theory of the leisure class: an economic study of institutions.* New York: Dover Publications.

————. 1958. (1904). *The Theory of Business Enterprise.* New York: Mentor Books.

————. 1975. (1914). The Instinct of Workmanship and the State of Industrial Arts. In Max Lerner. *The Portable Veblen.* New York: The Viking Press.

————. 1990. (1919). *The Place of Science in Modern Civilization and Other Essays.* New York: B. W. Huebsch.

————. 1919 (reprint). *The Vested Interests and the Common Man.* Montana: Kessinger Publishing.

————. 1983. (1921). *The Engineers and the Price System.* New York: B. W. Huebsch.

————. 1921 (reprint). *The Engineers and the Price System.* Montana: Kessinger Publishing

Wight, C. 1999. They Shoot Dead Horses Don't They: Locating Agency in the Agency-Structure Problematique. *European Journal of International Relations* 5 (1): 109-142.

Zizek, S. 1989. *The Sublime Object of Ideology.* London and New York: Verso.

————. 2000. From Proto-Reality to the Act. *Angelaki, Journal of the Theoretical Humanities* 5 (3): 141-148

————. 2001. *Did Somebody Say Totalitarianism? Five Interpretations in the (Mis)use of a Notion.* London and New York: Verso.

————. 2002. *On Belief.* London: Routledge

Masterless Engineers of Turkey:
An Institutional Evolution Corroborating
Veblen's Theory of Engineers [1]

Ahmet Öncü

Introduction

In *The Engineers and the Price System,* Veblen (1921) posited a set of persuasive theoretical arguments regarding the existence of a contradictory relationship between the material interests of technicians and businessmen. Nonetheless, he provided various reasons as to why a revolutionary "Soviet of Technicians" was a remote possibility in America. In substantiating his claim he had recourse to the notion of vested rights of "absentee owners" and how these were resiliently embedded in the "sentiments" of the "underlying population." In connection with this, he argued that "by settled habit" the technicians, just like other social groups and classes of American society, had been content with the leadership of businessmen. In this paper, I argue that Veblen's abstract line of reasoning regarding the incongruity between the material interests of engineers and businessmen has a sound theoretical basis. What Veblen contemplated as a possibility became an historical reality in the cultural context of Turkey - a country probably farthest removed from his concerns. The engineers of Turkey, by getting organized through a professional union (Union of the Chambers of Turkish Engineers and Architects (UCTEA)), have mobilized against business interests in the name of common people since the 1970s. This has ensued from the unique mixture of past and present social habits of thought in the agency of engineers of Turkey, resulting in -using Veblen's terminology- an anti-business engineering "point of view" or engineering "spiritual attitude" and a corresponding social and political identity, which has come to be known as "the revolutionary-democrat engineer."

In what follows, using Veblen's (2012/1919) cumulative causation methodology, I attempt to provide a theoretical answer for the origin, growth, persistence and variation of the anti-business engineering outlook in Turkey. My objective is to trace the trail of centuries old habits of thought in the present ideas and actions of the revolutionary-democrat engineers of the UCTEA. This inquiry may make a contribution not only to the Turkish studies beyond the limits of its subject matter but also to the growing importance of Veblen as a radical institutional social theorist. A better understanding of the peculiarity of the engineering point of view and its resultant identity in Turkey may help one to see why Veblen's claim regarding the potentially contradictory relationship between engineers and businessmen may become an actuality under certain institutional environments, and still why he did not expect the American engineers to rise up against their businessmen.

---

[1] This paper was originally presented with the title "Formation of an Anti-capitalist Engineer Identity and its Evolution in Turkey: A Veblenian Interpretation" in the *Veblen Symposium* held in Istanbul on July 6-7, 2012. A revised and extended version of this paper will appear in *Review of Radical Political Economics* with the title "On the Possibility of a 'Soviet of Technicians': Veblen's Cumulative Causation Applied to the Turkish Case."

A revolutionary "Soviet of Technicians": A remote possibility in America

In *The Engineers and the Price System,* Veblen (1921:69) when arguing against the possibility of a "Soviet of Technicians" in America, stated that

> [The technicians] still feel themselves, in the nature of things, to fall into place as employees of those enterprising business men who are, in the nature of things, elected to get something for nothing. Absentee ownership is secure, just yet. In time, with sufficient provocation, this popular frame of mind may change, of course; but it is in any case a matter of an appreciable lapse of time.

In other words, he thought that the technicians or the engineers had little or no serious social or political concern about lending themselves and their technical expertise to the "obstructive tactics" of businessmen to which he referred as "sabotage" (Veblen 1921: 8-9). In his mind there was no question that the American engineers were practically commercialized with a heartfelt devotion to the "pecuniary interests" of businessmen.

The question as to how such an idiosyncratic "spiritual attitude" had evolved among the American technicians has long been a topic of interest for those reflecting on Veblen's institutionalism and his multifarious theoretical heritage (Tilman 1996: 167-197). Many of his commentators provided a variety of reasons for why -contrary to his theoretical expectations - he was pessimistic about the American engineers' becoming anti-capitalist actors despite the fact that the country was fast approaching a catastrophe because of the sabotage of businessmen (Tilman 1996: 171). Among these, more convincing commentators have attempted to find the solution in Veblen's elaboration of the opposition between the spiritual attitudes or the points of view of "the Darwinian science" and "the natural rights philosophy" concerning the conceptualization of private property (Wenzler 1998). Between these two distinct spiritual attitudes there was "a difference in the basis of valuation of the facts" (Veblen 2012/1919: 39).

For Veblen, Darwinian science corroborated that all the facts required a non-teleological explanation. This was because goal setting and acting upon that goal was a possibility only in the case of human agency, the only agency being with a *telos* (Veblen 1994/1899: 9). Nature, lacking any agency, could therefore not have any purpose. Quite the opposite, however, the natural rights philosophers of the seventeenth and eighteenth centuries had argued for the existence of an impressive design, and thereby an intention in and of nature regardless of how humans had interpreted it. In the view of the natural rights philosophy, nature had a purpose over and above the agency of humans. Moreover, nature had been impacting on humans from a pre-social scheme of morality and compelling human civilization to abide by its principles. In this sense, human agency, if not an epiphenomenon, was only a derivative of the agency of nature.

The disparate epistemological assumptions of these two views on and about human agency and nature reflected explicitly in their treatment of the notion of private property. For Veblen, the Darwinian scientific approach treated ownership "as a social institution rather than a fact of nature," a conception which was objectionable for the natural rights philosophy (Wenzler 1998:19). According to the latter, ownership was "a 'natural right', in the sense that what a man has made, whatsoever 'he hath mixed his labor with,' that has thereby become his own to do with it as he will" (Veblen 1997/1923:49). Thus, a social category was reduced to and seen as an imperative of nature, and not an institution reproduced by and through cultural practices.

Veblen, following Darwin's "natural selection" methodology, wanted to develop a theory of social evolution that could address the origin, growth, persistence, and variation of institutions (Tilman 1996: 49-50, 2004: 589; Brette 2003: 456). He saw instincts and institutions or social habits of thought as units of selection in the process of cultural evolution (Brette 2003). In this context, he came up with his "cumulative causation" methodology. In Veblen's (2012/1919: 245) own words:

> [In] the Darwinian scheme of thought, the continuity sought in and imputed to the facts is a continuity of cause and effect. It is a scheme of blindly cumulative causation, in which there is no trend, no final term, no consummation. The sequence is controlled by nothing but the *vis a tergo* [2] of brute causation, and is essentially mechanical.

According to Rutherford (1998: 475-476), Veblen "was aware that individuals acted in a goal-directed manner, but he wanted to present institutional change as unintended result." Contrary to Rutherford, Hodgson (2004) claimed that Veblen's explanation of action and institutional change did involve intentionality. For him, "[i]ntentions can be causes, but intentions are always caused. The evolution of intentionality, and its development within each human being, has to be explained in terms of materialist causes and evolutionary selection" (Hodgson 2004: 349). When considered in connection with Hodgson's, Veblen's (2012/1919) depiction of the growth of culture as "a cumulative sequence of habituation" appears to be a theory of how past and present are mixed in the process of evolutionary selection. Veblen (1994/1899: 118) puts his theory in plain words in the *Theory of the Leisure Class* as follows:

> Institutions are products of the past process, are adapted to past circumstances, and are therefore never in full accord with the requirements of present . . . . At the same time, men's present habits of thought tend to persist indefinitely, except as circumstances enforce a change.

By departing from the premise that Veblen's theory is Darwinian in an epistemological and methodological sense, Brette (2003: 456-457) aimed to elucidate why and how Veblen's theory of institutional evolution had rested on cultural determinism in addition to technological determinism, as suggested by many of his readers. Brette supported his claim with reference to the self reinforcing nature of institutional system. His reading of Veblen's cumulative causation methodology signaled a fresh possibility for addressing the riddle of *cultural lag* reflected from the coexistence and persistence of past cultural practices with incongruent present material and technological conditions.

What makes Brette's interpretation crucial for the questions posed in this paper is the particular manner by which he explores the idea of institutional determinism in connection with technological determinism in Veblen's works. He states that "technological determinism," as conceptualized by Veblen, "must be qualified by the fact that, once established, institutions gain a certain autonomy and fall into a relatively coherent system that will, in turn, exert a determining influence on individual and social behavior" (Brette 2003: 463). Considered as such, the autonomous nature of institutions allows one to think of cultural diversity in processes of

---

2 *Vis a tergo* is a medical term that means "a force acting from behind."

developing, appropriating and using science and technology. This contingency ensuing from Veblen's institutionalism - which is so crucial for understanding the dissimilar engineering outlooks prevalent in America and Turkey- is persuasively articulated by Plotkin and Tilman (2011:78-79):

> At any given moment, science, its method, and its problems are products of cultural development; they are embedded within predominant cultural schemes and institutions. . . . If science, a realm of the most self-disciplined intellectual workers, is culturally mediated phenomenon, thoroughly enmeshed in society, industrial labor is no less exposed to the cultural mediation of experience. The industrial and mechanical workers who most directly undergo the rationalizing effects of technological processes are also products of cultural factors and powers. They too are prey to ...habits in their interpretations of experience . . . .

What Plotkin and Tilman (2011) argue here can be paraphrased as follows: The meanings of science and technology in the eyes of their practitioners are unequivocally mediated by the predominant spiritual attitude in society. Thus, we need to consider more carefully what Veblen might have meant by his somewhat uncommon notion of "spiritual attitude."

As we have seen previously concerning the Darwinian science and the natural rights philosophy, spiritual attitude is a result of a specific point of view that induces individuals to make an involved claim to the truth of a thing. If the natural rights view were predominant in society, private property would be affirmed and legitimized without any decisive questioning. In the case of the Darwinian scientific perspective with respect to the predominant spiritual attitude, private property would be seen as a social relation that has come into being by "the *vis a tergo* of brute causation" (i.e., the sum of the persisting past cultural practices that blindly impact on the present). In a different manner, the legitimacy of private property would come under critical scrutiny with the implication that it might cease to exist as a result of the conscious intervention of actors. Returning to Hodgson's claim regarding the caused nature of intentionality, one may argue that these two disparate spiritual attitudes cause two distinct kinds of intentionality. Given the existence of private property, the natural rights view causes a kind of intentionality on the part of actors that may induce them to preserve the current social and political arrangements. In contrast, the Darwinian science perspective causes a kind of intentionality that may stimulate actors toward changing the *status quo*. Thus, the predominant spiritual attitude carries out a selective control over particular institutions. Moreover, as Brette (2003: 464) argues, it may also "denature" or "degenerate" "them so as to make them coherent with itself."

Equipped with a basic understanding of Veblen's otherwise rich and versatile cumulative causation methodology, we can now turn to why he saw the emergence of a "Soviet of Technicians" posed against the obstructive tactics of businessmen as an unlikely prospect in America. For Veblen (1994/1899), the institutional evolution of American society resulted in the leisure class, conspicuous consumption, conspicuous waste, invidious comparison and pecuniary emulation as the fundamental pillars of the predominant spiritual attitude of common man. These institutions had come into being as a result of individuals' intentional actions geared toward gaining self-respect, social recognition, and hence social status (Powers 2005: 863). They fell into the relatively coherent cultural system to which Veblen referred as "business civilization" (Veblen 1958/1904). In business civilization, in order to be honorable one ought to be not only extremely rich but also exempt from industrial employment. Dowd (2000: 9) explains succinctly why this is particularly valid for Americans:

> We seek to convince others –and ourselves- of our worth by a demonstrably wasteful standard of living, and do what we can to become "exempt from industrial pursuits." To be sure, much of this is true because some wasteful consumption is pleasurable, and most industrial pursuits are poorly paid, monotonous, and even dangerous. But when our pleasure is derived from the attitudes of others (real or presumed) toward our consumption, and when we avoid working with hands even when such activities are not poorly paid, monotonous, or dangerous, it is emulation, or "honorific calculation," that motivates us.

For Veblen, it was the business point of view ensued from this particular code of social honor that appeared to engender the predominant spiritual attitude of common man in America. The latter came about as a consequence of the *vis a tergo* of institutional evolution of western European societies in line with the natural rights law formulated in the seventeenth and eighteenth centuries. This eventually led to the legitimization of liberal democracy in popular opinion via linking individually grounded human rights with basic freedoms.

In his account of the concept of freedom prevalent in Ottoman public opinion, Mardin (1988:25) provides a concise yet very lucid depiction of *the vis a tergo* of the scheme of individualistic conception of freedom in "Western Christianity." In Mardin's view (1988:24-25), an individualistically perceived idea of freedom does not only appear to be "an historical emergent" whose roots reside in the pre-medieval Christian publicists' longing for a "seamless society" but also a result of a series of "historical confrontations between social groups." He specifies four particular confrontations in this protracted evolutionary process. In chronological order these are the ones between (1) the pre-medieval Church and "autocrats", (2) the medieval Church and Empire (e.g., the confrontation between Innocent IV and Frederick II), (3) the late medieval feudal nobility and monarchy (e.g., Magna Carta), and (4) bourgeoisie and absolutist rulers in modern times. Mardin (1988:25) emphasizes that "a crucial shift occurs with Magna Carta: the collective purpose seen in early Christian ideas disappears and is replaced by matters relating to the 'control of the purse'." I should emphasize here that in Turkey the "control of the purse" came into being only in the twentieth century, an evolutionary difference that may explain the distinctiveness of its unique engineering outlook.

In his explanation of the social evolution of Western Christian societies, Veblen offered a compelling historical narration about how "the control of the purse," emphasized by Mardin, gained the upper hand in times of violent social confrontations, and defined the terms and conditions of social institutions from the perspective of the freedom to own property. He saw the late medieval "handicraft era" as the critical milestone in this unique path of cultural evolution. This era was characterized by the emergence of a "masterless man" who "escaped from the control of their feudal lords . . . by moving into protected cities" (Wenzler 1998:558). While this new persona was driven to productive activities by his "instinct of workmanship," he was at the same time interested in earning money for both survival and private accumulation. In this sense, he was both a craftsman and a petty trader. Because of this, for Veblen, "the habitual outlook and bias given by the handicraft system [were] of a twofold character –technological and pecuniary" (cited in Wenzler 1998:558).

What is critical for our discussion here is that the masterless man as a distinct actor in Western Christianity had unexpectedly legitimized "the control of the purse" or the natural rights law (i.e., the view that private property is a natural right). With the emergence of this novel character more and more people had come to believe that "the property possessed by a handicraft worker was morally equivalent to the amount of industrial labor that he had performed" (Wenzler 1998:559). A habit of thought that can be summed up as "If you are wealthy you are productive!" gained legitimacy among common people. Surprisingly, the culture of the handicraft era that had equated wealth with labor and thereby adapted to the demands of craftsmanship remained justifiable in the machine industry era – in essence, a cultural lag. In the machine industry era, businessmen or "absentee owners" as a faction of the leisure class established strict financial control over the industrial system through their ownership, and accumulated wealth via "force and fraud." This was at the expense of the industrious class involved in an impersonal as well as "interlocking" machine production process (i.e., the modern industrial system). Yet, despite the fact that they did not have anything to do with industrial employment, absentee owners remained to be seen as productive agents because of the enormous wealth that they possessed and controlled. In this sense, the businessman was (and still is) the degenerate form of craftsman. Thus, Veblen thought that the American engineers, because of their being just industrial employees without much prospect for becoming rich - or as Veblen put it, "public Merrymakers," not only had low self-esteem and social status but also had little chance to gain the backing of the underlying population who were sentimentally in "love" with businessmen. In other words, the dominant frame of mind prevalent in America was not particularly conducive to the formation of a revolutionary "Soviet of Technicians."

A revolutionary "Soviet of Technicians" in the service of common people: The case of Turkey

Returning to Turkey's engineers, one can argue that a revolutionary "Soviet of Technicians" in line with Veblen's depiction in *The Engineers and the Price System* has always been a possibility in Turkey since the second half of twentieth century. What is more; the spiritual attitude of the engineers of the Union of the Chambers of Turkish Engineers and Architects, which came into view in the late 1960s, is in sharp conflict with the business point of view. This spiritual attitude aligns with the ideas, principles and values of engineers largely referred to as "technical workers." In their own outlook, these engineers see themselves first and foremost as scientific experts and, because of their education and training, claim that they possess power over technology considered "a revolutionary force of production." Yet they also contend that the effective use of their scientific expertise over technology is obstructed by "imperialists" and "capitalists" or "the dominant forces" (*egemen güçler*), due to their sectional economic interests. In this context, they argue that governments of Turkey serve primarily imperialist and capitalist interests. Because of imperialism, capitalism and the ensuing political and economic dependence "people" (*halk*) and the country (*ülke*) are rendered culturally and socially backward and economically poor. This shows to them that technical workers are deliberately hindered from using their capacity to the fullest, and hence are prevented from fulfilling the requirements of their professional responsibilities at all levels of socio-economic planning required for social development. Thus they conclude: Under these conditions engineers must be politically active revolutionaries. The revolution in engineering must be a movement towards society captured by the motto "Engineering is in the service of society." The latter is a necessity tightly connected with the movement toward Turkey's democratization, which is a precondition for the elimination of social inequalities and injustices. Engineers, in order to fulfill their professional calling, must side with the oppressed and exploited laborers, namely the common people.

Obviously, behind the identity of the revolutionary-democrat engineer there is a prolonged process of evolutionary selection. We can begin with the origin of the word engineer, which is in Turkish *mühendis*. In the late eighteenth century, *mühendis* had been fabricated from the Arabic word *hendese* to refer to someone who knows and uses geometry in his occupation (Kunar, 1991). The first mühendis schools, *Bahr-i Hümayun* (1773) and *Mühendishane-i Berr-i Hümayun* (1795) were founded as military schools to generate a new group of officers who were supposed to know modern science and technologies developed in the west, and apply these in the organizations and activities of the state and the military. The underlying aim was to catch up swiftly with the technologically superior western states, and thereby reverse the decline of the Ottoman Empire and save the *Dar al Islam* (the land of Islam). In this sense, the engineer was intentionally created as a "savior" by the state with an unambiguous political mission. The origin of this persona overlapped with the end of traditional order and the beginning of the belated modernization effort called *Tanzimat*, i.e., the movement and process of the reorganization of the state and its relation to society by adapting modern western institutions.

Here an important detail should be briefly mentioned. Within the modernization process initiated from above, the state's creation of a group of technical officers with a secular educational background on the basis of modern science and technology led to a bifurcation not only in the state bureaucracy along the lines of modern/traditional, secular/religious and western/local axes but also within the *zanaatkar* (craftsman) community itself (Mardin 1994). The uniquely political creation of the engineer led to the social dichotomy referred to, by and large, as "*mektepli/alaylı*" (craftsman with schooling/ craftsman without schooling). In due course, the engineer had come to be viewed and approached deferentially as a *münevver* or *aydın* (enlightened and enlightener) with the fundamental responsibility and vocation of "saving the motherland." In this sense, seen as a social institution, the engineer in Turkey does not only appear to be the denatured or degenerated kind of ages old *zanaatkar* (craftsman or artisan) in the garb of the mysterious cloak *mühendis* but also a political actor beyond her/his professional field.

According to Er (1993), when the Turkish Republic was founded in the aftermath of the disintegration of the Ottoman Empire, there were only a small number of *mühendis* left in the country. On April 26, 1926, the Union of Turkish Master Engineers (UTME), the first organization of engineers was founded by 85 of these engineers as an alumni association without any legal authority over the engineering profession (Er, 1993). These engineers were all graduates of the *Mühendis Mekteb-i Alisi* (later to be *İstanbul Teknik Üniversitesi*), the only engineering school in Turkey at that time.

One of the founding members of the UCTEA, Muzaffer Binici's portrayal of the conditions that the engineers of the early decades of the Republican regime faced is noteworthy. The following quote provides more than a glimpse of how the engineers, just before the foundation of the UCTEA in 1954, would have posed themselves against the capitalists even if they had not taken on an anti-capitalist stand organizationally yet:

> In several public offices that did not want to hear the voice and suggestions of the *technique*, the inconsiderate management of responsible and authorized individuals caused a spiritual pain in our colleagues. Some of our co-workers who occupied technical positions did not hesitate to apply their personal judgments even if these opposed the principles of their profession. The pressure of *the unrestricted competition* caused frustration among *the contractor colleagues* who had devoted *their capital and professional life to public service*. Only a petition with a 16-kuruş stamp was needed to obtain the Certification of License; and *the capitalist contractor who had ruined the money, program and work of an organization could have easily found the opportunity to drag another public office through the same course of events.* There was not one single professional community that could have defended the rights of our colleagues from the day they began their careers to their posts in the civil service and eventually to an indifferent private life. (Quoted in Er 1993: 161, emphases are added)

The meaning of Binici's expressions is not difficult to decipher: Long before the foundation of the UCTEA, the engineers of Turkey had seen themselves as a special class of economic actors, who, in their own point of view, existed independently from the capitalist class. They thought that their autonomous social status had derived from their knowledge of "technique" or "state of the industrial arts," posing them as actors with the moral responsibility for being in the service of public. The latter would sometimes locate themselves in contradictory situations vis-à-vis the capitalist class whose main concern was pecuniary gain – as in the case of the conflict of interest between *the engineer* and *the capitalist contractor*.

Given the gloomy circumstances underlined by Binici, it is not surprising to find out that the official goal of the UTME was to put the various branches of the engineering profession together under the coordination of one single organization in order to defend "the rights of engineers." Because of the legal ban on the establishment of classed-based organizations during the first three decades of the Republic -which was effective until the mid-1950s- the UTME's goal did not initially come true. Then, on January 27, 1954, a proposal for the Code of Chambers prepared by the UTME and the UTMA (the Union of Turkish Master Architects) was suddenly promulgated by the National Assembly. Thus, after many bids and rejections, the Union of the Chambers of Turkish Engineers and Architects (UCTEA), one of the politically most influential professional unions of Turkey, gained the status of legal person.

The topic of "foreign" engineers was at the center of the founding members' "battle" for the rights of Turkish engineers. At this time, the Ministry of Public Works was having difficulty finding the needed technical personnel to work on large public projects. Because of the legally established salary scales, the Ministry could not offer a desirable wage to those engineers who might have wanted to work. When a foreign engineer applied to an advertised position, however, the Ministry could make an individual contract with this engineer and pay a more attractive wage. The following excerpt from the minutes of a meeting on the matter in 1953 may give some idea about why the Turkish engineers conceived the employment of foreign experts as an issue of *justice*:

If one of the engineers graduated from the same class gets a 60 TL daily wage and the other gets a 25 TL monthly principal salary, the Ministry of Public Works and those concerned must be responsible for explaining this *injustice.* An *injustice* has happened, as one friend did not give the salary of his own engineers to the 20 engineers that he brought [from abroad] in order to satisfy the needs of the country. *If engineers with the same qualifications got different salaries, this would cause a negative effect.* (Quoted in Er 1993: 54-55; emphases are added)

Binici expressed similar views in the same article from which I quoted previously. In this part of his reflection, he compares "modest, valuable and well-educated" Turkish engineers with foreign engineers by framing the latter as employees tied to "big interests." It is important to note that Binici refers to the Turkish engineers as "disappointed artisans":

In our country, which we are reconstructing now again after the great wars that had ruined and neglected her, with the disappointment of being just an onlooker we struggled against foreign elements' haphazard production of our national and local works. While in hotel corners, modest, valuable and well-educated Turkish *artisans* were trying to complete the small projects that they had obtained from here or there, foreigners in their fancy offices worked comfortably [on major public projects] that they got through big interests. (Quoted in Er 1993: 161-162 ; emphases are added)

Thus, as one would expect, in the years just after the foundation of the UCTEA - by laying a claim to being professionals with the knowledge of "technique" - the members of the UCTEA refused to be viewed as inferior to foreign experts. Their objective was to get organized within the Union and assert their distinct social and economic status in collective manner. Although the founding leaders succeeded in developing professional awareness among its members, they failed to create a strong sense of corporate collective identity under the UCTEA. They were mostly successful in acquiring cultural, symbolic and economic resources for their members. Nevertheless, they framed the engineer as an "artisan" with the knowledge of technique and claimed that "the fate of the country was the fate of the *mühendis*" (Er, 1993: 25).

In the second half of the 1960s, a group of young engineers and architects, who had become economically worse-off as result of the rapid increase in the number of engineers with the opening of new engineering schools, began to challenge the founding leaders of the UCTEA for being blind to the hegemony of capitalists over their work and submissive to receiving orders from them. At this time, just as in the rest of the world, socialism was not only popular but also triumphant in Turkey. Thus, by drawing from various kinds of socialist ideas and experiences circulating in the public, members of the UCTEA of the younger generation turned critical with respect to the power of the "dominant forces of society" over the "action fields of technicians" and redefined the requirements of their profession. They considered "the interests of the dominant forces of society" as the principal impediment facing "the attempt to satisfy the needs of all strata within society." In opposition to the impediment created by the "dominant forces," they thought they had to turn their face to society at large as there was "a huge demand for technicians" ensuing from the process of industrialization and social development. On the basis of such reasoning, at the beginning of the 1970s, the UCTEA had come forward to announce a new mission for the Union: "We, as engineers and architects of Turkey, are in the service of society."

The term society in the new mission referred to the ordinary people or the "common man" in Veblen's terminology. Considered on a global scale, this was indeed a very peculiar case. Majority of unions and associations of engineers around the world have come to terms with the political and social leadership of "vested interests" and conceived engineering and engineers as beings that are valued only insofar as they are of use to "business" (Meiksins and Smith 1996; Whalley 1986; Zussman 1985). The position of the UCTEA as an uncommon case rested on the understanding that the practice of engineering and engineers should become independent of the use to which they are put by business and be seen as beings that gain value to the extent that they open themselves up to the unmediated use of common people.

This radical break of the UCTEA with the hegemony of the vested interests gained further momentum after the 12 March 1971 military intervention. During the remainder of the 1970s, UCTEA fought against the constitutionally illegal actions of governments that were in the service of foreign and national vested interests and defended the democratic rights and freedoms of common people by participating in "the anti-fascist bloc." This was the fight within which the UCTEA transformed itself into a "revolutionary-democratic" organization, and for almost a decade participated in the political production of a democratic sphere in opposition to the oppression and exploitation of the vested-interests. [3]

The following excerpts amplify how determined the UCTEA was in acting upon the calling of the revolutionary-democrat engineer identity in the 1970s:

> We, progressive, democratic, revolutionary technical workers . . . Declare once again that [repressions] cannot stop the struggle of our people and its indispensable component, technical workers, for independence and democracy. (Birlik Haberleri (Union News), Issue 42, 25 June 1976)

> Technical workers have filled their struggle against the repression exercised by ruling classes with a political content by locating their professional problems within the totality of social problems at both national and international levels . . . The political content of the struggle has taken on a class character and the struggle of all technical workers has become a part of the struggle of all working masses. (Teoman Öztürk, President of the UCTEA, 1976)

After the 12 September 1980 *coup d'etat*, UCTEA as one of the leading organizations siding with the working masses and the coalition of the left, was literally crushed by the military regime. The leaders were arrested, persecuted and incarcerated. The Code of Chambers was amended to curb the political and economic power of the Union. All this happened while Turkish capitalism had been going through one of the deepest and most sever crises triggered by the global crisis of welfare capitalism or embedded liberalism. Just like in other cases, in Turkey too, the solution of the vested interests to the economic crisis was neoliberalism. As a pragmatic political project, neoliberalism aimed to dismantle the social state, and thereby free capital from the constraints of redistributive responsibilities, constructed once with the hope of inventing an equitable capitalism. It became all too clear that the fundamental mission of the emergent neoliberal state was to facilitate conditions for profitable business opportunities on the part of both domestic and foreign capital by atomizing individuals and casting them into, to use Marx's phrase, an "everlasting uncertainty." Under the conditions of political

---

[3] For the details of this epic period, see Öncü (2003).

oppression and neoliberalization, younger generation engineers of the 1980s found themselves alone with the task of building their lives as their "careers." All this led to the spread of individualism, careerism and an entrepreneurial spirit both among the administrators and the rank and file of the UCTEA.

In the 1990s the socially detrimental consequences of neoliberalism on the economically disadvantaged classes and groups became all too visible. In response to this, working class activism through labor unions revived and came forward with demands and aspirations in contradiction with the free market ideology of the vested interests. Thus all organizations representing the interest of the common people began to question and realign themselves in the face of growing opposition against neoliberalism. Insofar as UCTEA was concerned, two major contrasting points of view emerged and enrolled in a power struggle over the mission and the direction of the Union in this new era. The first point of view, in tune with the dominant neoliberal business spirit, defended a more limited political role for the Union. In this view, UCTEA should have exclusively acted as a professional organization and defined only the professional powers and responsibilities of engineers and architects. The second point view endorsed a more comprehensive political role for the Union in the social arena. In this view, UCTEA should have, in addition to functioning as a professional organization, first and foremost participated actively in the formulation of industrial and technology policies, possessed legal powers and responsibilities in the deliberations, policy formulations and implementations, and supervision processes in these areas. Moreover, the Union should also have gotten involved in other social and political processes that have had a crucial importance for the well-being of common people. Without doubt, the second view aimed to restore the mission of the Union prevalent in the 1970s, that is, "engineers in the service of society (i.e., common people)" represented by those who identified themselves as the "revolutionary-democrat engineers."

The conflict between the two factions came into open in *The UCTEA Democracy Program and the Democracy Convention* held in 1998. In the debates and discussions the revolutionary-democrats overshadowed the entrepreneurial faction and won the hearts and minds of the majority of participants. *The Convention* eventually stated the following definition for the organizational being of the UCTEA in the beginning of the new century - which is as active and spirited as ever today - as we saw in the summer of 2013 during the Gezi Revolt:

> The UCTEA aims at the preparation and implementation of science and technology policies that cater to the public interest, are oriented towards labor, and are integral and realistic. However, it is aware that under the present conditions it cannot accomplish this on its own. Therefore, it shall join forces with labor-based NGO's, other democratic mass organizations and political parties. It shall support their struggles. . . . (TDPDK, 1998: 53-54)

The *vis a tergo* of the revolutionary-democrat engineers of Turkey

Any attempt to reconstruct the institutional evolution of revolutionary-democrat engineer's identity in Turkey has to address the missing link between the concept of freedom and individualism in the history of Turkey until very recently. Turning back to Mardin's (1988) key article, one can argue that confrontations between social groups in the late-medieval and the early modern history of Turkey did not result in any significant "step away from the collectivist definition of freedom." In this part of the paper, by building from Mardin's work, I offer a brief sketch of the institutional heritage of the revolutionary democrat engineer identity. My account rests on the view that "the collectivist conception of freedom" as a cultural lag not only differentiates UCTEA from the majority of engineering associations and unions in the rest of the world but also constitutes the principal element of its spiritual attitude. In the point of view of the engineers of UCTEA, economic, social and cultural inequalities always have priority over individual freedoms and, first and foremost over the right of private ownership. Moreover, if these inequalities persist due to social and political arrangements they can justify state's active intervention into civil society in order to restore social justice. As we shall see, the engineers of modern Turkey inherited this spiritual attitude from the craftsmen of the Ottoman Empire organized into guilds.

What Aral (2004) argues in a recent article concerning the perception of the idea of "human rights" in the Ottoman Empire lends unequivocal support to Mardin's claim regarding the absence of an individualistic idea of freedom in Turkey's past. As Aral (2004:454) states, "The Ottoman system prioritized the benefits of collectivities rather than those of individuals, and emphasized justice rather than freedom." What is more, the idea of freedom, which had always been seen as secondary to social justice, was very much a spiritual notion rather than a rational one (Mardin 1988:25). Whenever it was uttered in a mundane fashion, it referred to the one who was not a slave (i.e., a reference to the legal status of a person). But if it had been used by reference to its deeper mystical connotations, it would have portrayed an ideal moral person according to the Islamic outlook. In this sense, it was considered an ontological state of the individual regardless of her/his legal status (Aral 2004:460). In order to be morally right, one must have prevailed over her/his worldly desires and passions and devoted her/his self completely to Allah. This was the true meaning of freedom in the eyes of the common people of Ottoman society. It was also a constant theme in the Islamic theology and jurisprudence -both before and after the Ottomans gained the leadership of Muslims- that a state whose members enjoyed uninhibited liberties of action could not realize a moral order, or what Mardin calls a "seamless society." Thus, while the rights law of the early modern Western Christianity rested on a rational view of individual freedom that one could allegedly comprehend through objectively observing and studying natural order, the one associated with the Ottoman Islamic tradition at that time was based on the God's revelation beyond any material or sensual experience. In other words, the latter was a collective representation of moral existence divinely exposed to humanity, which was the basis of a "*community-oriented* system of law. … No … polarity between state and individual exist[ed] in Islam" (Aral 2004:461).

For sure, no polarity existed between state and individual in the Islamic law understood as a moral doctrine. However, there existed not only polarity but also confrontation between state and individual as well as among individuals themselves as members of particular social groups in the practical world of Ottomans, which "was decidedly and unambiguously Islamic" (Faroqhi 2010:242). The Ottoman dynasty gained its legitimacy to reign first and foremost "through the practical services it rendered to the Muslim world. Sultans expanded the domain of Islam by conquering the land of infidel kings, and followed up their successes through the lavish provision of mosques and other charities" (Faroqhi 2010: 247). Secondly, they posed themselves as the rightful leaders owing to their purportedly divine role in the establishment of "just rule" in the world. "[T]his meant that the sultans claimed to protect their subjects, if necessary, against the administrators they themselves had appointed" (Faroqhi 2010: 247). The latter required a very delicate balancing act that was geared toward reconciling the Islamic law with the everyday rulings of the sultan (*kanun*). In other words, it necessitated an artful mixing of the religious precepts with secular rational imperatives.

Mardin (1988) suggests the use of "the idea of a tacit social contract" developed by Edmund Burke III so as to understand how this peculiar system of legal-rational authority within the boundaries set by the Islamic law had been rendered operational in the history of Ottomans. In Mardin's treatment, Burke's notion of "tacit social contract" refers to "the moral economy of Ottoman society, a concept that there existed socioeconomic arrangements in Ottoman society which provided a protective shield over Ottoman subjects, and which had to be respected" (Mardin 1988:29). Understood as such, at the heart of this contract was the dynasty whose symbolic force constituted the principal source of legitimization in all matters of the day to day rulings. In this sense, it was not the sultan *per se* but his lineage that had comprised the backbone of the Ottoman moral economy. The supremacy of the dynasty over the personhood of the sultan rested on a long-established point of view, according to which the sultan, due to his possible personal weaknesses, might fail to live up to the obligations of his leadership role. The Ottoman dynasty could never deviate from the principles of the divine revelation. "Basic to this view was the notion taken from a Quranic verse that the entire community was entrusted with ordering the good and prohibiting evil" (Mardin 1988:29). Beyond that, however, "Pragmatism was … the order of the day" (Faroqhi 2010: 251). This was very much a result of the structure of the religiously diverse Ottoman social formation within which the sultans as the rulers of the populace as a whole were supposed to establish a "just rule" for Muslims and non-Muslims alike.

Within the vast Ottoman Empire there were three distinct groups of economic actors: the farmers, the merchants, and the craftsmen. The farmers and the craftsmen, as "the classes who produced the essential necessitates of life," were subject to the regulations of the *hisba*. (İnalcık 1969:98). The *hisba*, constructed in line with what, following Mardin, we may call "the tacit social contract," was in practice a centrally administered market economy in which "a peasant or a craftsman should freely change the methods of production was not countenanced; his activities were permitted only within the limits of the ordinances laid down by the state" (İnalcık 1969: 98). What is more, the conditions of market supply and demand were under the strict control of the *İhtisap Ağası*, the head of the office of *hisba*. The latter was responsible for the requirement that the craftsmen were firmly regulated in their buying of raw materials and in the sale of their wares. In other words, "unrestricted" or "free competition" was not allowed in the Ottoman market economy. According to İnalcık, under normal circumstances, no craftsman was allowed to have a profit rate above 10 %. In this sense, the habitual outlook of craftsmen, if we use a Veblenian term, was not biased toward pecuniary gain. A well-demarcated legal and cultural boundary separated them from the merchants (*tüccar*) in that the latter was the only economic actor "who enjoyed conditions allowing them to become capitalists."

In Turkish *tüccar* is what in English is referred to as the big businessmen who own and control large sums of capital (*sermaye* or *mal*). As the moneyed class, the merchants "engaged in international and interregional trade or in the sale of goods imported from afar." Sure enough, controlling such a bulky "traffic" required not only huge amounts of accumulated wealth but also a vast network of business relations allowing the merchants to develop what Braudel once called the unique capitalist expertise, the capability of managing people from a distance, i.e. "absentee ownership." Unlike the merchants, the geographic span of the activities of the craftsmen was always local. In other words, they were local actors embedded in local traditions. They sold the goods that they themselves manufactured in the cities where they lived and worked. But that was not the only difference between these two social classes. The most critical difference was that merchants, unlike craftsmen, were "free" from the regulations of the *hisba*, and thereby "free to accumulate, by any means in [their] power, as much capital as [they] could" (İnalcık 1969: 98). As expected, their habitual outlook was entirely biased toward pecuniary gain. In the Veblenian sense, while the craftsmen made up the urban section of the industrious class, the merchants appeared to be a faction of the leisure class. Yet, similar to the other factions of the leisure class –namely, statesmen, officers and clergy- their wealth could have been confiscated by the state, if the manner by which they had accumulated their wealth had been perceived or framed as *unjust* according to the injunctions of "the tacit social contract."

As the most organized section of the urban industrious class, the craftsmen through establishing *taifas* (guilds) secured for themselves a notable political leverage so much so that "in many cases the very topography of the Muslim city, which was built essentially on the idea of a market, was determined by the needs of the guildsmen" (Lewis 1937:20). Although the Byzantine craft organizations of the fifth and sixth centuries appeared to be the predecessors of Ottoman *taifas*, the latter exhibited certain features that differentiated them from the former and came to be known more as a variant of the category of "Muslim guilds." Like their Byzantine counterparts, the Ottoman guilds were founded by petitioning for the permission of the state. The state in turn granted the license *from above* in order to regulate the markets and allot to each craft its place (Lewis 1937:21). In this sense Ottoman guilds were parts of the state organization and hence expected to perform some official duties of public control and supervision in their respective fields of production. Unlike their Byzantine counterparts, the Ottoman guilds, just as other forms of Muslim guilds in Islamic history, were also developments *from below*, formed not only in response to a state function but also to "the social requirements of the labouring masses themselves" (Lewis 1937: 36). When compared with the medieval Western Christian guilds where hostilities between the masters and the journeymen were pervasive because of the limited upward mobility opportunities for the latter, the Ottoman guilds were fraternal organizations without much "inner social differentiation" due to their being the heirs of the Islamic guild of the tenth and eleventh centuries. The latter "came into existence in its typical form as an artisan revolt against the rising commercial and financial capitalism of the day" (Lewis 1933: 37). In the thirteenth century, the last precursor of Ottoman guilds emerged in Anatolia (today's Turkey) that merged with Sufi and Dervish brotherhoods called *Akhis* -which in Turkish means chivalrous and generous:

> The Akhis first appear in Anatolia in the years immediately following the Mongol conquest. The period was one of general anarchy and disorder. The Mongols, who had destroyed the Saljuk State, failed to provide any effective alternative, and the administration crumbled away. During this period of crisis, the Akhis appeared as a strong widespread organisation, willing and able to control. With "solidarity and hospitality" as its code, the artisan class as its social basis and "the slaying of tyrants and their satellites" as its task, the Akhi movement spread rapidly in town and countryside. It was a movement at once social, political, religious and military. . . . the Akhis were not merely a professional organisation. They adopted as their duties the maintenance of justice, the prevention and punishment of tyranny .... (Lewis 1937: 28-29)

With the *hisba* system's eventual institutionalization, Ottoman *taifa* gained widespread legitimacy throughout the empire and took on the leadership responsibility of the industrious class as a whole (Rafeq 1991). The state was always being called upon by the guildsmen to resist "profiteering, fraud, and speculation" committed by the merchant class at the expense of the well-being of laboring masses (İnalcık 1969: 106).

Concluding remarks

"In the passage from medieval to modern times," writes Veblen (1997/1923:20), "certain profound and enduring changes took effect in the civil and political institutions of Europe." He then immediately adds:

> But all that had gone before was not lost, of course. Many things were carried over. As a matter of course very much of the institutional furniture of the Middle Ages has stood over and has continued to govern men's conduct and convictions very nicely in one bearing and another through the modern era . . . Regard being had to the very respectable body of such institutional holdovers, . . . the established order of law and custom is, after all, modern only in the sense that it has been modernised out of the past, and that its modernisation has necessarily been incomplete, in the nature of things.

These lines aptly summarize what has also happened in the case of the modernization of Turkey. In the passage from the Ottoman Empire to the Turkish Republic, a number of tremendous and permanent transformations materialized in the social and political institutions of Turkey. "But all that had gone before was not lost, of course. Many things were carried over." Unlike in the case of the modernization of Europe, however, "the institutional furniture" carried over got mixed with those imported from outside (i.e., "the West"). In this sense, Turkish modernization, while a continuation of the past, was also a divergence from it at the same time.

It is this mixed quality of the institutional baggage dragged into modern Turkey that makes social analysis of her both difficult and exciting all at once. It is difficult in that we are not provided with a handy theory readily available in sociology to deal with the peculiarities of the Turkish case, given that the latter has developed in a constant dialogue with the idiosyncrasies of European modernization. All of the key concepts of "western" sociology become problematic when they are used in the Turkish context without qualifications. Among these, the concept of individual appears to be the trickiest of all. If we pose the question as to whether the human individual should be granted certain incontestable "individual freedoms," we will be left in the dark by the answers of "common men" in the streets of Turkey even today. Their doubt over the notion of individually grounded freedoms appears to derive from the centuries old habitual spiritual attitude that sees uninhibited individual liberties as potential causes of social injustice. Of all the individually grounded freedoms, the ones associated with the unhindered right of private ownership are approached most cautiously because it is thought that these may lead to a social condition whereby one individual may gain at the expense of others, resulting in an immoral society.

As we have seen, in modern times this particular spiritual attitude is most prevalent among the engineers of UCTEA, who are indisputably the successors of the medieval craftsmen of the *taifa*. As the Ottoman craftsmen, they also feel extremely uneasy about the unrestricted market competition, which can only be legitimized by reference to the inviolability of private property. In the view of these engineers, free market is the opposite of social economy because it is the shortest way to the deviation from a high standard of morality and the loss of protection from the exploitation of the businessmen (i.e., the manipulation of market by the *tüccar* for pecuniary gain). Similar to their bygone *Akhi* "brothers," these engineers see themselves as agents responsible for "the maintenance of justice, the prevention and punishment of tyranny." So they mobilize their power over modern technology toward the protection of common people from "profiteering, fraud and speculation." Just like the olden *Akhi* guilds, their union, the Union of the Chambers of Turkish Engineers and Architects, is not merely a professional organization. Because of this very fact, the spiritual attitude of the engineers of the UCTEA has implications for the future fabric of Turkish society. Through their social, political and professional practices they have shown time and again that they deserve to be recognized as the masterless engineers who can act autonomously from "the established order of commercial profit and absentee ownership."

References

Aral, B. 2004. The Idea of Human Rights as Perceived in the Ottoman Empire. *Human Rights Quarterly* 26 (2): 454-482.

Brette, O. 2003. Thorstein Veblen's theory of institutional change: beyond technological determinism. *European Journal of History of Economic Thought* 10 (3) 455–477.

Dowd, D. F. 2000. *Thorstein Veblen.* New Brunswick and London.

Er, Ş. 1993. *Türkiye'de Mühendislik ve İTÜ Yüksek Mühendisler Birliği (Engineering in Turkey and the ITU Union of Master Engineers).* Ankara: Afşaroğlu Matbaası.

Faroqhi, S. 2010. The Ottoman Ruling Group and the Religions of its Subjects in the Early Modern Age:a Survey of Current Research. *Journal of Early Modern History* 14 239-266.

Hodgson, G. M. 2004. Veblen and Darwinism. *International Review of Sociology/Revue Internationale de Sociologie* 14 (3) 343-361.

İnalcık, H. 1969. Capital Formation in the Ottoman Empire. *The Journal of Economic History* 29 (1) 97-140.

Lewis, B. 1937. The Islamic Guilds. *The Economic History Review* 8 (1) 20-37.

Kunar, A. 1991. 'TMMOB ve "Mühendisler"in Oturma "Odaları"' (UCTEA and the Sitting "Chambers" of "Engineers"). *Birikim* 29 (9) 29-34.

Mardin, Ş. 1988. Freedom in an Ottoman Perspective. In *State, Democracy and the Military: Turkey in the 1980,* eds. M. Heper and A. Evin. Berlin: Walter de Gruyter.

———. 1994. *Cultural Transitions in the Middle East.* Leiden: E. J. Brill.

Meiksins, P. and Smith, C. 1996. *Engineering Labour : Technical Workers in Comparative Perspective.* London and New York: Verso.

Öncü, A. 2003. *A Sociological Inquiry into the History of the Union of Turkish Chambers of Engineers and Architects: Engineers and the State.* New York: Edwin Mellen Press.

Plotkin, S. And Tilman, R. 2011. *The Political Ideas of Thorstein Veblen.* New Haven and London: Yale University Press.

Rafeq, A. 1991. Craft Organization, Work Ethics, and the Strains of Change in Ottoman Syria. *Journal of the American Oriental Society* 111 (3) 495-511.

Rutherford, M. H. 1998. Veblen's Evolutionary Programme: A Promise Unfulfilled.

    Cambridge Journal of Economics 22 (4): 463-477.

TDPDK. 1998. *http://www.tmmob.org.tr/genel/bizden_listele_arsiv.php?bizden_kod=16&od=1*

Tilman, R. 1996. *The Intellectual Legacy of Thorstein Veblen: Unresolved Issues*. Westport: Greenwood Publishing.

————. 2004. Ferdinand Tönnies, Thorstein Veblen and Karl Marx: From community to society and back? *European Journal of History of Economic Thought* 11 (4): 579-606.

Veblen, T. 1994. (1899). *The theory of the leisure class: an economic study of institutions*. New York: Dover Publications.

————. 1958. (1904). *The Theory of Business Enterprise*. New York: Mentor Books.

————. 2012. (1919). *The Place of Science in Modern Civilization and Other Essays*. Fairford: The Echo Library.

————. 1921 (reprint). *The Engineers and the Price System*. Montana: Kessinger Publishing.

————. 1997. (1923). *Absentee Ownership: Business Enterprise in Recent Times: The Case of America*. New Brunswick, New Jersey: Transaction Books.

Wenzler, J. 1998. The Metaphysics of Business: Thorstein Veblen. *International Journal of Politics, Culture and Society* 11 (4): 541-578.

Whalley, P. 1986. *The Social Production of Technical Work: The Case of British Engineers*. Albany: State University of New York Press.

Zussman, R. 1985. *Mechanics of the Middle Class: Work and Politics Among American Engineers*. Berkeley: University of California Press.

Insubordination and the Technicians:
Thoughts on a Future Politics of Free Time

Sidney Plotkin

Throughout his work, Thorstein Veblen highlighted the costs of life under the "strong hand" of predatory chieftains. Human beings and the earth sacrifice much to sustain conspicuous empire of the few. Though Veblen was dubious about chances for an alternative, his *Engineers and the Price System* offers the prospect of a rational and humane social industrial economy managed by engineers. Considerable debate rages about Veblen's purpose. He was not, after all, a writer given to utopian thinking; his many books and essays crackle with unrepentant realism. His evolutionary outlook was insistently un-utopian, even anti-utopian. So why, late in his career, did Veblen choose to sketch an improbable "Soviet of Technicians"? [1] It is not as if he thought a rational economy was coming any time soon.

For all the controversy, the book's final chapter - "A Memorandum on a Practicable Soviet of Technicians" – actually offers a very clear statement of qualification. Veblen pungently observes there that the document's "purpose" is "to show, in an objective way, that under existing circumstances there need be no fear, in fact, no hope, of an effectual revolutionary overturn in America" (Veblen 1921: 132). Given its author's pessimism, the plan's vagueness is unsurprising. Why offer detailed counsel on such complex economic questions as valuation and price setting; distribution; or coordination of the various lines of production, when the chance to act on such plans is nil. Veblen's "soviet of technicians" exemplifies only the remotest possibility, a scheme without benefit of a chance.

Perhaps then leave it at that; it is pointless to ask or wish for more. Yet there may be some value in taking the idea seriously. Certainly the task of thinking through a more rational economic order is a worthy project. Moreover, because *The Engineers* frames Veblen's aspirations for technical rationality, it offers provocative counterpoint to his many arguments about the conservative cast of culture. But something more may be involved; an issue that extends well beyond economics. Veblen often wrote in his works about something that he called "the human spirit," frequently associating it with the idea of "idle curiosity" and its native creativity, playfulness and inquisitiveness. The question I'd like to pose then is this:

---

[1] Some critics believe the book exemplifies Veblen's political naivety; others his incipient technocratic authoritarianism; still others – and this is my view - think it was mainly intended as a satire that displays his deep political pessimism about the likelihood of progressive revolution in the US (Bell 1990; Tilman 1996; Knoedler and Mayhew 1999; Plotkin and Tilman 2011). Veblen probably believed the whole idea would be ignored. As he observed in a remarkable conversation with Stewart Chase shortly before he died: "Work of this nature...does not command attention, at least not yet" (Chase 1931: xii). In the end, because Veblen's intent is unknowable, we are left with the book's provocative if general design for a technocratic planned economy, the one place in his work where he begins to describe what production for generic human needs might look like in practice.

What might a rational economic order imply for a widened scope of freedom for "the human spirit'? On the face of it, technical rationality and "human spirit" seem to be alien, or at least quite different, categories. [2] Yet each informs an important dimension of Veblen's thought: his emphasis on technological development on the one hand, fascination with the sources of human curiosity and creativity, on the other. What can we learn by following the trail of this dualistic pattern?

So much has justifiably been made of Veblen's strongly Darwinian cast, his emphasis on the brute character of blind evolution, and his aversion to hedonistic or utilitarian theories of behavior, that it is easy to overlook the fact that Veblen saw human beings – individual human beings – as creative, thoughtful, and intelligent agents, as curious actors and doers. To be sure, Veblen was anything but an advocate of individualism. [3] He emphatically rejected the Austrian view of people as individualistic rational calculators. Neo-classical economics, he insisted, failed dismally to weigh the importance of social forces such as "habituation and conventional requirements" in human conduct (Veblen 1909: 239). Utilitarian theories of man as "a lightening calculator of pleasures and pains...a self-contained globule of desire" reflect a comparable failure (Veblen 1898c: 73-74). Individuals are never merely buffeted about by external or internal stimuli; they are active agents, they choose courses of action, although their choices and action emerge within frames set by native proclivities, established habits and prevailing institutions, each and all subject to forces of incontinent change. People deliberate, decide, and set purposes and ends for themselves, albeit from prevailing social repertoires. Conditioned by the past, sensitive to immediate pressures, human beings are also forever changing themselves – however slightly - by acting and reacting to the world as it impinges upon and is affected by their acts. Humans not only react; they act, and this "activity is the substantial fact of the process" of human behavior (ibid. 74).

Distinctively human activity is, for Veblen, irreducible to a single psychological formula. We are neither inherently rational nor utilitarian. Action draws from many factors. Ranking among the internal psychological elements Veblen thinks most provocative of human action are the "instincts" that he labeled "idle curiosity," "the instinct of workmanship," and "the parental bent." Each is part of the internal "spiritual" complement of human motivations that together and in myriad combinations work to influence what humans do (Veblen 1914: 86).

---

[2] For Veblen, the "instinct of workmanship" is a vital expression of the potential reciprocity of industrial rationality and the human spirit. See, for example, Veblen's notion of petty industry and individuality, p. 14 below.

[3] In writing of "the human spirit" and its various expressions, Veblen concerns himself with the subjective, teleological or purposive character of human consciousness, consciousness as it appears to and within the individual. He is neither offering a brief for individual rights nor an account of the juridical subject. He argues that as individuals act, so do they think, subjectively and purposefully, but always within social contexts (Veblen 1898b: 84; Kilpinen 2004). Because the larger evolutionary frame of his theory emphasizes the brute, non-conscious causes and effects of cumulative material and environmental change, it is sometimes easy to lose sight of Veblen's sense that the subjective or psychological standpoint of the individual must not be overlooked. Veblen, in short, neither omits individual consciousness as a factor in social life nor does he treat the individual simply as product of social, much less material forces.

Each instinct is, in turn, affected by the others, as well as by the culture, environment and historical ebb and flow. In short, Veblen offers a rich, multi-dimensional, dialectical view of the human actor, a dynamic and sociologically complex view of the human subject.

How then does this dynamic, animated aspect of Veblen's conception of what it means to be human stack up against the cold, implacable, mechanical rigor of the industrial system? Taking *The Engineers* seriously is a way of engaging Veblen's anthropological sense of the human within his larger view of industrial development. Reflecting on such issues is also a way of charting the scope and bounds of technical rationality and politics in Veblen's thinking. Involved here is a self-consciously utopian extension of Veblenian categories and analysis. Utopian – yes – clearly - so be it.

Economic Rationality and Time

Veblen believed a rational economic order would satisfy generic human interests; it would enhance human life on the whole, not constrict it. How much or even whether such a system might permit personal consumer preferences to shape output is not clear. [4] What is clear is that Veblen's preferred technocratic arrangement would not support investment and production decisions that reflect or to stimulate personal desires for "competitive advantage of one individual in comparison with another" (Veblen 1898a: 98). The overarching goal of Veblen's technocratic socialism would be to answer, rather than to amplify or expand "immediately organic functions" and needs (Veblen 1914: 86).

Let us assume for purposes of this essay that people have overcome all the vast impediments of culture and power that Veblen believes stand in the way of radical change. [5] Let us equally assume that a rational economy works on their behalf more or less as he envisioned. What implications might follow for the relationship between this economy and the active life of individuals, who would enjoy the remarkable opportunity to live beyond demands of economic necessity. [6] At least one crucial result would surely follow: to dispense with socially unnecessary status expenditure would dramatically reduce necessary labor time. My argument throughout rests on this key point. Its central claim is that Veblen's rational economic order, his economic planners, would have to make their peace with an expanded domain of free human activity, or risk running afoul of what Veblen called a popular "spirit of insubordination." "Time," as Marx once observed "is the room of human development" (Marx 1865: 422).

---

[4] Veblen does not in *The Engineers* - or anywhere else for that matter - spell out how his technocratic system will identify and prioritize generic human needs. Albeit very imperfectly, market pricing does coordinate demand and supply. Veblen suggests that panels of economists might help to perform this function in a rational order. However, given the less than impressive performance of orthodox economists in understanding or managing the crisis potential of capitalism, I for one hesitate to trust their reliability for this purpose in a post-capitalist order. The question thus remains very much open and very much problematic.

[5] More than anything else, it is Veblen's severe doubt about the chance for political change - not the technical difficulty of planning as such - that makes the present argument an essentially utopian effort in Veblen studies.

[6] For fascinating contemporary explorations of this issue, see Gorz (1985; 1988).

I start from the self-evident Veblenian proposition that a policy of building economic life around the principle of sufficiency would minimize socially unnecessary or "wasteful" expenditure of resources, labor and time. For Veblen, such "wasteful" expenditure of capital, labor and time, reflecting the distortion of predatory habit, absorbs the greater part of current economic expenditure and effort. Much of what we count as gross domestic product is in fact expenditure on a vast stock of goods designed to impress others with tangible evidence of status and power. This is, from a Veblenian perspective, sheer waste. [7] It results from a socially trained psychic eagerness for pecuniary display, the conventionalized habit of seeking symbols of invidious comparison, or in other words, items of "conspicuous consumption." Veblen's preferred economic system presumes a radically different kind of culture, an altogether different kind of "demand curve." He imagines a population agreeable to using economic means to serve generic, biologically driven metabolic needs - food, clothing, shelter, and health care - along with the material infrastructure essential to provide for these common goods. Such a population will have gradually lost the habit of using expensive things to signify yearnings for higher levels of dignity, status and power. Their economic life would serve intrinsically economic needs, not the social compulsion of individual status seeking.

Yet Veblen very well understood that "man does not live by bread alone." For him, reasonable people reasonably and efficiently served by their economy would nourish a host of immaterial ends and purposes, a vast range of projects governed by "the spiritual needs of man" (Veblen 1914: 86). Given "the relatively easy" labor load under such conditions, they would presumably pursue their peculiar cultural, social and spiritual needs outside the production system, in what Marx would have called their genuinely free time (Veblen 1892: 399; Marx 1973, 706). In short, I want to suggest and to underscore that what Veblen imagines with his "Soviet of Technicians" is not economic or technical rationality for its own sake, but the development of a rational economic system to support a robust, spiritually and aesthetically awakened life, what he termed "an enhancement of life and well-being on the whole." This is a vision, I contend, that anticipates a rising arc of human freedom, creativity and heterogeneity, and perhaps a little recalcitrance and conflict too (Veblen 1898a: 98).

Such a conclusion, while perhaps controversial, is a fair deduction to be drawn from Veblen's work. Indeed, it is foreshadowed in his discussions of primitive savagery, including his latter day quasi-anarchistic communities that continued to reflect savage norms. In other words, an economic order geared to material sufficiency would permit and indeed encourage

---

[7] Veblen's concept of waste is structural. That is, it entails considerably more than technical criticism of inefficiency, dissipation of scarce resources in contrast with their most effective utilization in production. For the technician, waste is the enemy of efficiency in any particular line of industry. Veblen certainly employs this technical concept of waste in his criticism of business enterprise. But "waste" as Veblen typically uses the term has a much more sharply critical social and political inflection. Waste specifies the predominant institutional bias of class-led social orders, their institutional tendency to drain off and consume the surplus product of their economies on behalf of the status and power aspirations of the "kept classes," at the expense of the needs of underlying populations. (Veblen 1923, 115) "Waste" is a matter of more than economic inefficiency; it is a matter of social and class injustice and injury. Indeed, it threatens survival of the species (Plotkin 2014). For Veblen's notion of cultural bias, see Veblen (1914: 177).

novel savage understandings of abundance. In the new order, abundance would no longer be conceived as an ever-expanding gaggle of symbolic goods, but as a surfeit of free time for pursuit of a full, robust, self-shaped life, variously understood and pursued by individuals, in their assorted and localized communities and cultures. Abundance would be savagely re-conceived as an abundance of freedom and time. What Veblen often referred to as "the human spirit" might then be emancipated from unnecessary labor to discover or to create new domains of expressiveness. Precisely the non-instrumental quality of "idle curiosity" would be released from its historical confinement by technical, industrial rationality. [8] Non-economic dimensions and possibilities of life would unfold in the arts, craftsmanship, spiritual renewal, and play. Humans would be radically liberated to discover and invent original forms and modes of self and communal expression. Unconstrained by pressures to work for the chronically dissatisfying purposes of invidious comparison, with their metabolic needs met, humans might re-discover the variety within and amongst themselves. In sum, a modernized savagery would offer the promise of a technically favored modernized anarchy.

Political Questions: Legitimacy

Needless to say, such arrangements are unlikely any time soon. We are not on the cusp of realizing our freedom from surplus labor; or at least as Veblen liked to say, "not yet" anyway. But even if this vision remains on the invisible far edge of political possibility, it is still appealing to think through some of the specifically political problems inherent in Veblen's ideal. Such a thought experiment is useful for several reasons. For one, it highlights aspects of Veblen's political thought, especially "the spirit of insubordination," which have not received adequate attention by scholars pre-occupied with the economic and sociological aspects of his writings. Moreover, thinking about incipient political tensions in Veblen's ideal helps to clarify potential dilemmas likely to be faced by governors of a well-running technocratic order, dilemmas and conflicts that reflect an inevitable chaffing between savage human spirits and industrial rationality, a potential for conflict hardly unknown to contemporary industrial societies at all stages of their development. In this way, a look at tomorrow illuminates an important aspect of Veblen's view of contemporary political discontents.

One such problem, for example, would be a continuing need for engineers to make legitimate their very claim to economic authority. For the new system to be faithful to popular will and democracy, values that Veblen embraced, it would have to possess a reservoir of popular consent and approval, and not only for the general structure of economic authority, but also for its institutions of conflict management and resolution. In other words, given a high likelihood of at least some disagreement about generic needs, priorities, and allocations, it is prudent to recognize that economic governance would have a necessarily or unavoidably political element.

---

[8] Veblen is uncharacteristically precise in stressing that "idle curiosity" concerns an interest in knowledge and ideas for their own sake, "apart from any ulterior use of the knowledge so gained." (1918: 4) See also Plotkin (2010).

How then would technocracy register its sensitivity to democracy, to popular will? How would relationships between managers and elected representatives be fashioned? What would the constitution of a democratic technocracy look like, or is such a concept inherently contradictory?

Late in his career Veblen seemed to toss such issues aside in a remarkably cavalier observation, one that seems to justify the belief of those who see his work as at best, politically naïve, or at its worst, downright authoritarian. In *Absentee Ownership* he proclaimed that a truly democratic industrial community could completely dispense with claims to legitimacy. An industrial republic, he observed, "would be nothing to bluster and give off fumes about; nothing better, in fact, than an unsanctified workday arrangement for the common use of industrial ways and means." Such a "commonwealth" would presumably draw its "sanctification," its legitimacy, from the fact of its sheer, self-evident, industrial and social rationality. Reason's justification, after all, is inherent in reason itself. Nationalism, patriotism, class and statehood having withered away, the community would neither urge nor require "sacramental value" (Veblen 1923: 28). Legitimacy, it would seem, is solely a political tool ruling classes use to justify their false claims to power. A reasonable, efficient economy would have no extra-material reason to justify its incipient rationality to society at large; its material rectitude would be plain for all to see, to understand and to embrace.

Much earlier and much more consistently throughout his writings, however, Veblen neither laughed away nor ignored questions of politics, consent, and legitimacy. Nor did he see reason in purely technical terms. As he said in *The Vested Interests and the Common Man,* published two years before *The Engineers,* "It is the frame of mind of the common man that makes the foundation of the modern world." The political corollary of this principle is not to be dismissed. Popular "advice and consent " are now "indispensible to the conduct of affairs among civilized men, somewhat in the same degree in which the community is to be accounted a civilized people" (Veblen 1921: 16). [9] Of course, Veblen fully understood that popular opinion was easily misled by veneration of ancient habit, especially when tutored in this direction by the business and political leaders and the hired opinion engineers of "ostensible democracy." Even more to the point, Veblen's impressive critique of Marx's theory of class struggle emphasized precisely why it is so important not to confuse the cumulative force and rationality of technological change, including its remarkable promise of human liberation from work, with politics, whose dynamic "moves on the spiritual plane of human desire and passion" (Veblen 1906: 414). [10]

---

[9] In fact, in one of his first published writings, Veblen stated unambiguously that "modern constitutional government" offers a revealing clue to the democratic organization of a future socialism, and such a political "system, especially as seen at its best among a people of democratic traditions and habits of mind, is a system of subjection to the will of the social organism, as expressed in impersonal law." (Veblen 1892: 404)

[10] For Veblen, Marx made the same error as the utilitarians: he tended to reduce class political behavior to a pleasure-pain calculus. He over-rationalized the process by which people arrive at their political conclusions; this despite the fact that Marx's view of the economic process emphasized, much more correctly in Veblen's opinion, blind and brute material development. (Veblen 1906: 411-417)

Politics deals in the sentiments, in passions and emotions; it trades on psychic dispositions and immaterial values. As it struggles to cope with the present, popular politics forever looks to recapture a heartfelt sense of the past, of tradition, custom and habit. A main corollary of Darwinian evolution, Veblen (1907: 441) argued, is

> that men's reasoning is largely controlled by other than logical, intellectual forces; that the conclusion reached by public or class opinion is as much, or more, a matter of sentiment than of logical inference; and that the sentiment which animates men, singly or collectively, is as much, or more, an outcome of habit and native propensity, as of calculated material interest.

Overcoming such political anachronism and sentimentality will be exceedingly difficult at best, perhaps impossible. [11] This is a main reason why Veblen was so pessimistic about chances for revolution. But even assuming that human beings could make substantial progress in this direction, their political behavior would doubtless retain elements of sentimentality and passion. The enduring emotional quality of political dispositions suggests why a progressive material system cannot ever wholly, convincingly, or democratically divorce itself from concern with the "the spiritual plane of human desire and passion," and thus with questions of popular approval, sentiment and legitimacy.

But by no means did Veblen consider such sentiments to be exclusively the legacy of bourgeois or predatory egoism. Such anachronistic habits will undoubtedly continue to matter, as they always do. But Veblen also alludes to "native propensity" as equally important to shaping political feeling and behavior. We can see something of this "native propensity" in the idea that humans are sentient creatures who move through life and act within their social settings by forming and pursuing their communally influenced but self-chosen ends. In other words, there is much evidence in Veblen's work of his sensitivity to human willfulness and purposefulness as characteristics essential to the human make-up. The very integrity of this purposefulness will undoubtedly push humans to demand justification or legitimacy, good *political* reasons, in other words, for social limits on their ability to chart their own directions in their own ways. Among the most vivid constructions of this idea in Veblen's work is his notion of a "spirit of insubordination." To understand its fuller implications, it is necessary to say a few more things about Veblen's sense of what it means to be human.

The Human Being: Intelligence, Agency and Exploit

As we have seen, Veblen considered the human being to be "in an eminent sense an intelligent agent...endowed with a proclivity toward purposeful action." Evolution gifted the species with a "discriminating sense of purpose" (Veblen 1898b: 80). Notice: Veblen refers not simply to purposefulness, but to "*a discriminating* sense of purpose." By this I think he means a well-honed capacity to differentiate or distinguish between various socially available goals or ends, and to choose amongst them those that most closely suits an individual's peculiar sense of

---

[11] Here we see how Veblen's theory embraced a synthesis of objective evolutionary factors and human subjectivity. Material factors move with incontinent force; human agents, embedded in a material word, respond to change with the habits they have inherited from the past, and in the process, however slightly or incrementally, change themselves. For humans, to make radical change is unlikely to say the least.

need or interest. Humans may widely diverge in the choices they make, "but the impulse" to "discriminate" among purposes "is a generic feature of the race" (ibid.: 80). It runs deep in the psychological and spiritual character of human beings to be discriminating or selective in their choices. Now, to be clear, Veblen does not equate human powers of discrimination with some notion of free will, or freedom in any simple, unconditional sense. But when he comes to define a chief critical concept of his work, the idea of "exploit," connections between discrimination and a notion of socially mediated freedom become unmistakable.

"Exploit" is Veblen's term for relationships of illegitimate control or power. In exploitative relations, an "agent" uses intelligence and strength to make another serve the exploiter's purpose. Exploit, Veblen writes, consists of "the conversion to his own ends of *energies previously directed to some other end by another agent*" (Veblen 1898a: 12-13, emphasis added). Where exploit unfolds, another human being's inner capacity to discriminate is surrendered to the exploiter, whose own purpose now prevails. Exploit is thus an absolutely crucial concept for Veblen. It denotes his critical understanding of the power relationship as a relation of physical and/or psychic domination. Exploit may result from force or fraud, from coercion or manipulation, or some combination of each. But whatever its techniques, with exploit, the exploited subject becomes an object; she loses the freedom to act in accordance with her own capacity to discriminate or to choose her own direction or purpose. [12] She is no longer so much an intelligent as an abused agent, her human power to choose sacrificed to an exploiter's power and purpose.

The case would seem to be very different if a legitimate authority asks the other's permission to establish purposes that diverge from the individual's own choices. In the latter case, the individual's rational, intelligent consent is the condition for altering or substituting society's aims for the individual's. Indeed, from this standpoint, Veblen's idea actually points back, at least minimally, to an essentially Lockean conception of democracy, a political system whose claims to achieve social purpose reflect the guidance and consent of the governed. Power is rendered responsible and legitimate when it is ordained and governed by citizens who endow it with their own intelligent, knowing, rational direction and concurrence. Democratic authority thus rests precisely upon recognition and respect for humanity's "discriminating sense of purpose." [13] Powers of social and individual discrimination can only converge fairly and justly though a rational politics of consensual government. Authentic democratic legitimacy demands such coincidence. "The spirit of insubordination," I want to suggest, is Veblen's way of talking about the intransigence of human beings with efforts to suppress their discriminatory powers beyond the limits of consent and the clear imperatives of social necessity. The "spirit of insubordination," in other words, is the most forceful Veblenian expression of human resistance to illegitimate power, a point I will develop below.

All this may seem surprising, even disconcerting. Critics and students of Veblen have regularly insisted that among his main contributions to political analysis is his stress on the

---

[12] Plotkin and Tilman (2011, esp. ch. 5). Use of the female gender is particularly apt in this connection because Veblen clearly believed women were the first members of the human race to suffer exploit (Veblen 1898a: 23-24).

[13] While Veblen veers away from discussions of the juridical subject, thinking about relationships between "the technicians" and "underlying population" suggests the potential value of such a concept even for, perhaps especially for, utopian political thought in a technocratic context.

power of ruling class ideas to enmesh underlying populations in ideological misunderstandings of their material interests. Pacification through processes of popular emulation - identification with leisure class values - offers the most potent means by which predatory orders obtain mass loyalty and subordination. His argument for the manipulative power of ruling class ideas and persuasion is so strongly etched that he often expresses the harshest skepticism about historical chances for a more rational economic order to emerge. People habituated to traditional emulative values will trade the historic possibility of freedom from toil in order to acquire more means of conspicuous consumption. Veblen (1898a: 111) underscores this point in one of the darkest, most portentous passages of *Theory of the Leisure Class.* In his words, as:

> increased industrial efficiency makes it possible to procure the means of livelihood with less labor, the energies of the industrious members of the community are bent to the compassing of a higher result in conspicuous expenditure, rather than slackened to a more comfortable pace. The strain is not lightened as industrial efficiency increases...but the increment of output is turned to meet this want, which is indefinitely expansible, after the manner commonly imputed in economic theory to higher or spiritual wants .

Capitalism absorbs and manipulates "the human spirit," twisting its yearnings for self-expression, its "higher or spiritual wants," into forms that can be answered only by the ever-expanding commodity form. No wonder serious students of Veblen like to rate him with Gramsci, as a comparable theorist of hegemony (Diggins 1990; Ross 1991). Such emphasis is eminently reasonable. But it is a view that can be taken too far, effectively obscuring other aspects of Veblen's political thought, which cut against this conservative grain. Veblen saw more than popular quiescence in politics and political behavior. He saw potential for militancy and insubordination too, a potential that would not disappear, even with the onset of a rational order. [14]

Anarchy, Necessity and Independence

Curiously, Veblen introduces "the spirit of insubordination" in his study of an authoritarian state bent on enforcement of the strictest discipline and subordination, *Imperial Germany and the Industrial Revolution* (1915). The idea appears within the context of an effort to describe Prussia's pre-feudal peasant culture, a quasi-anarchistic society quite unlike the military authoritarianism of the imperial state. Veblen's point was in part to dramatize the slow evolution of Prussian institutions, their halting transition from what he called northern European "pagan anarchy," into a long lasting militarized feudalism, one that directly and profoundly influenced the character and purposes of latter day Imperial Germany. But an important slice of Veblen's argument is often overlooked: notwithstanding the increasing militarization and centralization of the German state, its old anarchic habits of local self-government never disappeared. Furtively, awkwardly and subversively, they lurked within the interstices of modern Prussian

---

[14] Lest there be any misunderstanding, I do not dissent in any way from the claim that Veblen's main political emphasis falls on the side of power's ability to mold popular consciousness in its own image. But I regard this claim as an emphasis, a relative not an absolute claim. It does not preclude Veblen's belief in the lesser possibility of an oppositional consciousness developing against power. The latter chance, albeit improbable and largely inchoate, nonetheless deserves consideration in any assessment of the fullness of Veblen's political thought

life and politics, fueling potentially disruptive conflicts with authority. And this enduring influence was no accident; it reflected what Veblen saw as a basic feature of social development.

Human experience and self-consciousness first emerged and then evolved for the longest time within savage forms of community: small, poor, sedentary, and loosely governed associations of laboring people. With millennia to work upon its human subjects, savagery, with its largely anarchic habits of workmanship and self-rule, imprinted itself deeply on the human psyche. This experience left lasting deposits of habit and inclination. [15] These savage habits and dispositions would persist even amidst the increasingly predatory relations that abrogated savagery. Imperial Germany was a special case in many respects. But it was not unique in the fact that its cultural underbrush sheltered savage remnants. The *longue duree* of savage experience left lasting traces, anarchistic traces that were more than slight. Libertarian dispositions effectively approximated "native traits of human nature," so much so that Veblen believed "this anarchistic animus may well mark a generic bent of the human race at large" (Veblen 1915: 325, 328).

Northern European pagan anarchy is one later expression of savage culture. It re-emerged in lands bordering the Baltic and North Seas, substantially outside the predatory culture of antiquity. Comparable qualities and features would appear in the handicraft-based towns of the early modern era, especially in England. The vivid political experience of these municipal institutions would inspire the growth of modern liberalism and its ascendant figure - "the masterless man." [16] A set of close material and political connections and parallels bind such instances together, making them kindred forms of a common later savage type. Their cumulative effect is to support a vision and practice that inspires both communal strength and individual determination. These patterns, for Veblen, complement more than contradict themselves, at least up to a point.

Materially speaking, pagan anarchy was a petty industrial system; it worked "by manual labor;" "its scope" could not "exceed the manual reach of those engaged" (Veblen 1915: 325). Small-scale labor and hand tools permitted and encouraged individual and household self-reliance and autonomy. They stimulated a kind of rough-hewn economic independence to sprout up in and along the north European littoral, a sense of independence closely allied with a "spirit of insubordination." Veblen is quite unambiguous about the personal qualities that flowed out of petty industrial anarchy. In such simple orders, he insists, "The substantial fact is the personal force and temper of the human individual" (ibid.: 326; 1923: 48). Here, technical rationality and the human spirit flow easily one into the other. Hardly alien or estranged, each seems to be the condition of the other. [17]

---

[15] Veblen offers one sketch of savagery in the opening chapter of *Theory of the Leisure Class* (1898a); but chapter two of *The Instinct of Workmanship* (1914) adds much more detail, especially in regard to the maternal, female bias of primitive anarchy. On the importance of anarchy to Veblen's political thought generally, see Hodder (1956); Patsouras (2004); Plotkin and Tilman (2011).

[16] For the powers of late feudalism, the "masterless man" "was a graceless intruder and a good deal of a nuisance...an institutional misfit (whose) nearest modern analogy...would be a tramp, a drifter, a hobo, a species of Industrial Worker of the World at large, taking that term in its simpler more sinister meaning" (Veblen 1923: 45). He was, in short, the epitome of "the spirit of insubordination."

Of course, the pagan community certainly entitled itself to regulate the common affairs of its members. "The moral common sense of his neighbors" served as a broadly constraining limit on any individual behavior that defied community norms, a limit probably "fixed by the current apprehension of what is serviceable for the common good on the one hand and what is disserviceable, on the other" (ibid.: 329). Otherwise, it appears that people pursued and asserted their own peculiar courses of action, their own choices, to discriminate as they wished, undeterred by excessive or unnecessary social control. [18] As Veblen described the loose anarchic balance of community and liberty, "individual idiosyncrasy runs free so long as its' bearing on the common good is indifferent" (ibid.: 329). An inveterate claim to individual powers of self-discrimination, including freedom for idiosyncrasy, wove itself firmly through the fabric of pagan anarchy.

"Man's life is activity," Veblen observed, "and as he acts, so he thinks and feels." Moreover, "What men can do easily is what they do habitually and this decides what they can think and know easily" (Veblen 1898b: 85, 87). Pagan anarchy left people alone to act and to think as they saw fit, to discriminate freely and easily, at least within prevailing limits of economic common good. This widely acknowledged sphere of self-chosen action provided an experiential and material seedbed for the growth of claims to idiosyncrasy and eccentricity. People saw these as legitimate claims against the community. Again, as a person acts, so the person thinks and feels. Where the individual's behavior had little or no material impact on his neighbors, eccentricity, no matter how odd or strange, was tolerable. In this sense, the community's animating social principle was an attitude of "live and let live," especially for matters falling outside matters of material necessity. After all, even under relatively primitive conditions, human survival rested on serviceable economic cooperation, not necessarily strict conformity in every respect. Battles between individual and community were best kept to a minimum, of course. "Man," after all, is to be classed with those animals that owe their survival to an aptitude for avoiding direct conflict with their competitors" (ibid.: 86).

But despite human aversion to conflict, people were apparently prepared to defend their independence. Their inveterate expectation of freedom for idiosyncrasy was part and parcel of anarchic experience and habit; it was a social norm that demanded more than small measures of communal respect and tolerance. Individuals did not truck easily with what they took to be unnecessary or surplus social control. Anarchic experience led humans to develop a bent toward resistance and opposition against communal efforts to exercise power above and beyond the call of economic necessity. For "archaic anarchism," therefore, the reigning notion of justice swung between "individualistic" and "democratic" values. As Veblen explained,

---

[17] Only when the "industrial system" removes the human element from substantial roles in production do industrial rationality and "the human spirit" become increasingly disparate, if not antagonistic elements of social life. In this sense, a post-capitalist form of savagery would seem necessarily to involve radical re-direction of "the instinct of workmanship" away from necessary labor.

[18] Whether such individuals conceived or spoke of the space they reserved for themselves as "freedom" is quite beside the point. It is their perception of independence or self-direction that I am concerned with, not their vocabulary.

These are the two spiritual foci about which the orbit of right and honest living swings; and so long as this orbit maintains its balance it meets the demands of justice, because such is the moral bias native to man, as selectively determined in the archaic days when the extant types of human nature made good their survival. (Veblen 1915: 328)

On the one hand, communities should see to their economic needs – this is the core regulatory principle of any society anxious to survive; on the other, individuals will see to the preservation of their eccentricities under a policy of Live and Let Live. Here is the driving force of "the spirit of insubordination," the insistence on saying "No!" to excessive claims to power. This spirit of insubordination reflects the vigor of the individual's insistence "to live as good him seems," or, in other words, to discriminate among his own purposes in his own way and to fight for space within which to continue doing so (ibid.: 100, 327-329). [19]

Exploit, Modernity and Insubordination

The spirit of insubordination is central to Veblen's sense of the anarchistic value of "live and let live". It exists in direct political counterpoint to - indeed it is the direct negation - of exploit. To see why this is so helps to illuminate the normative strength of Veblen's concept.

As noted above, with social relations of exploit, one set or class of humans lose their powers of discrimination to another. Unlike a process of intelligible, transparent rational will formation by consent, with exploit, the predator either blocks consent entirely through coercion, or uses superior resources to load or bias the set of prevailing ideas in his favor. Exploit thus either excludes democracy or distorts and obfuscates its rational character. The result is that the exploited serve the predator's design, not their own. Throughout his work, Veblen stresses the overwhelming effectiveness of the ideological power to mislead. But the "spirit of insubordination" indicates a limit to domination. It marks a moment of resistance in Veblen's political thought. With the spirit of insubordination Veblen, *begins* - and I am not making a stronger case than that - to chart a human self-consciousness of self-chosen purpose, including the felt need to assert and defend it, a kind of recalcitrant will to freedom. Here Veblen proclaims the anarchist's negation to Nietzsche's will to power.

Insubordination is a rejection of unwarranted power that curtails human abilities to discriminate and choose. It is action aimed at preserving the inner integrity of human purposefulness; it demands respect for essential human powers of discrimination. [20] In short, the spirit of insubordination indicates that Veblen saw limits to repressive emulation. Upper classes do not have absolute power to mold underlying populations to their liking. People can seek to go their own eccentric way and to demand political respect for such seeking.

---

[19] At its most basic, simple level, the spirit of insubordination is manifest most conclusively in the libertarian credo: "live and let live." Indeed, at one point Veblen insists that "the ideal of insubordination" is exactly the active assertion of the "live and let live" principle, an ideal that has "eaten too close to the bone in the north-European hybrid to let him settle down into wholesome content without its realization" (Veblen 1915: 327).

[20] Strikingly, this zest for freedom might well be more spirited among women than men. Of this gender difference in the thrust toward freedom, Veblen notes "The impulse is perhaps stronger upon the woman than upon the man to live her own life in her own way" (Veblen 1898a: 358). Given Veblen's (1914, ch. 2) sympathetic observations about maternal anarchy, this gendering of the interest in freedom is not terribly surprising.

Because, for Veblen, anarchistic habits remain ever-present in human consciousness and culture, even if only in feint, tentative ways, individuals' spirit of insubordination remains a live factor in what can turn out to be a contested politics of power. It would not be too much to say that, for Veblen, "the spirit of insubordination" is the fighting spirit of popular self-rule. [21]

Clearly, the idea of a "spirit of insubordination" has normative implications. It invites critical thinking about distinctions between economically legitimate and illegitimate claims to power. Even more important, it compels thought about how such judgments should be decided and the criteria that should be applied. For much of Veblen's thinking about economic rationality, this crucial question looms in impersonal terms and centers on his structural concept of "waste". Thus in *Theory of the Leisure Class,* he is at pains to stress that the notion of "waste" should not be judged according to subjective or culturally informed criteria. Waste is to be determined on quite objective grounds. The test is "whether aside from acquired tastes and from the canons of usage and conventional decency its result is a net gain in comfort or in the fulness of life" (Veblen 1898a: 99-100). The requisite standpoint is generic; it is species-based: the issue is whether a given economic usage "serves directly to enhance human life on the whole...usefulness as seen from the point of view of the generically human" (ibid.: 99, 98).

Strikingly, Veblen never explains who should make such a judgment. He does not even say whether any individual or group, including his "Soviet of Technicians," should *ever* be in a position politically to make or to enforce it. In fact, I think that it makes much more sense to understand Veblen's idea of "waste" as a theoretical, critical category rather than as a tool or guide for policy analysis. After all, Veblen never advances more than a tentative case for judging generic need; indeed, he is forever reminding readers that his outlook deserves skepticism, debate, and re-examination. Consistently refusing to declare the truthfulness or authenticity of any of his arguments, he suggests their reasonableness, never their veracity. Veblen's theory of waste offers a heterodox critical standpoint against orthodox economics, not a political argument for any definite substantive alternative. Its implied scheme of value is critically suggestive, not directive. His offer of objective economic analysis is always governed, controlled and limited by the strength of his aversion to staking any claims to undisputable truth.

Veblen's offers an acute but self-limiting critique: it is powerful, but intellectually and politically constrained by a methodologically self-conscious refusal to promise more than he can adequately defend. That he speaks both radically and modestly is a major reason for his much criticized political quiescence (Plotkin and Tilman 2011: 30-38).

With the spirit of insubordination, however, we locate a major shift in perspective. Veblen moves from humanity's generic features toward interest in the conscious, subjective outlook and action of individual human beings, an expression of "the personal force and temper of the human individual." In the immediacy of conflict between power and the subject, factors excluded by his generic, species standpoint now become highly pertinent and active. We are dealing here with a recalcitrant and acutely subjective political consciousness, with the aroused

---

[21] Considered from the perspective of the spirit of insubordination, the great formal differences between democracy and anarchy matter less than their shared principle of faith in the ability of ordinary people to govern the community's direction without impinging on personal liberties.

agent, not the cold implacable environment. Thus the principle of "live and let live" inspires insubordination to take effect in personal, immediate and directly political ways. Insubordination is aggressive and assertive in its negation of power's claim. The subject acts. Here is a moment of political agency that resonates with efforts to unify belief and practice, principle and reality, behavior and institution. Far from his characteristically dispassionate, cool, aloof scientific standpoint, Veblen suggests the appearance of people who are fired by a spirit of resistance, who are ready to spit in the eye of power.

Insubordination is a noisy political declaration of individual desire to be insulated, protected against demands of socially excessive power. Most important, though its roots lie in what Veblen suggests is "a generic bent of the human race at large," its stubbornness as a form of individual self-expression stems – and this point is extremely important- from the cultural support it draws from libertarian and anarchistic habits of thought. These are ingrained in political culture, imprinted in a host of liberating forms, including the common law, political institutions, the philosophy of natural rights, or most recently, populist expressions of democracy (Veblen 1915: 328). The spirit of insubordination offers a dramatic, if admittedly rare moment of critical subjectivity in Veblen's political thought, one whose contemporary relevance looms large, however, and not least for those contemplating centralization and rationalization of economic and political institutions.

In a footnote in the "supplementary notes" to "pagan anarchy," Veblen makes this point crisp and clear. Referring to the spirit of insubordination, he admonishes economic planners to understand that:

> The ubiquity and persistence of this moral bent is by no means a newly discovered fact, of course. It is precisely this manifest ubiquity and persistence of it that makes this human trait – perhaps human infirmity – an invaluable premise in any inquiry into the practicability or expediency of any scheme of control or any projected line of collective enterprise. (ibid.: n.1, 328-329)

These remarkable words cannot reasonably be read as anything but a warning, a caution signal, to planners, regulators and controllers everywhere. Move forward gingerly with your designs for control, lest you step on the tripwire of popular insubordination. More is involved here than strategic advice to planners. Veblen is alluding to deep strains and contradictions, sources of pointed conflict embedded in the political culture of modern industrial society, reflecting a spirit that "has eaten...close to the bone" of modern peoples. [22] From an evolutionary perspective, millennia of life under the sway of savage institutions worked the spirit of insubordination into the very tissue of human nature, enough so that it "may well mark a generic bent of the human race at large." From a more immediate western perspective, the roots of modernity in institutions of the handicraft era made liberty and autonomy chief values of the emerging system of liberal capitalism, first in England, then elsewhere. [23]

---

[22] See note 17 above.

[23] Veblen (1915: 100) observed specifically for the English case that "the ancient animus of insubordination...took effect in the affairs of the commonwealth, threw the material interests and initiative of the individual into the foreground of policy, changed the 'subject' into a 'citizen,' and went near to reducing the State to a condition of 'innocuous desuetude' by making it a bureau for the administration of the public peace and the regulation of equity between private interests".

People once took such values seriously; they still do. But liberal capitalism changed its structure in three fundamental ways that profoundly unsettled possibilities for insubordination. From the technological side, of course, capitalism no longer rests on personalized handicraft, but on a cold, unforgiving industrial system, a structure of mutually and tightly interdependent technological functions and operations. These do not abide individual eccentricity. From the business side, liberal capitalism, of course, gave rise to the giant multinational corporation and its allied web of global financial institutions, all bound together in a vast planetary system of absentee ownership and pecuniary relations. Then of course there is the increasingly bureaucratized administrative state, with its powers centralized in executive hands, far removed from "the underlying population."

In all these ways, western civilization has developed technological, economic and political institutions that dragged people out of a history of social arrangements that more sympathetically reflected their incipient libertarian bent. If Veblen is correct - and there is plenty of evidence of popular unrest today – from Istanbul to Kiev, from Cairo to the U.S. Tea Party – to suggest that he may be - modern populations find themselves aching for return to smaller scale communities, for greater opportunities of self-government and a wider swath for their own independence and autonomy. This is why, in Veblenian terms, so many modern peoples – current resistance to political centralization of the European Union also comes to mind - chafe at efforts to consolidate, unify and coordinate absentee institutions. It appears that they have indeed "been restlessly casting back for some workable compromise that would permit their ideal of 'self-government' by neighborly common sense to live somehow in the shadow of that large-scale coercive rule that killed it" (ibid.: 326-327).

Herein lies the problem: for "it happens that insubordination is the vital principal of this defunct system of self-government," while modernity rests precisely on subordination of individual to system: technological, financial, and political (ibid.: 327). Contradictions between ancient anarchistic legacies and contemporary social imperatives demanding predictability and control, lead Veblen to predict continuing stress, discontinuity and conflict in the evolution of modernity. Human beings are ill suited by spirit and temperament to the industrial world they have made. The springs of alienation and estrangement run very deep. As a result, for such a regime, it is hard to anticipate any "enduring continuity of popular welfare." Indeed, to the contrary, "the life history of such a culture" will more likely "be marked by catastrophic disturbances and recurrent collapse" (ibid.: 327). Veblen may be accused of exaggeration here; but I am inclined to think he is correct to believe that the spirit of insubordination is anything but marginal to enduring chances for global stability.

Insubordination testifies to a central political fact. For all the effort to engineer consent, to persuade individuals of the technological and commercial inevitability of globalization and remote power, contemporary ruling classes seem between unable and overrule a strong, recurrent bent favoring popular autonomy and self-governance. Its equally stubborn denial by elder statesmen and absentee owners continues to plague modern political and economic institutions. Episodic bouts of unrest, resistance, conflict, rebellion, recalcitrance and insubordination follow. This is because, for Veblen, a profound strain of psychic and political dissatisfaction runs through modern western culture. This is a strain of discomfiture not only with recently wavering levels of material betterment; but even more profoundly, there is deep dissatisfaction with the whole institutional system of absentee controls. It is a *distinctly political problem* - a problem of profound disequilibrium facing centralized structures of political authority and power. What seems from systemic perspectives to be a need for ever more centralization seems from individual perspectives to be an unceasing quest for ever more socially excessive and irresponsible organizational power. In this contradiction lies the fuel of episodic political stress, for conflict between rulers and ruled (see e.g. Veblen 1914: 18).

Insubordination and Radicalism

Veblen is more than a theorist of manipulation. He understands popular resistance too; its source is "the spirit of insubordination." This "spirit" has features that amplify its political importance for contemporary society as well as for a more rational one in the future. But there are aspects of the concept that control its application to any particular current case. These aspects or qualification should not be underestimated.

For one thing, Veblen does not describe "the spirit of insubordination" as the underpinning of any particular political ideology, except perhaps anarchism. It should not be seen as the rage of the right or the left so much as an expression of an indefinite popular anger. No ideological persuasion has a monopoly on the potential to abuse power; popular resistance frequently opposes such abuse wherever it appears, and who is to say that such popular anger will itself not turn hostile or violent. Veblen never excludes that possibility. More, whereas ideological goals tend to be experienced more or less subjectively, the agent's conscious self drives the spirit of insubordination only in part.

Inasmuch as insubordination may be a "generic feature" of the race, it resembles that peculiar mix of native psychology and ingrained habit that Veblen called "instinct." And while all instinctive action contains elements of purposive intelligence, the degree of conscious intent varies (ibid.: 30). At a minimum, the spirit of insubordination rebels against the immoderate power claims of rulers. To this extent, deliberate purpose is involved. People choose to stand against power: resistance is never merely tropism. But the generic bent from which the will to fight emerges, its savage legacy, remains obscure and opaque. As modern citizens do not readily perceive or understand their savage inheritance, the deep roots of their political irritation remain unintelligible, pre-conscious, an expression of their "native propensity." The spirit of insubordination is perhaps best understood then as a kind of inchoate political motive, which, as with political motivation generally, is more a "matter of sentiment than of logical inference" (1907: 441). In other words, for Veblen, insurgent political consciousness is never quite fully in tune with its sources. [24]

---

[24] As Veblen (1919: 174) once observed of Americans, "The common man does not know himself as such, at least not yet... The American tradition stands in the way".

All this suggests that for insubordinate citizens, non-conscious or pre-conscious and habitual factors combine in variant ways with deliberate intelligence to inform and spur political opposition. Therefore, because of its' opaque and less than fully deliberate character, insubordination is unlikely to be effective in changing the scope, character or bias of institutions. People will register their anti-power feelings; they will question and even defy authority. They may even induce more or less cosmetic policy or institutional changes. But this is a long way from saying that ordinary people constitute an historical subject capable of bringing about fundamental social and political change in deliberate, purposive, much less class conscious ways. Characteristically, Veblen's account of human behavior tends to toward pessimism about the effects of conscious action on social change. [25] As with other forms of instinctive action, the spirit of insubordination expresses the force of non-conscious or pre-conscious influence on consciously chosen purpose and action. With the aid of this concept we can see how Veblen believes savagery continues to animate, excite and disrupt contemporary politics; but we should refrain from overestimating its subversive power. Its capacity to incite fundamental change is dubious at best. [26]

Lacking explicit ideological content, often vague and shifty in its demands, and limited in its probable effects, the spirit of insubordination might well be charged with being a characteristically imprecise and weak Veblenian concept. Indeed, it is indefinite and inexact, and only vaguely or generally predictive, if at all. It lacks clarity, refusing reduction to anything like mathematical or statistical calculation. The idea is, at one level, simply a statement about the likelihood of populist resistance in advanced industrial societies, and one does not need Veblen to be assured of that. Veblen frustrates desires for guidance or indication about the more specific conditions, circumstances, probability, direction and scope of insubordination. Moreover, he is just as unwilling to be specific about its agents: will they be composed of a class, an interest group, a social movement, a political party, a loose gaggle of angry individuals, any and all of these? Indeed, if the spirit of insubordination expresses contradictions between long evolved human traits and current systems of order, might it not also find some expression among ruling elites? Indeed, perhaps it will; recent outbreaks of conflict among Turkish elites suggest as much. These are legitimate and important questions, and we might expect Veblen to offer some clues. But he does not.

---

[25] In his last major work, *Absentee Ownership*, Veblen is especially insistent about this point: deliberate human action, caught up as it is in ingrained habit, is poorly suited to make basic change. Basic changes in habit and institution tend to come about from "forced movements" in material circumstances, not as a result of "shrewd initiative and logical design - even though much argument may be spent in the course of it all." Indeed, whether a society or civilization manages to survive at all "appears to be a matter of chance in which human insight plays a minor part and human foresight no part at all" (Veblen 1923: 18-19; 1914: 25).

[26] In another essay, it may be worth pursuing the lead that Veblen's spirit of insubordination bears comparison with Francis Fox Piven's idea of "disruptive power," the ability of ordinary people "to disrupt a pattern of ongoing institutionalized cooperation that depends on their continuing contributions." (Piven 2008: 21). Like Veblen, Piven suggests that popular insurgency can make gains for ordinary people, but these victories are vulnerable to erosion when resistance fades. Most important, like Veblen, Piven has few illusions about the lasting revolutionary implications of popular insurgency. Also see Euchner (1996).

Still, it is possible to turn such criticism on its head. After all, it is not hard to see connections between demands for scientific prediction and calculability and elite political interests in conflict management and containment. Clearly, the last thing Veblen was interested in was to tender advice to ruling classes about how better to rule. This was a job for political scientists, as he understood the discipline, and he wanted no part of it. [27] In the end, what Veblen hoped to achieve with his concept, I suspect, was to reaffirm a central thesis of his most important theoretical work, *The Instinct of Workmanship*. This is the idea that the generic bent of human nature leans back toward the relatively simple industrial and social design of savagery. This legacy makes contemporary human beings restive with demands of modernity. Thus throughout the span and scope of spreading modernity, there will "persist an ineradicable sentimental disposition to take back to something like that scheme of savagery for which their particular type of human nature once proved its fitness" (Veblen 1914: 20). We are, again, as a species unsuited to, estranged from, the world we have made; "the spirit of insubordination" is a political expression of that profound cultural, historical, and in some sense, biological unease. Unlike Marx, Veblen does not believe that just because humans make or produce their world, they are destined to achieve some ultimate historic purchase on its comprehension or suitability. Some level of alienation is enduring for Veblen; history will not expunge it. [28]

If there is sociological or political value in such an observation, maybe it lies in its refutation of all claims to a passive end to history, ideology, or politics (Fukuyama 1992). Indeed, as recent events have shown, the power of advanced industrial society to contain forces of crisis is somewhat more modest than social thinkers such as Herbert Marcuse and Daniel Bell predicted a half-century ago (Marcuse 1964: xliv; Bell 1960). Examples of insubordination and bloody elite response have mounted throughout the modern world during the last half-century, episodes of unrest that persist into the present one. System stability has proven to be more elusive than mid and late twentieth century thinkers expected. Perhaps then we should not be too quick to underestimate the predictive power of Veblen's concept.

If Veblen can be accused of intellectual faults, underestimating the crisis potential of advanced industrial society is not one of them. To the contrary, he identified at least three sources or channels of significant strain and crisis. First, and most obviously, there is the inherent instability of modern financial and credit systems (Veblen 1904: 1923). At the same time, at the sheer material level of brute economic process, he stressed the extreme fragility of advanced industrial and technological systems, whose tightly interlocked networks of production and communication remain acutely vulnerable to disruption, energy crises for example, or increasingly, cyber attacks, or an eventual environmental breakdown. Finally, and perhaps least well appreciated among scholars of Veblen's work, is the theme we have explored in this essay: simmering political tensions over loss of popular control to an absentee-managed economic order.

---

[27] For a provocative view of the failures of political science as predictive science, see Stevens (2012).

[28] Indeed, Marx had his own doubts about the ultimate extinction of alienation. See below, p. 147.

Veblen never equated crisis potential at any moment with a definitive projection of economic or political breakdown. A nerve-racking ambiguity and uncertainty hovers about his assessment of future trends. On the one hand, the system of absentee ownership maintains a loose pattern of high echelon governance of high echelon governance by investment bankers, the US Federal Reserve, and a host of international financial institutions. On the other, Veblen sees no necessary and determined connection between economic or industrial crisis and popular political rebellion. Financial, economic or technological crises of various types may run their course, with occasional bouts of popular irritation largely checked by established institutions. By the same token, economic success or technological effectiveness does not guarantee political stability either. To the extent that political sentiment can generate its own dissatisfactions, material progress may not be enough to ward off protest, resistance, and a host of insubordinate behaviors. Turkey is a contemporary example; China offers another; so are Egypt and Syria; and so is the United States – although these cases obviously represent very different levels of intensity.

The Limits of Economic Rationality: Free Time and Insubordination

Most important for the purposes of a future society, simmering contradictions between technological interdependence, political centralization and the incipient savagery of the population mean that conflict and crisis will remain enduring issues even for a rational economic order governed by engineers. The essential point is this: Veblen's rational technocracy cannot expect to be apolitical. Engineers should not believe that they could immunize their system against the risk of insubordination. In fact, the more coldly rational and interdependent the system of production, the more the strain of labor is relaxed and attenuated, the more such a society will feel pressure to de-couple its economic order from the spontaneity of social life. There are several Veblenian reasons to support such a conclusion.

First, the instinct of workmanship, a passionate psychological and spiritual attachment to craft, will surely prompt people to search for novel outlets once the planning process rationalizes and objectifies industrial life. Veblen occasionally made this point in distinctly positive ways, expressing a vivid sense of the opportunity for freedom opened by a system geared to economic sufficiency. As he explained in *The Instinct of Workmanship*,

> It seems to be only after the demands of the simpler, more immediately organic functions, such as nutrition, growth and reproduction, have been met in some passably sufficient measure that this vaguer range of instincts which constitutes the spiritual predispositions of man can effectively draw on the energies of the organism and so can go into effect in what is recognized as human conduct. The wider the margin of disposable energy, therefore, the more freely should the characteristically human predispositions assert their sway. Veblen (1914: 86)

Once the labor mandate is relieved, and human beings can deploy their energies more freely, "conduct will be guided by what may properly be called the spiritual needs of man" (ibid.). Under these promising conditions, the purposive strain in human personality will seek to create spaces and domains that fall outside the hyper-mechanized, automated economy. What Veblen called "the human sprit" will presumably aspire to fashion ever more free spaces in which to pursue its penchants toward craftsmanship, community and curiosity. Art, play, intellectual work, perhaps religion and myth making too, might flourish. A whole new popular creativity might reflect the delight and gratification to be discovered in playful reconstructions of life and art. It is impossible to know what kind of culture a technologically liberated order might foster; but it is an exciting prospect to contemplate. At the same time, politics, the working out of solutions for continuing problems of social, economic and environmental adjustment, might itself become a subject of free agency, creativity and participation. Democracy would be less the show it currently is and more the ongoing work of sharing in communal decisions and burdens it is supposed to be.

The larger, more pressing point here is that if the whole of Veblen's thought is to be taken seriously, the fuller development of industrial or technical rationality must not be seen as an exclusive matter of economic thinking, calculation or control. The full development of economic or industrial rationality will raise the most provocative questions of substantive rationality: what will people make of themselves when they no longer to need to attend mainly to satisfaction of their "more immediately organic functions"? How free will they become to answer such questions for themselves, in their own way? What will "fulness of life" mean when industry is geared to support free activity rather than status driven consumption? The full development of technical rationality will thus confront society with the most promising but complex human questions.

If the logic of this is argument has merit, it points to the conclusion that the engineers must be prepared to leave individuals and communities alone to work out plural answers to the central issues of their day-to-day existence. The technicians must tolerate coexistence with the advent of a kind of modernized quasi-anarchism in their midst, an impetus toward self-direction for which an efficient economy is but the historical pre-condition.

One implication of the co-existence between quasi-anarchy and technical rationality might well be the need for a re-conceptualization of the concept of "waste." Perhaps another way of seeing this point is to ask the following question: will a rational economic order reduce waste to something approximating zero or would it in fact face needs to re-define waste altogether? What would waste mean in a rational economy?

Under capitalist conditions, waste constitutes output that is devoted to competitive emulation, social needs for symbolizing the superiority of one individual or group or class to another. Waste is deployed in the race for invidious reputability, the endless production of more for purposes of conspicuous consumption. It is the economic loss that serves production of chronically unsatisfying output. It is the sign of a system engineered to produce and enlarge dissatisfaction, economic and psychological futility. Waste exemplifies the dysfunctional function at the core of capitalism. A rational order would abandon pursuit of futility, putting in its place the goal of optimizing economic and material sufficiency: metabolic, organic satisfaction. Not less than that, to be sure, but not more than that either. Assuming steady progress toward eliminating physical and material inefficiencies in discrete lines of production, and especially if we equally presume a green economic attitude that looks to systematic recycling of resources, waste of tangible materials and energy would diminish; indeed it would trend toward zero.

Socially necessary labor time would likewise trend toward zero. But whatever pursuits people choose to follow in their resulting free time would hardly be waste. The production of such free time would in fact become the primary purpose of increasing economic efficacy. The chief systemic aim of a rational order would not be output of more things, but the systemic production of free time itself, an ever widening domain of opportunity for individuals and communities to develop their own freely exhibited capacities and purposes. Freedom to discriminate and choose among purposes and activities would be radically extended. No longer consumed by futile pursuit, life would be lived in ways that exceed our imagination. "Man's life" would then truly be *his* "activity."

In a rational economic order, the opposite of waste would not be efficiency; it would be freedom. In this context, the chief critique of a rational economic system would not be its economic inefficiency, but any attempt by engineers to regulate behavior or "free time" beyond an economic, social minimum. For example, they might invoke the objective demands of science itself as a rationale to justify such control. The technical system is after all cold and implacable, as Veblen warned, compelling the individual to follow its dictates. Marx made a similar point about the ambiguity of science and technology in a post-capitalist context, a view that anticipated Marcuse's critique of technology as ideology and that also bears on the possibility of a repressive form of technocracy that floats through Veblen's work. [29] As waste and necessary labor time lessen, savage expectations and habits would vigorously reemerge. Popular expectations would incline toward rising expectations of relief from material pressures and from unnecessary constraints on time and freedom.

Savage habits and outlooks will be rekindled by the promise of an economy of sufficiency. In this increasingly liberated setting, the spirit of insubordination would doubtless remain a key check on attempts to exercise undue power. It is reasonable to surmise that members of the community will take with the utmost seriousness the sense of serviceability for the common good as the exacting standard of any proposed regulation. If they sense threats to their liberties, however, they will assert themselves. [30]

Accordingly, the concept of structural waste has a significant social and political meaning only in relation to predatory, emulative, self-expansive systems of status and power oriented production. The concept of "waste" can have no meaning or relevance to the use of free time in a rational order. The technicians will have to respect the fact that anarchy, liberty, and idiosyncrasy are central values of modernized savagery. Communities and neighbors may judge the eccentric as they wish – but in whatever modernized form a new order re-emerges, short of threats to the material common good, the principle of non-interference must prevail over the principle of control. If it does not, insubordination will rear up. Make no mistake: it will trouble the technicians.

---

[29] See McLellan (2006: 279); Marcuse (1964); Plotkin (2013).

[30] For Veblen, of course, there will be no u-turn back to savagery, although the sentimental dispositions of humans will nonetheless be forever looking back to simpler, less taxing times, accounting for what he called our "refractory penchant for elementary savage modes of life," and our at best "slight facility" for adjustment to what passes for civilized life (Veblen 1914: 21, 334).

The spirit of insubordination is not a concept reserved for understanding the societies we know. For Veblen, it is a generic political bent that will continue to demand recognition and respect in a future society whose outlines we do not yet know. Indeed, Veblen's idea of insubordination is hardly negated by a fuller realization of technological rationality. Even though the machine may yet release us from necessary labor, its managers will have to tread wearily and cautiously. There will likely continue to run through even the most advanced industrial community feelings of "maladjustment and discomfort," feelings of irritation and/or undue control. Perhaps such sentiments will take the form of calls for some kind of "return to nature." Or perhaps, they will result in insubordination (Veblen 1914: 319).

References

Bell, Daniel. 1960. *The End of Ideology, The Exhaustion of Political ideas in the Fifties.* Glencoe, Ill: The Free Press.

_____. 1990. Introduction. *The Engineers and the Price System* by Thorstein Veblen. New Brunswick, New Jersey: Transaction.

Diggins, John Patrick. 1990. *Thorstein Veblen, Theorist of the Leisure Class.* Princeton: Princeton University Press.

Euchner, Charles. 1996. *Extraordinary Politics.* Boulder, Co.: Westview.

Fukuyama, Francis. 1992. *The End of History and the last man.* New York: Free Press.

Gorz, Andre. 1985. *Paths to Paradise, On the Liberation From Work.* Trans. By Malcolm Imrie. Boston: South End.

_____. 1988. *Critique of Economic Reason.* Trans. By Gillian Handyside and Chris Turner. London: Verso.

Hodder, H.J. The Political Ideas of Thorstein Veblen. *Canadian Journal of Economics and Political Science* 27 (3): 347-357.

Kilpinen, Erkki. 2004. How to Fight the 'Methodenstreit'? Veblen and Weber on Economics. Paper delivered at *The meetings of the International Thorstein Veblen Association.* Carleton College. Northfield, Minnesota.

Knoedler, Janet and Mayhew, Anne. 1999. Thorstein Veblen and the Engineers: A Reinterpretation. *History of Political Economy* 31 (2): 255-271

Marcuse, Herbert. 1964. *One-Dimensional Man, Studies in the Ideology of Advanced Industrial Society.* Boston: Beacon Press.

Marx, Karl. 1983. (1865). *Value, Price and Profit.* In *The Portable Karl Marx,* ed. Eugene Kamenka. New York: Penguin.

_____. 1973. *Grundrisse, Introduction to the Critique of Political Economy.* Trans. With a Forward by Martin Nicolaus. New York: Vintage.

Patsouras, Louis. 2004. *Thorstein Veblen and the American Way of Life.* Montreal: Black Rose Books.

Piven, Francis Fox. 2008. *Challenging Authority, How Ordinary People Change America.* Lanham, Md.: Rowman and Littlefield.

Plotkin, Sidney. 2010. Veblen's *The Higher Learning in America* and the Ambiguities of Academic Independence. In *Transforming Higher Education, Economy, Democracy, and the University.* ed. Stephen J. Rosow and Thomas Kriger. Lanham, Md.: Lexington Books: 37-63.

_____. and Tilman, Rick. 2011. *The Political Ideas of Thorstein Veblen.* New Haven: Yale University Press.

_____. 2013. Veblen, Europe and Utopia. *History of European Ideas.* *http://dx.doi.org/10.1080/01916599.2013.805045*

_____. 2014. Misdirected Effort: Thorstein Veblen's Critique of Advertising. *Journal of Historical Research in Marketing* 6 (4) (2014): 501-522.

Ross, Dorothy. 1991. *The Origins of Social Science.* Cambridge: Cambridge University Press.

Stevens, Jacqueline. 2012. Political Scientists Are Lousy Forecasters. *The New York Times, Week in Review.* 24 June. *http://www.nytimes.com/2012/06/24/opinion/sunday/political -scientists-are-lousy-forecasters.html?_r=1&pagewanted=all*

Tilman, Rick. 1996. Veblen and the Industrial Republic. In *The Intellectual Legacy of Thorstein Veblen, Unresolved Issues.* Westport, CT: Greenwood.

Veblen, Thorstein. 1919, 1947. (1892). Some Neglected Points in the Theory of Socialism. In *The Place of Science in Modern Civilization and Other Essays.* New York: B.W. Heubsch.

_____. 1931. (1898a). *The Theory of the Leisure Class. With a Forward by Stewart Chase.* New York: The Modern Library.

_____. 1964. (1898b). The Instinct Of Workmanship And The Irksomeness Of Labor. In *Essays In Our Changing Order.* ed. Leon Ardzrooni. New York: Augustus M. Kelley.

_____. 1919, 1947. (1898c). Why Is Economics Not An Evolutionary Science? In *The Place of Science in Modern Civilization and Other Essays.* New York: B.W. Heubsch.

_____. 1978. (1904). *The Theory of Business Enterprise.* Intro. Douglas Dowd. New Brunswick, New Jersey: Transaction.

_____. 1919, 1947. (1906). The Socialist Economics of Karl Marx And His Followers I. In *The Place of Science in Modern Civilization and Other Essays.* New York: B.W. Heubsch.

_____. 1919, 1947. (1907). The Socialist Economics of Karl Marx And His Followers II. In *The Place of Science in Modern Civilization and Other Essays.* New York: B.W. Heubsch.

_____. 1919, 1947. (1909). The Limitations of Marginal Utility. In *The Place of Science in Modern Civilization and Other Essays.* New York: B.W. Heubsch..

_____. 1990. (1914). *The Instinct of Workmanship and the State of the Industrial Arts.* Intro. Murray G. Murphey. New Brunswick, New Jersey: Transaction.

_____. 1954. (1915). *Imperial Germany And The Industrial Revolution.* Intro. Joseph Dorfman. New York: The Viking Press.

_____. 1993. (1918). *The Higher Learning in America.* With a New Inroduction by Ivar Berg. New Brunswick, New Jersey: Transaction.

_____. 1964. (1919). *The Vested Interests and the Common Man.* New York: Augustus M. Kelley.

_____. 1990. (1921). *The Engineers and the Price System,* Intro. Daniel Bell. New Brunswick, New Jersey: Transaction

_____. 1997. (1923). *Absentee Ownership, Business Enterprise in Recent Times: The Case of America.* Intro. Marion J. Levy, Jr.. New Brunswick, New Jersey: Transaction.

Sabotage With a Smile: Waitrose and the Common Man

Anita Oğurlu

Are we returning to a world of plantations—*Latifundia* the spacious estates of Rome as they were once known—or did we ever leave them? As a second-generation Norwegian immigrant farm boy raised in Minnesota, Veblen was acutely aware what independent farmsteads meant for United States business enterprise. American farmers believed themselves to be 'self-made men' who were self-reliant and free from the invisible hand of the market. Independent farmsteads in North America rather than *Latifundia* in Latin America accounted for one of the major differences in technological advancement of the northern continent over its southern counterpart. Nations like Guatemala, Honduras, Colombia and Ecuador were labeled 'Banana Republics' for their reliance on one commodity export, usually fruit or minerals, realized through the subjugation of landless peasants forced into slave labor on plantations or in mines. Railroads were laid to transport bananas before people. Coercive and predatory politics in these nations stemmed from their *Latifundista* collaborating with foreign absentee landlords and politicians to ensure joint business interests succeeded at all costs. [1] Latin American, African and some Asian nations' lack of diversified economies made them the butt of American jokes. Politics and business enterprise stop for no one, least of all the common good of humanity. Post-1980 neoliberal policy and its subsequent agricultural technologies, fertilizers, modified crops and primitive methods of land acquisition, coerced rural folk to flock to cities after big money. Peasants had no choice but to flee guerrilla and counter-guerrilla struggles in some countries. Those who remained on the land faced bankruptcy. In this manner, neoliberal policy appears to have left fields open for today's neo-*Latifundia* partnered with foreign business enterprises like *Monsanto, Cargill* and large supermarket chains. But business enterprise holds little prejudice toward geography. Gone are the days of Veblen's 'self-made' men in America.

Food is our existence and dictates everything; our culture and how we live, how healthy we are, how we use our water, our wealth distribution, the level of social unrest in our megacities and our economic robustness in services and industrial enterprise. Food production and practices of food marketing continue to evolve. Particularly in industrialized nations, supermarket chains of the 1960s bloated into Big-box stores of the 1990s with packaged and processed goods abounding the shelves. Today some chains are downsizing to mid-size stores, as on-line purchase and delivery service implies one is saved from the inconvenience of grocery shopping. The fast food revolution has evolved into one of slow food. We are increasingly aware what we eat is often unhealthy and seldom produced with environmental or ethical consideration. As Veblen believed, we have an 'economic conscience' that catches us up. For example the French farmer José Bové attempted to drive his tractor into a *McDonalds* in Paris (1999).

---

[1] Practices of *The United Fruit Company* (Chiquita brand today) supported paramilitary groups, evicted and raised entire villages, bribed government officials in Colombia and smuggled drugs into Europe.
http://www.democracynow.org/1998/7/7/the_chiquita_banana_story Retrieved 20.12.2012.
In *Canto General,* Pablo Neruda wrote a poem titled "La United Fruit Co."

Chef Jamie Oliver campaigned for 'Feed me Better' programs in UK school canteens (2005). [2] Turkish consumers gratuitously exchanged non-genetically modified seeds (2010). [3] President Evo Morales kicked *Coca Cola* out of Bolivia (2012). [4] Some demand food is locally produced with respect for the 'well-being' of the worker, grower and/or producer—the cult of 'Fairtrade' brands. Some individuals cultivate inner-city community gardens but the feasibility of such projects remains limited. The masses still continue to purchase food at supermarket chains. In short, technology and industrial production rule our food consumption. We are conditioned to accept the fact that old agricultural methods and community production cannot ensure food security for the masses in the future. Naturally, business enterprise steps in to save the day.

Business enterprise has always exploited food production and consumption. [5] Prescient to increasing global food demand business enterprise, under the auspices of the new food regime or food security—in full cooperation with politicians—IMF and World Bank policies have secured and will continue to secure food as a business interest. Even as cultural trends toward food have evolved, business enterprise has evolved with them. Taking *Waitrose* as a case study, a successful and upscale UK supermarket chain, this chapter will illustrate how business enterprise engages the employee, consumer, producer, government and nation(s) into a highly evolved and seeming sophisticated food regime. Through the exploitation of cultural habits, rituals and beliefs, the new food regime works both in and across cultures. First, I begin with an overview of John Lewis, founder of *John Lewis* and *Waitrose* business enterprises. Then I introduce his son, Spedan Lewis, and his novel approach to ownership. In the second part, a *Waitrose* employee will guide a behind the scenes discussion of this unique business enterprise and culture. Based on its success, *Waitrose* has been deemed an exemplar business model by the British government. But what is 'culturally engineered' into a 'price' at *Waitrose*? In the third part, I briefly review neoliberal agricultural policy, in relation to but not unique to Turkey, under the EU regulations of CAP (Common Agricultural Policy) and what implications these policies have for the Turkish grower-producer. Whilst the food regime applauds new and efficient means of feeding the masses, it appears to permit and authorize inefficiency and a substantial waste of resources, especially troubling when 'common man' is increasingly less likely to have access to the 'full-dinner pail.' [6] The chapter concludes with Veblen's cautions and insights on business civilization and common man. Despite the global food regime promise to feed millions, might we actually lose our ability to feed ourselves?

---

[2] *http://www.jamieoliver.com/media/jo_sd_history.pdf* Retrieved 20.10.2014.

[3] This process takes place at an event called "Takas Masası" at Bayramiç, Yeniköy. *http://www.bayramicyenikoy.com* Retrieved 20.12.2012

[4] *http://www.businessinsider.com/bolivia-to-ban-coca-cola-starting-december-21st-2012-8* Retrieved 20.10.2014.

[5] For an excellent account of the grain industry in North America and its affect on the world food supply, see Dan Morgan. 1980. *Merchants of Grain*. London: Penguin Books.

[6] Veblen's use of the term "common man" is not gender specific. "Full-dinner pail" is Veblen's metaphor for a salary or wages paid by business enterprise

The John Lewis Legacy

John Lewis, one of eight children born into abject poverty in mid-nineteenth century London, made his fortune selling drapery and upholstery to the growing bourgeoisie from their capital accumulation across the British Empire. Undercutting competitors with low prices, Lewis opened a small shop on Oxford Street in 1864. When British legislation allowed for the destruction of small shops (row houses), the *John Lewis* Department Store located on Oxford Street in central London, was founded. Hiring mostly married men with family responsibilities they tended to be subservient. Many of them worked over seventy hour weeks. Employees either slept on the shop floor or crammed into overcrowded substandard quarters and paid outrageous rent in these nearby hostel/dorms owned by Lewis. [7] Infamous for his unexpected visits to the shop floor, if Lewis found an employee with money in their pockets they most likely were fired on the grounds they'd stolen from his business. Obviously employees refrained from complaint against such austere business practices. On occasion Lewis spent brief periods in jail when competitors made spurious accusations about his alleged shady real-estate dealings.

Lewis had two sons, Oswald and Spedan of which the latter was the kinder and gentler. At the turn of the century, Spedan sought to reform his father's harsh 'pecuniary' business practices. In a recent book *Spedan's Partnership: The Story of John Lewis and Waitrose* (2010) [8] it is reported Spedan got the brilliant idea of creating a fairer form of capitalism. Around the same time Harry Gordon Selfridge, a retail magnate from the U.S. arrived on the scene, opening his *Selfridges* Department store (1909) and swiftly became a competitive business concern for John Lewis not to mention the more established *Harrods* (1834). Selfridge had been innovative in attracting customers across England by paying their day train fares into London to shop at *Selfridges*. Each man was obliged to get the better of the other by various means and forms of sabotage. Veblen's 'sabotage' notion is helpful to assess the Lewis business enterprise and how it pertains to the evolution of *Waitrose*. Sabotage can work to the benefit of whoever uses it against another. Veblen explained sabotage as follows: '...all such peaceable or surreptitious maneuvers of delay, obstruction, friction and defeat, whether employed by the workmen to enforce their claims, or by the employers to defeat their employees, or by competitive business concerns to get the better of their business rivals or to secure their own advantage.' [9]

Perhaps to secure his own advantage Spedan considered, 'whether a more humane and inclusive way of doing business could mitigate the destructive effects of capitalism on society...' [10] But would Spedan's 'fairer form of capitalism' by inviting employees to be 'partners' and

---

[7] His practices resemble those of large Chinese factories today, accused in the western media as being inhumane by forcing their factory workers into factory dorms, working them almost seven days a week.

[8] I have approached this book with some caution, as it is often common practice on behalf of business interest to make use of or even on occasion commission such a book to be written and used as an artifact for cultural engineering and myth making about capitalism, in this case British capitalism. Peter Cox. 2010. *Spedan's Partnership: The Story of John Lewis and Waitrose*. London: Labatie Books.

[9] Thorstein Veblen. 1965/1921. *The Engineers and the Price System*. New York: Reprints of Economic Classics, Sentry Press.: 3

[10] Cox (2010: 33).

'entrepreneurs' in the business enterprise, suffice to coerce them (sabotage) away from solidarity with their fellow common man at a time of massive social unrest in 1911? With pre-revolutionary Russian uprisings and WWI only three years away, Spedan's idea was hailed exemplar, revolutionary and scandalous! Some politicians backed him. In 1909 Liberal opposition leader David Lloyd George resembled Spedan's sentiment at an East London speech:

> Who is the landlord? The Landlord is a gentleman... who does not earn his wealth. He does not even take the trouble to receive his wealth. He has a host of agents and clerks to receive it for him. He does not even take the trouble to spend his wealth. He has a host of people around him to do the actual spending for him. He never sees it until he comes to enjoy it. His sole function, his chief pride, is stately consumption of wealth produced by others. What about the doctor's income? How does the doctor earn his income? The doctor is a man who visits our homes when they are darkened with the shadow of death: who, by his skill, his trained courage, his genius, wrings hope out of the grip of despair, wins life out of the fangs of the Great Destroyer. All blessings upon him and his divine art of healing that mends bruised bodies and anxious hearts. To compare the reward which he gets for that labor with the wealth which pours into the pockets of the landlord, purely owing to the possession of his monopoly, is a piece if, they will forgive me for saying so, of insolence which no intelligent man would tolerate. [11]

George most adequately defined 'absentee landlord' to an agitated common man as if he had read it from the pages of Veblenian treatise. But the difference between Veblen and politician George is that the latter used rhetoric to sabotage common man, yet again. Veblen, on the other hand, took capitalism, business civilization and politics to be of a predatory domain that utilize intrigue, strategy, deception and gamesmanship for its ends. [12] Moreover, Veblen's observation of British governance was most astute. 'Grown wise in all the ways and means of blamelessly defeating the unblest majority, the gentlemanly government of the British manage affairs of this kind much better. They have learned that bellicose gestures provoke ill will, and that desperate remedies should be held in reserve until needed.' [13]

Having survived virtually unscathed from economic circumstances that saw over 25% unemployed in Britain, in 1937 Spedan acquired ten small grocery shops, formerly established in 1904 as *Waitrose* by three partners; Wallace Waite, Arthur Rose and David Taylor. These *Waitrose* partners had already secured a good reputation (niche) by selling better quality foods, in this case beneficial sabotage for common man, but only as a means of differentiating *Waitrose* from other British food merchants engaged in despicable practices. 'Bread was whitened with alum and contained sand and ashes. Tea was glazed with black lead, and 'red' Gloucester cheese was brightened with red lead. Gravel, leaves and twigs were added to pepper.' Lead, copper carbonate, lead sulfate, mercury bisulfate and Venetian lead were added to confectionaries. *Waitrose* 'refused to adulterate the food'. [14] Championing ethical business, Spedan enhanced his reputation by evolving his *Waitrose* enterprise as a means of outdoing rival competitors (sabotage). Spedan's business continued to succeed and was now well poised for the nascent post-war boom where food would become the focus.

---

[11] Ibid.: 35.

[12] Sidney Plotkin and Rick Tilman. 2011. *The Political Ideas of Thorstein Veblen*. New Haven and London: Yale University Press: 99.

[13] Veblen (1965/1921: 86).

[14] Cox (2010: 97).

Working with Spedan was better than working for his father John. Common man, no longer an employee, was invited to become 'partner' or 'entrepreneur' in the business enterprise. The scheme was called the *John Lewis Partnership*. When the business did well so did its 'partners.' Based on annual profits, Spedan's notion of the partner 'bonus' was paid as a fixed percentage across the board to each and every partner proportionate to their wage. This 'bonus' persuaded partners to take on responsibility for the Vested Interests. In short, it created loyalty. Spedan's business enterprise engaged the employee in a unique culture of inclusion or what Gideon—writing on corporate America in the 1990s—termed 'cultural engineering'. 'This is the basic building block of the culture [...] using individual strengths for the good of the company...' by capturing employees "hearts and minds" through regular "rituals and ceremonies."' [15] Normative controls under the tyranny of John became obsolete when one became a 'partner' with Spedan.

Kunda believes artifacts play an essential role in culture making. The internal transparent communication system titled *The Gazette: Of the John Lewis Partnership*, as a artifact, encouraged not only new ideas but also that discontent and grievances openly be expressed on its pages. All partners were granted freedom of speech in 1930s Britain when many workers were hostile toward bosses. Veblen remarked such worker hostility is normally kept under control. 'Now, the Guardians of the Vested Interests are presumably wise in discountenancing any open discussion or any free communication of ideas and opinions.' [16] Oddly, Spedan did just the opposite. Encouragement to publish criticism against the business enterprise became a vehicle of emancipation. One needn't be fired. One was responsible enough to voice an opinion, even in a business world hostile to its workforce. Still implemented today, *The Gazette* marks the heritage of cultural tradition at *Waitrose*. Veblen appears to be justified in his thoughts on the use of tradition and ritual as coercion in politics and business. Kunda agrees the use of ritual is key. '[R]ituals—ranging from the mass spectacles of modern politics to the seemingly inconsequential routines of everyday social interaction—are collectively produced, structured, and dramatic occasions that create a "frame", a shared definition of the situation within which participants are expected to express and confirm sanctioned ways of experiencing social reality. Such displays have the power to affect participants profoundly.' [17]

Spedan purchased large estates in the countryside at Leckford and Odney. Partners were invited to an annual gathering where they could partake in a set of rituals in the countryside with absentee landlord Spedan. Privileges seldom granted outside of *John Lewis* or *Waitrose*, partners must have embraced the honor. Over time the ritual became integral to *Waitrose* cultural heritage. It represented an emotional side of the 'cultural engineering' coin and Veblen's robust argument as to how habits built on predatory notions of terms like honor, status, social-esteem, prestige, rank and class, tend to coerce common man. But there had to be a 'rational side' to the coin too. Fairness was realized through published pay rates, regular staff council meetings,

---

15 Gideon Kunda. 1992. *Engineering Culture*. Philadelphia: Temple University Press: 72.
16 Veblen (1965/1921: 84).
17 Kunda (1992: 93).

weekly profit posting, elected members by shop assistants, transparent bookkeeping, shared knowledge, bonus pay and holidays. In addition, conscientious objectors against the war were not to be fired. Too good to be true? During the first two weeks of WWII, 300 out of 6,000 partners were promptly fired. They were, however, given promissory notes of reinstatement after the war.

Despite major economic crises in the twentieth century, two World Wars—inclusive of the 1940 German bombing of the *John Lewis* Department store—Spedan expanded the *John Lewis* and *Waitrose* business enterprises, even keeping unions off the doorstep, although union membership was not banned. Partners gradually came to believe unionization offered no benefit over *John Lewis Partnership* culture. It might harm fellow partners. 'Strikers wouldn't be sacked but they might have Partnership privileges withdrawn.' [18] Spedan foresaw or reacted to potential sabotage on behalf of common man by pre-empting employee sabotage with his own form, to get the better of them. Placing worker against worker or rather partner over worker, solidarity in strike action weakened. The privilege of partnership coerced workers away from unions only to defend 'fairer capitalism.' But not all partners were dupes. On two occasions *John Lewis* employees went on strike: in 1920 and 1931 when Britain suffered over 25% unemployment. Partners were promptly fired and replaced. Remaining partners were given an ultimatum. 'Take your pick, pay cut or redundancies […] with evidence of unemployment and hardship only too visible […] the Partners buckled down without much public complaint in the Gazette.' [19] Partners signed an oath they weren't members of the communist or fascist party of Britain. Despite social unrest (1960s), 24% inflation (1975), IRA bombs and strikes (1980), partnership reigned. 'How dare you? Get back to work before you damage our—our—business. And you people who (we pay to) run our business, get your act together.' [20] Veblen cautioned: 'It is still the unbroken privilege of the financial management and its financial agents to "hire and fire."' [21] Ironically, fellow partners pressured other fellow partners back to work.

Waitrose Today

In *The Guardian* newspaper on 15 January 2012, Deputy Prime Minister Nick Clegg announced British business should follow the '*John Lewis* Economy' as a twenty-first century business model. The *John Lewis Partnership* has over 80,000 employees.[22] *Waitrose*, with over 282 locations, has 4.2% of the British food market and 2% of the British economy. Currently *Waitrose* is the sixth largest supermarket (UK) with targets to open four hundred new branches across the UK by 2017. With net income over £123.3 million, it is the fastest growing chain of supermarkets said to challenge *M&S* (*Marks & Spencer*) and *Sainsbury's*. UK salaries from the shop floor clerk to CEO work on a pay ratio of 75–1 compared to most FTSE U.S. corporations where the pay ration is 150–1. The partnership bonus averaged 16%

---

[18] Cox (2010: 111).
[19] Ibid.: 84.
[20] Ibid.: 207.
[21] Veblen (1965/1921: 70).
[22] Figure is inclusive of both *John Lewis* and *Waitrose* employees.

over fifty years and is paid annually in March as an equal percentage across all salaries. 'We hire people and pay them at the market rate at all base levels, we don't pay individual bonuses', reports Managing Director Andy Street. The 2012 Olympics in east London saw a Stratford store open, whereby one quarter of its employees (273) were trained and hired from the long-term unemployed; a generous gesture. '*John Lewis* is loved by consumers and government and represents a fairer form of capitalism for suppliers, the community, the long-term unemployed and salaried employees.' [23] The *John Lewis* Economy is a beacon of truth; proof fairness does exist in British capitalism.

What Goes into the *Waitrose* Price?

Twenty-one year old Mr Brown [24] became a Fresh Foods Partner at *Waitrose* in October 2011. With Mr Brown's comments, I explore what goes into a *Waitrose* price. A college student living in London, he believes *Waitrose* a fair employer and best pick in supermarket franchises. Originally from the north, he sees himself a radical socialist, who supports unions and believes in democracy. Mr Brown was interviewed three times over a month for his position at *Waitrose* and considers himself lucky to be taken on. Hired at entry level, he was a bit cynical about *Waitrose*, believing it to be a large corporation only interested in profit. His thinking echoes Veblen's, in that, an element of mutual distrust always exists between the business enterprise and common man. Throughout the course of my interview Mr Brown exhibited some vulnerability. I sensed a struggle between his 'economic conscience' and having fallen prey to 'coercive exploit.' Although oscillating between congratulatory and critical remarks, he eventually admitted: 'We're all notionally respected Partners. "Mr. Brown to check out." Well, it's quite nice really, isn't it, to be called "Mr."'

Latifundia belong to *Waitrose* culture even when it advocates honest food, honest price, quality, high-quality farms, only line-caught fish, pigs reared outdoors and eggs from free-range chickens. *Waitrose* seems to trigger our 'economic conscience' for a more just world without waste. 'We encourage African farmers with help in forming co-operatives […] we don't drive our British farmers into the ground. But all this comes at a price, just a little extra. Are you prepared to pay for it'? [25] *Waitrose* marketing is highly sophisticated. Visuals, packaging, slogans backed by corporate responsibility campaigns, certainly allude to the common good of community and humanity. But, is it actually so? *Waitrose* supports Fairtrade, should the scheme apply to fairness. Fairtrade produce has become popular with up-market customers, willing to pay extra for these goods. [26] Franchises seek to exploit the trend and now offer more Fairtrade sugar, tea, coffee, fruit and other goods on their shelves. Fairtrade allegedly pools farmers into cooperatives, but in turn they are rapidly being pooled into new Latifundia with increasingly harmful affects on small peasant farmers, often left destitute. It is uncertain how much money returns

---

23 *http://www.bbc.co.uk/iplayer/episode/b01fb0pp/HARDtalk_Andy_Street_Managing_Director_John_Lewis/*
24 Mr Brown wishes to remain anonymous.
25 Cox (2010: 264).
26 *http://www.guardian.co.uk/environment/2012/feb/27/uk-consumers-go-bananas-fairtrade*

to the farmer/worker as viable wages. Adversely, profits may end up in the hands of the supermarkets. [27] Whilst the extra price is supposed to fund education, health services and infrastructure, the worker and/or farmer continues to earn a substandard wage in many countries. *Waitrose* is proud to operate its own banana 'cooperatives' in Ghana. But, under what conditions? To an observant customer, *Waitrose* shelves might appear like the United Nations of food. Produce like snow peas and baby corn arrive from unexpected countries thousands of kilometers away, like Zambia. More striking is the subtle division of labor and produce by nation. Garlic—Argentina; carrots—South Africa; green beans—Kenya and Italy; mandarin oranges—Uruguay; limes—Mexico and so on. In some instances there are several national suppliers; blueberries—Morocco and France; grapes—Morocco and Egypt. Should one supplier nation suffer a natural disaster or unfortunate political unrest, like in the overthrow of a government, another supplier nation can deliver. Shelves will always be plentiful.

Companilismo is also a pillar of *Waitrose* culture. Pride in British produce and goods—or any regional produce or goods for that matter—is a belief system carried over from Middle Age Europe. *Companilismo* means attachment to a city or regional custom and tradition played out as a spirit of rivalry between towns and communities. [28] Cultural beliefs like, the finest cream from Devon; famous prosciutto from Parma or fine sparkling wine from Champagne, France are all forms of *companilismo*. However banal, these once rivaling regionalisms are habits that remain with us today. Veblen would have noted it part of these regions' cultural inheritance. Although the EU is a geographical polity transcending nation-states, protectionism is rooted in older regional *companilismo* structured to benefit EU business interest vis-à-vis CAP (Common Agricultural Policy). Subsidies privilege a few countries in the EU namely Holland, Denmark, France, Germany and Italy over less fortunate EU member states like Bulgaria, Greece and Romania. The former have superior food culture status over the latter deemed sub-standard. Poor quality food comes from those 'others' outside the food regime security circle. These other regions must be increasingly monitored. *Companilismo* works to sabotage rival competition as those nations-producers deemed of inferior quality do not make the list of the finest suppliers exclusive to *Waitrose*. For example, it is in Britain's best interest *Waitrose* support British meat/poultry and fruit/vegetable producers. Slick television campaigns show images of prize cattle and stoic, British farmers laboring against the driven snow to Elvis Presley's 'Love me Tender.' The *Waitrose* endorsement boasts: 'Through good

---

[27] "One UK Sainsbury superstore, in November 2010, had 76 product lines for coffee and 53 product lines for Fairtrade coffee. The most expensive coffee was nearly four times the price of the cheapest, £21.20 per kg, compared with £5.36. Many of the more expensive lines were Fairtrade. Some of the objective characteristics were stated, such as organic, Arabica, produced in Costa Rica, but there was no indication of most of them. Most of them would have been blends of at least half a dozen different qualities and different growths, produced by different suppliers." Peter Griffiths. 2011. Ethical Objections to Fairtrade. *Journal of Business Ethics* July 2011. *http://www.griffithsspeaker.com/Fairtrade/why fair trade isn.htm* Retrieved 20.12.2012

[28] Loyalty to a region influences community economy. In Italy, loyalty incited rivalry between regions known as protecting the Bell Tower. *Companilismo* is also associated with family feuds and local wars. Football rivalry is another form of *companilismo*.

[29] *http://www.voutube.com/watch?v=b ENjI39vbM* Retrieved 20.12.12012. Foot-and-mouth disease across the UK in 2001 saw millions of livestock culled during the restructure from independent farms to large-scale production.

times and not so good times… we have always supported the toughest breed of all… the British farmer.' [29] Exploiting British sentiment—to pacify the public during an economic downturn—gives the impression *Waitrose* allegedly protects and respects British jobs. Such tactics indirectly foment British nationalism. Veblen's notion of 'invidious comparison' becomes apparent as customers make conspicuous selections of cheeses, wines, olives, meats, and the like, as a display of prestige and social status. Cheese must be matched with the correct wine; an exhibition of power, honor, social esteem, rank and class.

Royalty is the backbone of British business civilization, aptly fitting Veblen's ideas on predation, prowess and tradition. Queen Elizabeth II is officially supplied groceries, wine and spirits by *Waitrose* under a Royal Warrant. Lest we forget, common man is a subject of the Queen and the Queen needs to have an affiliation with her subjects. An official seal legitimizes the *Waitrose*—Royalty affiliation. The Royal Warrant is lavishly printed on every shopping bag as a symbol of prowess to sabotage vulgar competition. Royal Duchy Originals, an organic food brand established by Prince Charles, later became a *Waitrose* acquisition. Known or unbeknown to customers, habitual shopping endorses Royalty, hence the Commonwealth, along with past and present strategic relationships and alliances to empire. *Waitrose* opened branches in the Middle East; Abu Dhabi, Bahrain and Muscat in 2014, paving the way to India. For years, small grocers in India have been vigilant in keeping out large supermarket chains fully aware they destroy their livelihoods. Plans to launch a flagship *Waitrose* supermarket in New Delhi are underway since rescinding an Indian law prohibiting them in December 2012. The location will span over four football fields and displace over 8,000 inhabitants but will hire 300 graduate students. [30] Despite Indian protests overseas, charities at home distract common man. Purchase of an exclusive *Waitrose* wine labeled 'One in a Millione' funds the building of schools in Sierra Leone. In addition, every partner at *Waitrose* is given a corporate membership to English Heritage sites like the National Trust, national museums, Tate and Tate Britain and country houses. Mr Brown is free to fraternize with mid to upper classes. He gets discounts on theatre tickets but not on rock concerts or films: lower-class activities of common man.

A *substandard wage* is where Mr Brown as Fresh Foods Partner begins, although paid the market rate for his labor. Contracts commence on a part-time basis and consist of three three-term contracts before a partner is hired full time. Entry-level pay is £7.18/hour. Should the partner pass to a third term contract the pay is £7.49/hour. Mr Brown is near completion of his third-term contract. 'Personally I think that's a really good wage. For the kind of manual labor I do, there are a lot making less. It's not a living wage. A living wage is £9/hour in London. But you're not going to get that for shifting boxes around. Minimum wage is £6.18/hour. Others work for much less. Undocumented workers get £2/hour as they did at the Diamond Jubilee.' Mr Brown's statement oscillates between what Veblen termed 'irksomeness of labor' (abhorrence of work) and 'instinct of workmanship' (pleasure of work). As *Waitrose* heritage respect him as partner, Mr Brown is bound to feel worthy of the pay. But instincts tell him he'd prefer a proper job. Best not to demand more. It's not real work, is it? MBA graduates, parachuted in,

---

[30] *http://www.thedailysnooze.co.uk/2012/09/waitrose-to-india/*

earn considerably more as partners and have titles like Section Managers, Department Managers and Branch Managers. Behind the shop floor, numerous forms of cultural engineering are underway. Mr Brown explained: 'There are a lot of signs around... pick up this... and that cost us a £20 loss a week. That's your bonus you're wasting.' Kunda noted: 'Ritual gatherings where the organizational ideology is enacted causes members to "internalize the culture" and infuses them with the right "mindset" and the appropriate "gut reactions."' [31] Despite the fairness with which *Waitrose* treats its partners, the fact remains unions are frowned upon. Mr Brown commented about the issue. 'I am a member of USDAW. [32] They allow me a union membership but significantly they don't recognize a union. They don't do wage bargaining or anything like that. You become a member of the union yourself. One thing that is significant about *Waitrose* and its partner ownership is that once you say that everybody is an owner then the worker kind of disappears, because there can never be any workers notice board because everybody's a worker.' Mr Brown's statement captures the core of 'coercive exploit' under such a unique business enterprise—a sophisticated form of sabotage against common man to destroy their 'spirit of insubordination.' Veblen saw this spirit as one that '...stands against power: it renounces hierarchy, disrespects authority, and opposes mastery [...] claims self-respect based on individual autonomy and independence.' [33] Mr Brown admitted: 'I've not talked to anybody else at work about being unionized. No one discusses it. Maybe they are. Maybe they aren't, which is weird. You are constantly told about how much *Waitrose* is a partnership and its for the collective benefit.'

Waste and the improper use of resources are conspicuous at *Waitrose* although every measure is taken to minimize them. The conspicuous nature of waste is the perception *Waitrose* minimizes waste while in reality they generate tremendous amounts of it. Interestingly, the cost of waste is already built into every price. Mr Brown admitted anything with the slightest defect or one day over its due date, goes directly into the bin, hence straight into the landfill. 'I go through the fruit and veg and if there's anything that looks a bit dodge you take it out, put it in a basket and write it all off in the end. Have it taken off the system and thrown in the bin at the back. We don't have a compost bin. The other day, to give you an example, I wrote off an 18 pound lobster because it was a day out of date.' At internal communication meetings called 'Partner Voice' *Waitrose* partners are encouraged to offer innovative ideas. 'It was suggested that some items, as long as they're not kept in the fridges, like apples, might be kept for partners and sold to them at a nominal rate. Partners could get apples for ten pents.' Mr Brown's economic conscience got the better of him again. He seemed somewhat concerned about the amount of food that went straight into the landfill. Trucks wait on the premises surrounded by fences making it impossible for anyone to enter the secured area. He commented on a chocolate cake he had to destroy one morning when he was rather hungry himself. Taking into account Veblen's concern about inefficiency and waste in industrial production, consider the *Tesco* supermarket

---

[31] Kunda (1992: 93).
[32] Founded in 1947 the Union of Shop, Distributive & Allied Workers is the fourth largest union in the UK.
[33] Plotkin and Tilman (2011: 206).

franchise (largest in UK) has 2,975 locations and *Sainsbury's* over 1,000. Assuming they have similar practices when you multiple this waste by the number of supermarket chains in Britain alone, it becomes apparent systemic waste due to sabotage tactics between competitors, is of astounding proportion. As food regime engineers are trained to minimize waste and maximize production, Veblen believed they might become critical of inefficiency and waste. 'Their class-consciousness has taken the immediate form of a growing sense of waste and confusion in the management of industry by the financial agents of the absentee owners.' [34] With austerity measures still unfolding and a living wage for many British seemingly impossible under capitalist governance, will any common man or engineer along the food chain come to ask: 'What about it?'

Neoliberal Food Security

As outlined in the chapter introduction, post-1980 neoliberal policy has dramatically transformed Turkey and the entire globe, to accept policies and comply with the food regime under the auspices of agricultural development. Turkey has been, for most of the twentieth century, self-sufficient in terms of her own food production thanks to her diverse climate and abundant water supply of the Tigris and Euphrates rivers and three seas (Black Sea, Marmara Sea and Mediterranean Sea). Home to diverse produce in seed grains, rice and lentils, she also produces tea, most fruits, vegetables and nuts. She has a long tradition of animal husbandry and fishing. For most of the twentieth century, farms were small and under-industrialized compared to those in the U.S. and Canada. But that was once upon a time. Since the 1960s, many rural folk left their communities to find work and better pay in the rapidly developing manufacturing and industrial sectors in the western half of the nation. Policy change in Turkey chose business interests over the welfare of common man. This section will examine what happens to those who produce the foods found in many supermarkets like *Waitrose* at the other end of the food chain. Emphasizing the effects of policy change, I will examine five areas. 1) Policy reform as EU accession; 2) Seed laws and synthetic crops; 3) Contract farming, land inheritance and *Latifundia*; 4) Direct payments and national interest; 5) CAP and EU conformism.

Policy reform as EU accession has been and continues to be the proverbial carrot to coerce Turkey to comply with foreign policy dictated by the IMF, World Bank, WTO and EU. In 1963, Turkey signed the Ankara Agreement, paving the way for accession to the EU. In 1970, she signed the Additional Protocol to Ankara Agreement to further streamline agricultural policy with Europe. What occurred post-1980 and following a second wave of policy reform post-2002, is an ever-increasing coercive exploit—on behalf of business enterprise—to de-regulate and privatize the Turkish economy, inclusive of agriculture. There appears to be two points of view. Defenders of CAP believe policies have little adverse effect on developing economies and without such legislation countries might be worse off in agricultural development. [35]

---

[34] Veblen (1965/1921: 71).

[35] Alan Matthews. 2008. The European Union's Common Agricultural Policy and Developing Countries: The Struggle for Coherence. *European Integration* 30, (3): 381-399.

Others believe little thought was given to how reform might eventually have a long-term negative effect on the Turkish economy and society as a whole. [36] Veblen cautioned government places business over human interest as '…the nation's law givers and administration will have some share in administering that necessary modicum of sabotage that must always go into the day's work of carrying on industry by business methods and for business purposes.' [37] With policy in place, corporate business enterprise teamed up with the local bourgeoisie to introduce genetically modified seeds. On behalf of selective and unbalanced investment, *Cargill* focused on sugar beet and maize production. It promptly raised quotas on sugar beet from 5% to 35% as a long-term objective to establish contract farming of maize in Orhangazi near Istanbul. Strategically located near the Marmara Sea, it makes a suitable transportation route. In Ayd?n's view: 'The ability of US transnational agro–food companies to develop new crops to substitute tropical products with temperate or synthetic products has undermined the ability of developing countries to establish balanced and articulated national economies.' [38]

Seed laws and synthetic crops enforce a division of produce and labor by nation. *Waitrose* shelves are exemplar of such production. Nations often supply only one or several specific crops under the food regime. Increasingly, pre-specified crops determine a national product for export. As a result, local food crops become increasingly extinct. In Turkey's case, any missing produce—take beef for example—is supplemented with expensive foreign beef imports flown in from as far away as Uruguay. In the case of fruit and vegetables, will common man be permitted to plant a garden as an alternative strategy for food? The 2001 Sugar Law and 2006 Seeds Law favor agri-business enterprises like *Cargill, Monsanto* and *Dupont*. Supported under intellectual property rights, these genetically modified seeds end the use of local seed varieties. Legislated before the Bio Security Law, public health has been rendered defenseless. Ambiguous and misleading, the Seeds Law is far-reaching. Any farmer who produces crops with uncertified seeds will be fined up to 3,000 YTL. [39] Substandard seeds are confiscated. A rouge dealer marketing uncertified seeds may face fines up to 10,000—25,000 YTL and be banned from trade for up to five years. 'It regulates seeds for field crops, vineyard and garden plants as well as all forest plant species and propagation material. The main principles, aims and objectives of the 2006 Agrarian Law are full of contradictions. Its article 4 states the main aim of agrarian policies is to increase the level of welfare in agriculture through rural development, by improving agricultural production in accordance with internal and external demands…' [40] In Turkey, common man is not entirely oblivious to such 'coercive exploits' of sabotage. As Veblen believed possible of the human 'spirit of insubordination', common man devises strategies to avert the laws. In Turkey, local seeds were swapped for other local seeds without any monetary exchange: common man sabotage against business enterprise.

---

[36] Zülküf Aydın. 2010. Neo-Liberal Transformation of Turkish Agriculture. *Journal of Agrarian Change* 10 (2): 149-187.

[37] Veblen (1965/1921: 19).

[38] Aydın (2010: 150).

[39] Ibid.: 173. Three thousand new Turkish lira is approximately £1,000 fine, a substantial amount for a small farmer.

[40] Ibid.: 173.

But it was a short-term tactic, as laws were inevitably enforced. Hence governments—especially those of alleged semi-developed nations—face a contradictory position as food regime policies are meant to seemingly develop their national agriculture but also simultaneously hinder efficient food production and overall development of the nation.

Contract farming, land inheritance and Latifundia imply a global shift toward plantations. Gradual impoverishment of common man leaves little option but to accept the new food regime. Contract farming is the first step. Mid-size farmers are persuaded into becoming 'entrepreneurs'—as in the *Waitrose* partnership scheme—by expanding small plots, taking on debt to purchase seeds, fertilizers and equipment to accumulate larger crop yields. But this 'entrepreneurship' appears to be a far riskier endeavor than the 'partnership' at *Waitrose*. Specified crops are enforced under the Ministry of Agriculture and Rural Affairs (MARA). Only those who cooperate will be given contracts. Smaller farmers have few options whilst the mid-size farmers seek to become 'self-made men'—free from the invisible hand of the market—a cultural appeal once belonging to the American farmer. But such aims increasingly bind farmers to banks and finance capital—a 'rentier' form of accumulation collaborating with speculative capital. There's no guaranty all mid-size enterprises prosper. Banks accumulate more land from mid-size entrepreneurs forced into bankruptcy. Estates (*latifundia*) form and the small-mid size farmers abandon agriculture altogether. In addition, new legislation is in the pipeline to restrict inheritance of land so as not to interfere with expansion of large-sized plots. With such legislation common man will lose the right to family land inheritance. 'Contract farming gives indirect control of farming to agribusiness firms. During the colonial period, it was popular for international capital to establish big plantations to produce cash crops for the world market.' [41]

Direct payments and national interest appear an exciting opportunity to direct cash. But, is this yet another ambiguous incentive? The EU capitalizes on the direct payments scheme to ensure against over production. Good arable land is left dormant or in grass when farmers, inclusive of absentee landowners, are paid *not* to produce. Uncultivated land, in a time when media constantly informs us the world cannot meet food demand, is exemplar of waste and inefficiency. Furthermore should over production occur, in the case of poultry in Britain, second grade quantities are shipped overseas and dumped on developing nations. These markets are given a provisional discount on inflated tariffs (sometimes reaching 1,000%) to export produce like bananas back to the UK and EU. Unfair tariffs obviously meet the national interests of Britain before they meet the national interests of developing nations. Turkey, as a non-EU member, is subject to tariffs and does not benefit from direct payments of the type above. Turkey's former 'price support system' of state run agriculture co-operatives and unions was replaced with direct payments, placing responsibility on the producer not buyer. 'Being the sole buyer of the crop through the contract, the firm is in a position to refuse any crops deemed to be below certain standards.' [42] Keyder and Yenal writing on tomato producers involved in contract farming for export markets state:

[41] Ibid.: 178.
[42] Ibid.: 178.

stipulations regarding the pricing of the output seem to be vague and complicated, and the schedule for payment is not clear. For instance, the unit price of tomato is pegged to the average market price of dried tomatoes at the time of delivery, and the price of corn is determined through a complex calculation based on specific coefficients for specific varieties of seeds and the minimum price that is set by the government. Furthermore, it is stated clearly in all contracts that the buyer shall not pay any compensation to the grower for harvest failures due to natural or any other causes. [43]

The signed contract, in itself, is a form of sabotage. Although Turkish tomatoes are sold internationally to major export markets like Russia, Europe and Middle East, I did not find Turkish tomatoes in *Waitrose*. Instead, I found British, Italian and Portuguese varieties. British tomatoes were brightly marked with the British flag either on the packaging or the sticker on their red skin.

CAP and EU conformism seek to exploit Turkish agriculture for the global food regime as in some of the examples cited so far. Notwithstanding Turkey, produce in the global food regime must increasingly conform to CAP. Standards are most evident when examining the packaging of produce. Courgettes from Spain are packaged with the size specified '14–20 cm' under the 'Organic Certification UK5' title. 'Display before' and 'best until' dates are indicated. A *Soil Association* logo appears on the packaging, to confirm organic standards have been met. [44] A supplier code number is marked on packages. As I discovered of British produce, a specific name may appear like Chris Wall, in the case of tomatoes. Chris Wall is not a little independent producer, I imagined. [45] Packaging acts as a pseudo-passport. Any customer grievance about the product is easily traced from the customer receipt, back to the coding on the package and immediately to the supplier. Moreover, should the produce not meet specifications, one centimeter too long in the case of courgettes, a buyer holds the right to reject the produce and waiver payment. *Waitrose* fresh produce is impeccable thanks to the aesthetic criteria that is enforced. Size, shape, skin color, smell, weight, taste and texture must conform to CAP standards. Germany has been ridiculed for its 'cucumber regulation' even stipulating the curvature of the vegetable. After all, sudden deaths were sparked by e-coli in 2011 due to substandard cucumbers. [46] EU producers benefit from generous government subsidies, which take over 47% of the budget allotted for only 5–7% who work in agriculture. In 2013, the EU reduced the CAP budget to 33% down from 71% in 1984. [47] Privileged EU producers will face increasing competition with *latifundia* beyond the EU polity. Hence, plant passport and animal identification systems spell stringent controls. Mr Brown is briefed as Fresh Foods Partner that it is 'illegal to ticket

[43] Çağlar Keyder and Zafer Yenal. 2011. Agrarian Change under Globalization: Markets and Insecurity in Turkish Agriculture *Journal of Agrarian Change* 11 (1): 71.

[44] Organic standards are the rules and regulations that define how an organic product must be produced and are set by EU law. Anything labeled 'organic' that is for human consumption must meet these standards as a minimum. The standards cover all aspects of food production, from animal welfare and wildlife conservation, to food processing, to packaging. *http://www.soilassociation.org/whatisorganic/organicstandards* Retrieved 20.12.2012.

[45] Chris Wall is the son of a family business Eric Wall Ltd., established in 1977. Company greenhouses encompass over 28 acres (70 hectares) in Sussex and rows of tomatoes spanning 53.1 kilometers.

[46] *http://www.bbc.co.uk/news/world-europe-13624554*

[47] Edina Lendvai. 2011. Different Views of EU Agricultural Policy. Annals of Faculty of Engineering Hunedoara, *International Journal of Engineering* 9 (3): 170.

the wrong country on a product.' Turkey, well known for her tomatoes, is currently the fourth largest grower in the world. [48] But as Turkish tomato producers conformed to EU standards, in order to sell their produce, the quality of their local seeds was compromised after buying seeds from Israel. To weed out any remaining independent production, in general, the Turkish government has set coercive measures in place. The 'system will rely on data, forcibly collected from Turkish farmers in a scheme of financial aid. Once everyone is registered, a complete control can be monitored on animal quality, seeds, production, etc. in accordance with what the EU health and safety check standards to manage what it wants grown, seeds and size of holdings.' [49] Turkish legislation follows that of Europe.

Learning from Veblen

In June 2012, outsourced cleaners went on strike in front of the Oxford Street *John Lewis* department store to demand a living wage of £8.30 from the current legal minimum wage of £6.08. [50] In addition, they face 50% redundancies. Partners inside go about their work with little intent to disturb the peace. They have their upcoming bonus in mind. Veblen's theory on joint enterprise was correct. 'Collective ownership of the corporate form that is to say ownership by a collectively instituted *ad hoc*, also falls away as being unavoidably absentee ownership, within the meaning of the term.' [51] Veblen's suspicions of those trained for business might prove equally sound. 'To avoid persistent confusion and prospective defeat, it will be necessary to exclude from all positions of trust and executive responsibility all persons who have been trained for business or who have had experience in business undertakings of the larger sort.' [52] Is this an overstatement? *Waitrose* and the '*John Lewis* Economy' have been exemplary in selling high quality, fair and honest goods, produce and services. British government has been most congratulatory of their efforts to set high standards in the name of British capitalism. If only all business enterprise would convert! Little wonder British government applauds 'fairer capitalism' in 2012, as did David Lloyd George in 1909.

By way of Veblenian 'dispassionate common sense', this chapter attempted to illustrate that despite the 'fairness' model of *Waitrose*, it appears that incoherent and contradictory outcomes occurred and continue to occur. Waste and inefficiency are rife in the global food regime and clearly take precedence over the best interests of common man. Fairness doesn't come into play. Some gain handsomely while common man is 'got the better of.' Caught in the middle is a middle-upper class—largely unaware or little interested in harsh realities—the habitually loyal customers of *Waitrose*. Common man seems to go along, for now, with various forms of sabotage or 'coercive exploit', as Veblen defined and I've emphasized, of national governments in close collaboration with business enterprise. Mr Brown, happy to be called 'Mr' does

---

[48] *http://en.wikipedia.org/wiki/Tomato*
[49] Aydın (2010: 174).
[50] *http://london.indymedia.org/articles/12457*
[51] Veblen (1965/1921: 157).
[52] ibid.: 146.

exercise Veblenian 'economic conscience' from time to time but he is not well poised to rebel as a *Waitrose* 'partner'. While common man in Britain and elsewhere did exercise their spirit of insubordination against such exploit, as of recent, such discontent is increasingly turning to the far Right for a voice. Veblen wouldn't have been surprised. He knew business exploit is always war-like and that workers can be coerced by nationalist sentiment. So as business enterprise continues to provide humanity with food in the new food regime, will it lead to feast or famine? This chapter indicates it may lean to the latter. Veblen knew where the problem lay. Lieutenants in business enterprise inherit wealth by a 'decent livelihood in industrial *absentia*' it is nothing other than "to get something for nothing, at any cost."' [53]

---

[53] ibid.: 162.

References

Aydın, Zülküf. 2010. Neo-Liberal Transformation of Turkish Agriculture. *Journal of Agrarian Change* 10 (2): 149-187

Cox, Peter. 2010. *Spedan's Partnership: The Story of John Lewis and Waitrose.* London: Labatie Books.

Griffiths, Peter. 2011. Ethical Objections to Fairtrade. *Journal of Business Ethics* 105 (3): 357-373.

Keyder, Çağlar and Zafer Yenal. 2011. Agrarian Change under Globalization: Markets and Insecurity in Turkish Agriculture. *Journal of Agrarian Change* 11 (1): 60-86.

Kunda, Gideon. 1992. *Engineering Culture,* Philadelphia: Temple University Press.

Lendvai, Edina. 2011. Different Views of EU Agricultural Policy. Annals of Faculty of Engineering-Hunedoara, *International Journal of Engineering* 9 (3): 169-172.

Matthews, Alan. 2008. The European Union's Common Agricultural Policy and Developing Countries: The Struggle for Coherence. *European Integration* 30 (3): 381-399.

Plotkin, Sidney and Rick Tilman. 2011. *The Political Ideas of Thorstein Veblen.* New Haven & London: Yale University Press.

Veblen, Thorstein. 1965. (1921). *The Engineers and the Price System.* New York: Reprints of Economic Classics, Sentry Press.

Veblen's Contribution to Democratic Change

Ross E. Mitchell

Introduction

Fiercely adept at dissecting societal mores and unravelling productive and pecuniary dynamics that distinguished industry from business, institutional economist Thorstein Veblen (1859-1929) spent inordinately less time theorizing politics in the context of democratic transformation. [1] This in stark contrast to some of his predecessors and contemporary counterparts such as Alexis de Tocqueville, Karl Marx, John Maynard Keynes, John Commons, John Dewey, and Wesley Mitchell. Yet a closer read of Veblen clearly shows he had much to say about institutional and evolving factors of *change* that influence and direct political and capitalistic systems alike. Given his radical epistemological approach in the social sciences and his somewhat understated influence on American policies of the early twentieth century such as Franklin Roosevelt's New Deal (Vaughan 1999), it is somewhat surprising that Veblen's political ideas have been relatively overlooked. This important omission has been recently well-captured and thoroughly analyzed in *The Political Ideas of Thorstein Veblen* (2011), authored by two critical thinkers, Sidney Plotkin and Rick Tilman. While Veblen's works rarely mention politics and he likely was no liberal democrat, Plotkin and Tilman make a convincing argument that he had unmistakable democratic sympathies and understandings.

My paper examines Veblen's thought on the potential for democratic political change from below for a "rational" economic order. It bears mentioning that any "rational" change from below may, in fact, be quite irrational, spontaneous, unanticipated, yet still capable of accomplishing desired change. Notwithstanding the unlikely scenario of any significant political transition occurring in an orderly fashion, direct or face-to-face, participatory decision-making tends to be relatively inefficient and infrequent beyond small-scale settings. The imperatives of global technology mandate levels of expertise that defy possibilities for direct democracy.

Such a situation was not lost on Veblen, who critically, albeit resignedly, accepted the liberal model of representative or parliamentary democracy. While Veblen did not offer much enthusiastic hope for change from below, three recurring themes are worthy of reflection: "conspicuous consumption," "the masterless man" and "the spirit of insubordination." These subjects are discussed at length in this paper, along with other Veblen terms and premises, including the "parental bent" and the interplay of the "vested interests" and the "common man."

---

[1] A master of wit and idiomatic language, institutional economist Thorstein Veblen's (1859-1929) diverse writings on evolving societal periods and mores, war and peace, business and industry, and technological change illustrate an impressive and expansive body of work. Veblen used psychological (behavioral), sociological, and anthropological critical theory to inform his analysis, but his unorthodox behaviors and writings led to dismissals at the University of Chicago and Stanford University. After his post at the University of Missouri, Veblen took up various positions in Washington and New York City, serving for a time as one of the editors of the Dial, a radical journal of literary and political opinion, as well as on the formative staff of The New School.

Veblen's largely pessimistic epistemology that business interests (in his acute sense of cynicism, "shenanigans" and other predatory behaviors) ran against community norms of solidarity and fairness; and to the detriment of workmanship, the triumph of pecuniary dealings over earthly toil and grind would likely continue. The Great Depression along with the lingering global recession of recent years makes us wonder if democratic ideals and norms can coexist within the framework of a neoliberal capitalistic model. Since the 1960s groundswell of social and political change, the underlying population continues its long struggle to regain control over their own health and welfare, their communities, and the environment. Time has shown that the insatiable profit motive has tended to obfuscate and hinder such attempts. As pointed out by Thomas Jefferson, "The end of democracy and the defeat of the American Revolution will occur when government falls into the hands of lending institutions and moneyed incorporations." [2] Such a prophecy seems borne out by the global financial crisis of 2008 and beyond, resulting in the collapse of large financial institutions, the bailout of banks by national governments, and downturns in stock markets around the world. Global recovery is still ongoing.

During this economic malaise, the "Occupy Movement" spontaneously took off in 2011 in the United States and quickly spread worldwide. [3] Are such civic movements a sign of the latest reflection of popular dissatisfaction of the domination of predatory corporations and complicit nation-states, ahistorical in content and tone? Or are these just modern manifestations of sporadic discord against the ruling classes since time immemorial? Such global economic control has predominated for some time and history suggests will likely continue to do so. While collective voices and perspectives are attempting to create healthy forums for democratic renewal of what some believe to be oligarchic and predatory institutions and norms, a "people-first" democracy seems unlikely today. Even a scaled-down version of a friendlier or more direct form of democracy may not be enough to overcome dominant interests of business and political circles.

Is there anything that a read of Veblen can add to this context? The purpose of my paper is to explore whether concepts of the masterless man and the spirit of insubordination could be both catalyst and culprit for grassroots democratic change in a predatory world. After discussing some of Veblen's ideas germane to this topic, a section on the Occupy Movement follows, interweaving an understanding of this international phenomenon from a Veblenian perspective. I discuss a Canadian example of the legendary "Masterless Men" to provide some empirical and historical context on the Occupy Movement. Finally, I end with some suggestions of the application of Veblen in an emergent arena of civil disobedience during a time of global economic uncertainties and struggles.

---

[2] This quote has not been verified, and may have been adapted from Paul Leicester Ford's 1892 *The Writings of Thomas Jefferson*, 10 vols, 1892-99, New York.

[3] Turkey was also part of the Occupy Movement. On December 5, 2011, hundreds of students gathered near campus of Boğaziçi Üniversitesi in Istanbul to protest the increasing commercialization of spaces on campus as well as for affordable and healthy food for everyone. Following the rally about 100 students began to squat the campus Starbucks outlet for several days (see *http://ism-global.net/starbucks_occupation_bosphorus_uni_dec5*).

An Emergent New Order of Business and Politics

Capitalism as (Conspicuously) Consumptive and Wasteful

While Veblen's work has relevance to both environment and society (see Mitchell 2001), Veblen's approach to consumption and waste was less about the environment and more about the cultural consequences and implications of contemporary capitalism. [4] Consumption for its own sake, with all the attendant exploit and waste that it entails, becomes a defining feature of modern culture under corporate capitalism. Veblen was both skeptical and critical of this development. He describes advertising and marketing, enshrined by pecuniary interests as a way to encourage both consumption and waste. One of the main consequences of marketing consumption to the masses is the transformation of sheer consumption and waste into an "honorific endeavor."

One only has to tour a modern landfill, visit Disneyland or Las Vegas, take in a rock concert, or visit a mall to see that consumption and waste are inextricably linked to marketing and mass media; certainly of a scale sans precedent. Reduce, reuse, and recycle may be the ecological mantra, but environmental altruism is hard to maintain when consumers are continually bombarded with the advertiser's mantra of "Sale!" and "Buy!" and climate change from unchecked industrial development is a modern reality. Veblen wryly notes how savvy marketers generate the desire to purchase in his "invention is the mother of necessity," a play on the ancient maxim "necessity is the mother of invention." Advertisers are but one side of the coin; people's emulative behaviors show that, just as readily, we vicariously (and in some cases, voraciously) shop to consume, or just to shop. As Veblen described so well in *The Theory of the Leisure Class* (1899), we buy to possess, to display, to emulate, to "satisfy" some other desire, but not necessarily out of an intrinsic need for survival. For example, we may choose to "upsize" our soft drink or popcorn at the cinema generally not out of hunger but perhaps just because "we can" and it's presented as a deal – for an extra buck we get more, including refills! But for some there is a nagging sense of guilt in this wanton display of conspicuous consumption, not to mention the extra calories or environmental "bads" that come with the choice. This moral pejorative is the "economic consciousness" that Veblen spoke of, or a test to judge the wasteful patterns of production and consumption. It motivates us to ask, "Does our use of resources serve 'directly to enhance human life on the whole?'" (Plotkin and Tilman 2011:91). The same test could apply to conspicuous consumption and leisure.

With the rise of capitalism in the modern era, marketing of resources and their derivatives became the new "propaganda of the faith," only less efficient (a reference to his comments on religion in *Absentee Ownership* 1923). Marketing and advertising is also the institutional mechanism that that connects his writings on the leisure class to the middle classes; its cultural mechanism is the absolutely decisive significance of emulation, which is central to Veblen's understanding of how society works. The middle and working classes emulate the honorific

---

[4] It has been argued that Veblen contributed to an understanding of environmentally related fields; for some diverse examples, refer to the 2007 book edited by Ross E. Mitchell, *Thorstein Veblen's Contribution to Environmental Sociology: Essays in the Political Ecology of Wasteful Industrialism*. Edwin Mellen Press: Lewiston, NY.

waste and consumption styles of the upper strata, so that waste and consumption broaden out from the leisure classes to become a defining feature of the whole culture of capitalism, not just that of its leisured strata.

The importance of emulation also frames Veblen's underdeveloped conception of political power. As he described it, emulation was so effective at keeping the underlying population in check that state coercion was less necessary. If the masses can be kept entertained and compensated well enough to maintain a certain level of satisfaction, perhaps they would be less likely to protest or rebel. As discussed below, reluctance to publically express dissent is changing as people everywhere appear to be tiring of the corporate agenda. Business and political leaders promise that continued economic growth will generate more wealth, thereby increasing employment, improving quality of life, and providing better education and healthcare. One is reminded of Dr. Seuss's cautionary tale *The Lorax*, "Business is business! And business must grow, regardless of crummies in tummies, you know." [5] The global economy is fueled by such growth in China and India, among other emerging productive powerhouse nations, who increasingly engage in emulative behavior with the same desire for material or "status" goods as those living in highly developed countries.

How does democracy fit into this pecuniary scenario? While often relegated to the sidelines in the business of business to paraphrase Milton Friedman, democracy is benignly complicit at best and generally a willing partner for the Captains of Industry. Early in his career, while Veblen manifested some hope that constitutional democracy and the rule of law could temper all that was ugly in power politics, his contempt for politics was all but total by the time he wrote his last book, *Absentee Ownership* (1923). Tactics of salesmanship, propaganda, deceit, secrecy, and manipulation were "legitimizing" political power, especially of the populist variety which was often publically supported, but this also ran counter to any claims of rationality or decency (Plotkin 2010). The irrationalities of consumption owing to envy and emulation as Veblen saw it at the turn of the twentieth century have entrenched themselves in a global economy and complicit nation-states; the "New Order of Business" as Veblen called it long before Reaganomics and Thatcherism of the 1980s.

The Masterless Man

Veblen's "masterless man" was a term he used for serfs and peasants, who rejected the grip of feudal control during "the handicraft era" in Europe. This period lasted from about the fourteenth to the late eighteenth centuries, and was marked by the decline of feudalism, growth of urban commercial towns, early industrialization, and appearance of the modern state system (Plotkin 2010). The masterless man became a social phenomenon: a nascent middle class of small craftsmen, inventors, petty shopkeepers, drifters, vagabonds, and the like, who challenged the predatory political relationships and militarized values of feudal society. Their "spirit of insubordination," as discussed below, symbolically demonstrated by throwing off their shackles of feudalism, inaugurated a surge of freedom and technological progress, as they searched for a better life in the emerging commercial and industrial towns of Western Europe.

---

[5] The crummies were a gastrointestinal disease suffered by the Bar-Ba-Loots, bear-like creatures who lived in a forest filled with Truffula Trees.

The masterless men, as Veblen observed, were not altruistically motivated. They did not wholly forgo opportunities to become masters themselves once shop was set up. Wives were treated as property, slaves worked the plantations, native lands were confiscated, and old emulative behaviors continued as they strove to accumulate wealth and fortune. Yet their time was limited. The advance of technology and the consequent massive increase in the scale of work would eventually make the masterless man seem outdated, at least in the sense of a brash, independent individual seeking adventure and risk for pecuniary ends. While exceptions exist, even today (consider ostentatious billionaires Richard Branson and Donald Trump), the anonymity of instantaneous electronic trading and predacious, collusionary corporate politics is the new normal. Impersonal market conditions predominated as pecuniary and productive relations separated, with a slow but sure decline in the independent worker and workmanship (Edgell 2001:124). Technological efficiency and market effectiveness began to trump "self-help and "self-determination." The rise of the corporation and its shareholders as an amorphous but legally entitled "person" became the new order of business.

With the demise of the masterless man, or perhaps more accurately the transformation of masterless men into corporate leaders working in institutionalized or bureaucratized iron cages, what was to become of "the common man" comprised of farmers, factory workers, teachers, store owners, and other ordinary folk? Veblen notes that in his day, Americans were still quite far from obtaining a clear idea of their predicament:

> Evidently the cleavage due to be brought on by the new order in business and industry, between the vested interests and the common man, has not yet fallen into clear lines, at least not in America. The common man does not know himself as such, at least not yet, and the sections of the population which go to make up the common lot as contrasted with the vested interests have not yet learned to make common cause. The American tradition stands in the way. This tradition says that the people of the republic are made up of ungraded masterless men who enjoy all the rights and immunities of self-direction, self-help, free bargaining, and equal opportunity, quite after the fashion that was sketched into the great constituent documents of the eighteenth century. (Veblen 1919: 174)

The common man had not "awakened" to the fact that he or she was not "masterless," and as a result was unlikely to change the situation over the short term. Even if they were aware of these "clear lines," there seemed not much that could be done to ameliorate things. Veblen noted that common cause was capable of being taken up by union leaders, farmer cooperatives, and even sympathetic political or business leaders, but America in his day was still many decades away from the civic rights protests of the 1960s.

The Spirit of Insubordination

Another concept explored at length in their book, and more thoroughly advanced in Plotkin's paper "Thorstein Veblen and the Politics of Insubordination" and presented at a 2012 conference in Turkey, [6] include Veblen's use of "the spirit of insubordination". This can be seen in such works as *Imperial Germany and the Industrial Revolution*, *The Higher Learning in America*, and *The Engineers and the Price System*. Veblen's "spirit of insubordination" was a tool that the underlying population had yet to wholeheartedly adopt and employ to their advantage.

---

[6] Veblen, Capitalism and Possibilities for a Rational Economic Order, Yıldız Technical University Auditorium, July 6-7, 2012, Istanbul, Turkey.

The way Veblen posits the spirit of insubordination is not as an "instinct" but rather an assertion of difference, or a sentiment of living one's life her or her own way. This so-called "passive resistance" was a grassroots or individual movement, which in the handicraft era developed into the liberal version of the masterless man: "Insubordination has potentially democratic consequences, bursting out in such familiar acts of popular sabotage as strikes and protest movements" (Plotkin and Tilman 2011:148). But as described earlier, and as Veblen also remarked, insubordination was not allowed to fester and spread unattended. Authorities tend to keep dissenters in check.

Typical of Veblen's writings, he leaves unanswered how the spirit of insubordination might serve a practical end, or could be accommodated within a tolerant system of representative governance; or even more crucially, used to enhance the life process. Protests by themselves don't put food on the table, but in theory represent a spark for positive change. Veblen's underdeveloped notion spirit of insubordination could benefit from additional insight. In Karl Polanyi's (2001) classic work, *The Great Transformation*, he introduced the concept of the "counter movement," the idea that the chaos and poverty caused by marketization, which restrains the market through political and institutional change, can lead to popular resistance. If this is true, then the popular motivations for the global Occupy Movement as introduced below make sense. It is perhaps no coincidence that world protests about the market have so quickly followed the global recession.

As Veblen noted, there was little that the average person could do to stop the vested interests. Taking action into his or her own hands could only lead to trouble: "he will find himself in the wrong and may even come in for the comfortless attention of the courts" (Veblen 1919:177). In some instances, and indeed in more or less massive formation, this movement of dissent has already reached the limit of tolerance and has found itself sharply checked by the constituted keepers of law and custom (Veblen 1919:180-181).

Business Takes Care of Business

Pecuniary self-interest led such individuals to raise prices through industrial delays and obstruction, which was nothing less than "sabotage" or the "conscientious withdrawal of efficiency" as explained in *The Engineers and the Price System* (1921). Veblen takes pains to distinguish sabotage from the "violence and disorder" or "passive resistance" of disaffected workers against the "similar tactics of friction, obstruction, and delay" which were used to secure advantage over business rivals. Industrial sabotage was carried out to artificially boost prices up while keeping volume down to obtain the largest possible profits. As shown in this quote, Veblen understood well the controlling, monopolistic power that large business firms and later corporations demonstrated:

> It is argued, by one and another, that the country's business concerns have entered into consolidations, coalitions, understandings and working arrangements among themselves - syndicates, trusts, pools, combinations, interlocking directorates, gentlemen's agreements, employers' unions - to such an extent as virtually to cover the field of that large-scale business that sets the pace and governs the movements of the rest; and that where combination takes effect in this way, competition ceases. So also it will be argued that where there has been no formal coalition of interests the business men in charge will still commonly act in collusion, with much the same result. (Veblen 1921: 77)

174

Sabotage and delay were an essential part of the toolkit of business and political leaders, but were occasionally used to advantage by union syndicalists too. There are times in various societies, including capitalism, when the economic institutions hold back economic performance. Capitalism actually sabotages production at certain times and in a handful of times has occasionally been replaced by other systems (e.g., communism, totalitarianism), although these other alternatives have generally not worked out. As Churchill's oft-repeated refrain goes, democracy is the worst form of government, except for all the others that have been tried. He could have said the same of capitalism.

Veblen's cynicism and pessimism for meaningful change to the system was less obvious in *The Engineers and the Price System* (1921), although still present. Indeed, there was some concern for the future if the system was sufficiently challenged:

> ... the date may not be far distant when the interlocking processes of the industrial system shall have become so closely interdependent and so delicately balanced that even the ordinary modicum of sabotage involved in the conduct of business as usual will bring the whole to a fatal collapse. (Veblen 1921: 77)

In the twenty-first century, when corporations rule the global market, the gains from technical efficiency (or as Veblen put it, reducing the level of "derangement" while increasing productivity) does not necessarily benefit the workforce. It is just as likely that a powerful firm will be able to bring more pressure to bear on employees and unions in negotiations. The greater the size, the more likely corporations are able to weather the storm of discontent, leaving workers in a disadvantaged or more vulnerable state. The pervasiveness of powerful groups such as the Captains of Industry over social and political issues was an important metric in Veblen's day, a power dynamic which continues today. According to Veblen, even the labour unions were not always working in the best interests of the general public.

In short, "getting something for nothing" was the ultimate objective of the "vested interests," which the community had come to accept as part of life. The "irksome of labour" in exchange for "free income" as earned by the vested interests was the price to pay by the common man to maintain family and material comfort. As excerpted from the *Vested Interests and the Common Man*:

> Approximately the whole of this remaining margin of free income goes to the business men in charge, or to the business concerns for whom this management is carried on. In case the free income which is gained in this way promises to continue, it presently becomes a vested right. It may then be formally capitalised as an immaterial asset having a recognised earning-capacity equal to this prospective free income. That is to say, the outcome is a capitalised claim to get something for nothing; which constitutes a vested interest. The total gains which hereby accrue to the owners of these vested rights amount to something less than the total loss suffered by the community at large through that delay of production and derangement of industry that is involved in the due exercise of these rights. In other words, and as seen from the other side, this free income which the community allows its kept classes in the way of returns on these vested rights and intangible assets is the price which the community is paying to the owners of this imponderable wealth for material damage greatly exceeding that amount. (Veblen 1919: 35-36)

Veblen separated out those who held wealth, thus control, from the rest; namely, those lacking sufficient wealth and who were dependent or controlled by the first class:

> So that the population of these civilised countries now falls into two main classes: those who own wealth invested in large holdings and who thereby control the conditions of life for the rest; and those who do not own wealth in sufficiently large holdings, and whose conditions of life are therefore controlled by these others. It is a division, not between those who have something and those who have nothing as many socialists would be inclined to describe it but between those who own wealth enough to make it count, and those who do not. (Veblen 1919: 160-161)

His dig at socialists here is subtle recognition of the fine line between having wealth or not, versus having enough wealth to be able to *control* how the rest of us live. Power and money are mixed together in this milieu that ultimately affects us all. The political response to the worst financial collapse since the Great Depression during the global economic crisis of 2008 until now is a shining example of the uneasy alliance between government and financial institutions tackling the disaster. Indeed, the 2007-08 financial crisis spurred the largest federal bailout in the history of the United Sates, and led to a rewriting of the rules of government.

Having laid some of the foundation for Veblen's approach to capitalism and democracy, we now move to the next section: the Occupy Movement as an analytical point of departure to Veblen. Before delving into the subject, I discuss some of the contributing factors and drivers of the movement, including the relationship between democracy and capitalism, and the evolving distribution of wealth in the United States.

A Veblenian Take on the Occupy Movement

Democracy and Capitalism

The notion of capitalism is relatively straightforward. As Marx explained it, capitalism is understood to be an economic system that emphasizes private ownership of the means of production. In other words, a privately controlled economy manipulated by the invisible hands of market and the forces of supply and demand. In contrast, democracy is a rather complicated and messy business; rules of the game are predisposed to change, typically from above but also surprisingly at times from below. Individual citizens have the numbers, hence the votes. In theory, bad leaders can be replaced and bad policies can be revoked. Yet even in a democracy the majority of money and power is class-based; these are held by a few, a trend that only has intensified in this neo-liberal era. This is partly a reality of the "representativeness" of most modern, complex democracies. It also goes back full circle to the synergistic overlap of capitalistic and democratic goals.

Democracy and the rule of law are important considerations in a westernized political system. People must be able to protest, demonstrate, and organize when their interests or health are damaged. That means guaranteeing the rights, assembly, and association. The media must be free to report protests and to investigate pollution incidents and corruption, and so they must enjoy complete editorial freedom from government and commercial pressures. Free elections are needed with multiple candidates, so that representatives who don't respond to public pressures can be booted out. There must be an independent legal system with equal access for the poor.

Such conditions are not a given for all democracies, and messy situations do regularly occur. It is not a given that evolutionary change will "clean up" the mess. Not surprisingly, the vested interests resist with all their power any attempt to change the institutions that give them their wealth and power. Only an immense effort can overcome such resistance. Common people will expend that effort in the case of a clear crisis that is directly harming them. This may be occurring now, as will be discussed shortly; yet even in a crisis, it is not a given that the common people will triumph over the vested interests. Major evolutionary change comes about only when stars align; if institutions are harmful to economic performance, if this is clear to the great majority of the common people, if they are willing to fight about it, and finally if the strength of the common people can overcome the vested interests (Sherman 2004).

Wealth Distribution and the Vested Interests

Wealth distribution has been extremely concentrated throughout American history, as well as most of the capitalistic world. In the nineteenth century, the top 1% owned 40-50% of the wealth in large port cities like Boston, New York, and Charleston (Domhoff 2005). The wealth distribution flattened somewhat in the aftermath of the New Deal and World II, as increased employment and some progressive income tax rates took some money from the rich to help with government services. Further decline in the 1970s occurred, largely due to a fall in stock prices. By the late 1980s, however, the wealth distribution was almost as concentrated as it had been in 1929 as explained earlier. Wealth continued to edge up before the economy crashed in the late 2000s and ordinary people got pushed down again (Domhoff 2005).

Today, a downward shift in living standards is being experienced by most of the American population and the world for that matter. Unemployment is high almost everywhere and the housing market has either already crashed in many cities and regions or appears about to soon. Some observers say that bankers, stockholders, and corporate executives have become so powerful that they are able to influence and control politicians, rig the market and economic system in their favor, and eliminate competition. Veblen would not have been surprised at all. In *The Vested Interests and the Common Man*, Veblen (1919: 125) described "democratic sovereignty" as having been converted "into a cloak to cover the nakedness of a government which does business for the kept classes." By the time the global recession hit in 2008, the pursuit of the almighty dollar appeared to have drowned out any other moral considerations. Enron, Goldman Sachs, the oil industry, and mortgage companies have all been accused of moral bankruptcy in recent years, and the list continues to grow.

Since the civil rights reforms of the 1960s and an emerging social and environmental awareness into the 1970s, unprecedented economic and environmental catastrophes have become the norm. Billions of people, the overwhelming majority of humanity, are suffering due to a concentration of wealth and resources by a minute but very powerful minority. Ultimately, short-sighted greed has proven to be humanity's most severe disease. If free markets are truly the best way for nations to grow from poverty to prosperity, this has not occurred evenly, not only in non-Western countries but even within the backyards of Western nations. One does not have to spend much time in large urban centres of North America to see homelessness and other forms of destituteness and decay.

The impersonalization of work with financial gain as the overriding objective and a society of complacent consumers are steadily wearing away Veblen's instinct of workmanship and parental bent. The latter was a proclivity to a communal orientation with values of community pride, self-sufficiency, and solidarity. More work equates with more money, more goods, more stress. Work for many has become less pleasing, "irksome," even though it may serve to (temporarily) satisfy some self-defined degree of conspicuous consumption. Low job security provides a greater incentive to acquiesce to employer's demands for longer hours but at great cost to humans and nature alike. Competitive or "pecuniary" individualism in many modern economies has undermined our social and environmental fabric (Mitchell 2007).

The Occupy Movement

The Occupy Movement is in essence a protest against the powerful by the powerless. By occupying physical spaces of urban centres, those involved are attempting to assert their collective voices, the rich and influential will listen. The first Occupy protest is commonly referred to as "Occupy Wall Street." It began September 17, 2011 in New York City's Zuccotti Park. By early October, Occupy protests had taken place or were ongoing in over 95 cities across 82 countries, and over 600 communities in the United States (Wikipedia 2012). Protests spread from New York to Chicago, Boston, Washington, Los Angeles, San Francisco, and other cities across the United States. They also began popping up in small cities. The Occupy Movement was initiated by the Canadian activist group Adbusters [7] and partly inspired by the Arab Spring, especially Cairo's Tahrir Square protests, and the Spanish Indignants. The movement commonly uses the slogan "We are the 99%" and organizes through websites such as Occupy Together. [8] Considered by some as a "democratic awakening," it remains difficult to distill its demands.

Although most popular in the United States, Occupy has seen protests and occupations in dozens of other countries and on every continent. Since Occupy Wall Street, there have been hundreds of Occupy movement protests worldwide over time, some turning violent. A list of proposed events for the October 15, 2011 global protests listed events in 951 cities in 82 countries. [9] For the first two months of the protest, authorities largely adopted a tolerant approach towards the movement, though this began to change in mid-November with over a dozen camps being cleared in both the United States and Europe. By the end of 2011 authorities had cleared out most of the major camps. On May 1, 2012, the Occupy movement marked a resurgence with a May Day general strike that took place in cities across the United States, including New York, Washington D.C., Chicago, and Los Angeles.

While the number of activists remains small, the movement has caught international attention. The faces of the protesters are diverse, making the movement look less like suburbia and more like America. While some may argue this point, the movement in essence transcends gender, race, religion, and other demographics, except for one – class. Those who have engaged

---

[7] The Adbusters Media Foundation is a Canadian-based not-for-profit, anti-consumerist, pro-environment organization founded in 1989 by Kalle Lasn and Bill Schmalz in Vancouver, British Columbia.

[8] See *http://www.occupytogether.org/*.

[9] See *http://en.wikipedia.org/wiki/Occupy_movement*.

in the protest are mostly from lower and middle income classes. The Occupy Movement is comprised of the unemployed; students having trouble making tuition payments; families facing home eviction; people lacking adequate health insurance; groups facing discrimination based on race, gender, or sexual preference; homeless people; children and the elderly; and so on.

While their agenda was not crystal clear, the Occupiers called for economic reforms to bring stability to people experiencing recent and/or long-term financial disadvantage. Improved quality of life was the fundamental motivation for the movement, and attention is drawn to the *inequality* faced by many: inequality of incomes, of opportunity, and of power. Its famous slogan, "We are the 99 percent," highlights the widening chasm between the superrich, who combine lives of luxury with enormous political influence due to powerful lobbying and generous donations to campaigns, and everyone else, struggling to provide a decent life for their children. A few quotes from speakers at October 28, 2011 Occupy Portland provides a sense of what the main concerns were [10]:

> We are not controlling Wall Street; we have been bought and sold. … we have been made into chattel.
> A corporation is a person [according to the courts], but a person without a heart.
> It's time to stop the war against the middle class.
> Change your bank, go to a credit union.
> Economic justice needs to be extended to all.
> We are the majority, and we are tired of business as usual.
> The 99 percent knows the system's not fair, but the 1 percent know it too, so that's 100 percent.

Neatly summed up in Howard Beal's line from the 1976 movie *Network*, "We're mad as hell, and we're not gonna take it anymore!" The "business as usual" rhetoric for many has worn out its welcome, a trend that Veblen noted was already occurring during the late nineteenth and early twentieth centuries.

The Occupiers also called for a variety of ecological reforms, electoral changes to ensure fairness, and the improvement of the American infrastructure. If we leave out some of the more controversial demands by some, such as the elimination of free trade and the complete opening of national borders, their agenda is calling for a "kinder" society (Mason 2012). The Occupy Movement has also brought attention to the impact of the Global Recession of 2008, of which effects are still being felt throughout the globe. It has raised awareness that poverty is not viewed solely as a statistic but as a very real situation where families suffer from poor nutrition, inadequate housing, and limited access to quality health care.

The Occupy Movement is not the only recent social event in North America for protesters targeting the wealthy elite. In Quebec in early 2012, one-third of the province's post-secondary students walked out on their classes. For months, Montreal was the site of daily, occasionally turbulent, street demonstrations by protestors of all walks of life who mixed street theatrics, including nudity, pot banging, and costumes, with determined savvy and gumption. Quebec's student uprising began as a battle over tuition fees but evolved into a broader ideological and social struggle. Many of the tactics and goals of the Occupy Movement found common ground in the Quebec student protests. Other events around the world have also built on the momentum experienced in the Occupy Movement.

---

[10] See *http://www.americancurrents.com/2011/10/occupy-portland-part-4-you-know-maybe.html.*

Veblen and the Occupy Movement

So how does one apply and reconcile a Veblen analysis with the Occupy Movement? In Veblenian terms, the movement appears to pit the common masses against the minority vested interests. The Occupy Movement seemingly places itself outside and against the system and questions whether existing democratic institutions are truly aligned with popular views. It is interesting that the opposition between the 99%, the true or authentic people, and the 1%, the plutocratic elites, was already found in the Veblen who, in his *Theory of the Leisure Class* (1899), condemned the "conspicuous consumption" of parasitic elites.

Veblen's spirit of insubordination is also enmeshed in the direct actions taken by the Occupiers. Rebellion is the inevitable result of a social order unwilling to accommodate or even acknowledge working-class demands, ideas, and feelings. The justified expression of working-class anger, in turn, produces a more inclusive and democratic social order. Occasionally violence is an undesirable outcome of this insubordination, although as Ghandi and other pacifists have shown, including the 2011 Arab Spring movement, violence is not always necessary to effect major change. Quite the contrary, the Occupy Movement likely represents a manifestation of the parental bent in its values of sharing and communal organization.

The movement also appears to be comprised of Veblen's masterless men, those individuals who are realizing that they can make an impact in unconventional ways. But "masterless" in the positive sense of the term; namely, the sense of independence and qualities of self-help and self-determination that Veblen's masterless men possessed. The frustration with being controlled by a feudal lord led to a breaking point as the masterless men hit the open road in search of better opportunities. Leave aside for now the problematic that Veblen found with the masterless men; namely, that once they became established their conversion into masters themselves soon began. The masterless man was about action – not depending on someone else to act on one's behalf, making independent decisions and acting to improve one's chances. Similarly, the Occupy Movement *is* direct action. In the context of this form of protest, a direct action may be a strike, boycott, or other form of refusal. It could be sharing food, sewing clothing, or building a tent. It may also take a more "offensive" approach such as a form of disruption at the point of production or destruction; sabotage in the "act now" sense. Regardless, direct action is against the existing economic and political institutions and for new social relations. It does not recognize the existing power structures, and this is precisely what makes it effective by many accounts.

The Occupy Movement is, for now, without a leader. The sentiment appears to be that a leader is not necessary to be successful. Perhaps this form of direct democracy is not so foreign. Veblen also questioned the wisdom of political or other institutional attempts to organize society on the basis of central planning. Veblen suggested that the popular inclination "to live and let live" raised questions about "the practicability or expediency of any given scheme of control or any projected line of collective enterprise."

Example of the Masterless Man

Could Veblen's masterless man be both catalyst and culprit, or friend and foe, for grassroots democratic change in a predatory world? A glimpse into a spontaneous, anti-hierarchy occupation of public land from the province of Newfoundland, Canada is useful to highlight here for comparative purposes. This example comes from an online article written by Hans Rollmann (2011).

While Newfoundland was also a participant in the 2011 Occupy Movement, it may be a surprise for many that an Occupy "camp" was part of Newfoundland's history. In 1750, led by an Irish deserter named Peter Kerrivan, some oppressed soldiers, sailors, and fishers decided to turn their back on their exploitative working conditions, and the backbreaking labour they were expected to perform for their rich employers, and for which they received little compensation or justice. They left their jobs and wandered off into the area of Butter Pot, on the Avalon Peninsula, where they established an "Occupy" camp (or in the terminology of the day, an "outlaw society"). Calling themselves the *Society of Masterless Men*, they formed their own free camps and survived by hunting, fishing, and living off the land, as well as trading with local communities. As their numbers grew, so too did the alarm of the authorities. Local merchants and businesspeople complained that the Masterless Men were ignoring government authority, and that they were organizing "riotous and unlawful assembly of people." The authorities investigated and decided the best solution was to build more prisons, and send in the Royal Navy to chase out and arrest them. By this time, the band had grown quite large and they knew the land well. Three separate military expeditions failed to capture them. The band is credited with having built the first roads in the region, both in order to move around the wilderness quickly as well as to serve as decoys to confuse the authorities. For the next 50 to 100 years the Masterless Men and their kin roamed the hills of Butter Pot, eventually becoming absorbed into the local communities and outports.

The Masterless Men had no agenda, no list of demands, no media or exit strategy. Neither were they altruistically motivated as Veblen described. Bandits and rebels they may have been but they simply wanted to enjoy their freedom, live without exploitation, and enjoy the fruits of their labour. They terrorized nobody but the merchants who were appalled at seeing them earn a free living, in fact "getting something for nothing." Their independence, self-reliance and willingness to challenge exploitation and the unduly harsh rule of government authority left its imprint on Newfoundland's outport communities. These values continue to be honoured and cherished today, and represent an important part of Newfoundland's heritage. A quote from Rollmann (2011) is worth repeating here for its Veblenian sentiment:

> It's hard to square the Occupy protest camps, with their wireless, generator-run internet and their library yurts, with the band of free Irish outlaws living in the hills of Butter Pot, but they share a common thread: the courage to say enough is enough, and to turn their back on a system that exploits them. I'm still not sure that I fully like the Occupy movement, but I do know that that courage is something far too many of us have lost, and something we must regain if we are indeed to build a better world in the face of what this one is becoming.

Conclusion

What would Veblen say regarding the potential for democratic political change from below for a rational economic order? Veblen may have lamented the way the common man was getting the short end of the stick, but he offered no radical solution. While the Occupy Movement is not an extension of a Veblenian form of proselytizing, he would not have been surprised at its rapid emergence and spread given today's communication technologies and the impact of globalization to inform and effect change. He made clear again and again that the common man was reaching the limit of its power to make change. Not that the type of transformation that Marx, Polanyi, and others called for was impossible for Veblen. The conditions at the time of his writings were such that the modern political-economic system that had taken root in the United States was here to stay for a while. Even so, for Veblen, evolution and transformation were always a possibility, indeed an inevitable outcome.

Has the Occupy Movement failed? This fervent movement spread like wildfire all over the world in a matter of weeks, garnering support and media attention as fast as one could tweet to his or her followers. Protesting the fact that much of the wealth in the United States (and the world in general) is concentrated in a small group of people, the "1%," while the majority of people, the "99%," are languishing in varying levels of dissatisfaction, if not poverty, Veblen would likely have been befuddled that so little has changed. Yet the spirit of insubordination, if anything, is stronger than ever. True, from an outsider's perspective, the movement seems less focused and possibly even less vital than the 1960s civil rights movement, when minority and gender rights along with the Vietnam War protests were the burning issues of the day, and the movement was guided by charismatic leaders such as Martin Luther King. Much more work, irksome though it may be, is needed to convert the amorphous collective energy and goodwill first felt around the globe during 2011 into something more lasting.

The Occupiers established that they were discontented about the state of things and as such, and decided to have an Occupation. But after the initial shock-wave of excited rebellion dissipated, people began to ask a very, very important question: "What do we want?" We know why they were protesting, but what objectives are the Occupiers, both former and current, seeking to accomplish? It remains to be seen whether the Occupy Movement will benefit society and make the protests more than just an angry blip in history. The movement appears to have petered out in many locations. In some cases the Occupy Movement is being replaced by other forms of civil disobedience and direct action gatherings, aided in the process by social media such as Twitter and Facebook. In our wireless, tuned in society, organizing the masses for spontaneous social and political events is a cinch; keeping up the momentum and enthusiasm is where the challenge lies.

The Occupy Movement and its mantra of a "people-first democracy" may not be enough to overcome dominant hierarchical interests - the greedy profiteers, exploiters, and speculators commensurate with Veblen's absentee owners. It remains to be seen what role individuals or communities will play in a spirited renewal of life and hope in a social and ecological awakening. But as this paper has tried to illustrate, the positive side of the masterless man may represent a need for both individual and collective voices and perspectives to help create a healthy forum for renewed democratic institutions, and for a kinder corporate face.

When the people occupied Zuccotti Park and renamed it Liberty Plaza, they did not ask permission nor demand that they have the park. They simply "took it" and transformed it into the world that many of us want to live in, one based in mutual aid, trust, self-determination, and self-management. Perhaps the Occupy Movement offers us the choice between Veblen's era of barbarism and a radically better democratic society. The desire of the vested interests to preserve the status quo leads to barbarism. The desire of the common people for a better life may perhaps lead to a more democratic society in both the political and economic spheres. Time will tell which system ultimately wins the struggle.

Epilogue

Ironically, almost a year after the 2012 Veblen conference in Istanbul where this paper was presented, protests began in Taksim Square. On May 28, 2013, the Islamist Justice and Development Party (AKP) government ordered the Istanbul Metropolitan Municipality to move into Gezi Park in order to remove some trees and clear the ground for the construction of a new shopping mall in Taksim Square. When it was clear that the park was slated to be bulldozed, peaceful demonstrations and sit-ins were organized. The resultant police crackdown on the demonstrations sparked a broader uprising against the government, triggering a wave of protest across Turkey against (then) Prime Minister Recep Tayyip Erdogan and his AKP.[11] Violence injured thousands and led to at least three deaths, including of a police officer. People began chanting "Everywhere is Taksim, everywhere is resistance," calling on Mr. Erdogan's government to resign. Erdogan, who was democratically elected and has been in power for a decade, continues to be defiant.

Similar to the Occupy Movement in the U.S. and the Indignados in Spain, the Turkish uprising had no leader. It brought together people from all walks of life, with different political affiliations and agendas, and different ethnic and religious backgrounds. Protesters included students, professional associations, labor unions, the main opposition party, small left-wing parties, anti-capitalist Islamists, Kurdish politicians, soccer fans, environmentalists, and others. Likewise, Turkey's uprising is also youth driven; most of those on the streets are young adults and students, with no history of political activism.

For many, the largest popular revolt in the history of the Republic of Turkey had begun (Öncü 2014). The power of this movement may be in mobilizing tens of thousands of apolitical or cynical young people. People have joined the protests for reasons that may be more about social freedoms than financial oppression. They protested the increasingly conservative orientation of the AKP party, especially after the election victory in 2011, and as a consequence thereof the restriction of freedom rights in Turkey. These include freedom of speech, freedom of the press, and so on. Protesters also raged against alcohol consumption and abortion restrictions, sexual discrimination, and other aspects. As elsewhere, from Newfoundland's Avalon Peninsula and New York's Zuccotti Park, Veblen's contributions to understanding and acting on this new order of business have struck a civic chord in Turkey. As Professor Öncü (2014) suggests, this anti-capitalistic movement by the Gezi community, in a country "where difference differs with itself," may be a defining moment of freedom. A fitting locale for rethinking grassroots democracy through the lens and spirit of Veblen.

Acknowledgements

I wish to express my sincere appreciation to Dr. Ahmet Öncü and the Chamber of Electrical Engineers for their financial support which made possible this paper and its presentation at the symposium, Veblen, Capitalism and Possibilities for a Rational Economic Order, Yıldız Technical University Auditorium, July 6-7, 2012, Istanbul, Turkey.

---

[11] Current President of Turkey who previously served as the Prime Minister from 2003 to 2014.

References

Domhoff, G. W. 2005. Wealth, Income, and Power. Who Rules America? University of California at Santa Cruz. *http://whorulesamerica.net/power/wealth.html*.

Edgell, S. 2001. *Veblen in Perspective: His Life and Thought*. Armonk, New York: M.E. Sharpe.

Mason, S.E. 2012. The Occupy Movement and Social Justice Economics. *The Journal of Contemporary Social Services* 93 (1): 3-4.

Mitchell, R.E. 2001. Thorstein Veblen: Pioneer in Environmental Sociology. *Organization & Environment* 14 (4): 389-408.

_____. 2007. Absentee Ownership and Resource-Dependent Communities: Veblen and Beyond. In *Thorstein Veblen's Contribution to Environmental Sociology: Essays in the Political Ecology of Wasteful Industrialism*, ed. R.E. Mitchell. Lewiston, New York: Edwin Mellen Press.

Öncü, A. 2014. Turkish Capitalist Modernity and the Gezi Revolt. *Journal of Historical Sociology* 27 (2): 152-176.

Plotkin, S. 2010. The Critic as Quietist: Thorstein Veblen's Radical Realism. Symposium: Apology for Quietism, Part 4. *Common Knowledge* 16 (1): 79-94.

_____. and R. Tilman. 2011. *The Political Ideas of Thorstein Veblen*. New Haven [Conn.]: Yale University Press.

Polanyi, K. 2001. (1944). *The Great Transformation: The Political and Social Origins of Our Time*. New York: Beacon Press.

Rollmann, H. 2011. On Occupy Camps, Hello Kitty, and the State. Or, how Newfoundland Invented the 'Occupy' Movement before Wall Street... Newfoundland and Labrador: The Independent.ca. *http://theindependent.ca/2011/11/15/on-occupy-camps-hello-kitty-and-the-state*.

Sherman, H. J. 2004. Political Economy of Evolution: Remarks upon Receiving the Veblen-Commons Award. *Journal of Economic Issues* 38 (2): 315-326.

Vaughn, G.F. 1999. Veblen's Possible Influence on the New Deal Land Utilization Program as Evidenced by his Student Claud Franklin Clayton. *Journal of Economic Issues* 33: 713-727.

Veblen, T. 1967. (1899). *The Theory of the Leisure Class: An Economic Study of Institutions*. New York: Funk & Wagnalls.

_____. 2005. (1919). *The Vested Interests and the Common Man*. New York: Viking.

_____. 1921. *The Engineers and the Price System*. New York: B.W. Huebsch.

_____. 1967. (1923). *Absentee Ownership and Business Enterprise in Recent Times: The Case of America*. Boston: Beacon.

Wikipedia. 2012. Occupy Movement. *http://en.wikipedia.org/wiki/Occupy_movement*.

Contributors

Gülenay Baş Dinar is Assistant Professor in the Department of Economics at Abant İzzet Baysal University in Turkey. Dinar completed her Ph.D. at Hacettepe University and her undergraduate studies at Abant İzzet Baysal University. She examined the theories of Veblen, Keynes and Minsky about financial instabilities in her Ph.D. dissertation. Her research interests are political economy, economic methodology and history of economic thought.

William M. Dugger is Professor of Economics at the University of Tulsa. A founding member of the Association for Institutional Thought and a member of both the Union for Radical Political Economics and the Association for Evolutionary Economics for over 40 years. He has published ten books and written widely in the heterodox journals. He has been the President of the Association for Evolutionary Economics, Association for Social Economics and Association for Institutional Thought. He has served widely on the editorial boards of heterodox journals.

Faruk Eray Düzenli is Associate Professor of Economics at St. Mary's College of Maryland. He is a member of the editorial collective of *Rethinking Marxism,* and a co-editor of its *Reviews* section. His recent publications include "Surplus-Producing Labor as a Capability: A Marxian Contribution to Amartya Sen's Revival of Classical Political Economy" (*Cambridge Journal of Economics*), and "Did Marx Fetishize Labor?" (*Rethinking Marxism*).

Michael Hudson received his Ph.D. in Economics from New York University in 1968. His dissertation was on American economic and technological thought in the nineteenth century. He received his M.A. also from New York University in 1963 in economics, with a thesis on the World Bank's philosophy of development, with special reference to lending policies in the agricultural sector. He was philology major with a minor in history at the University of Chicago, where he received his B.A. in 1959.

Hudson previously taught at the New School in New York City. He is currently Professor of Economics at the University of Missouri at Kansas City (UMKC). He has been economic advisor to the Icelandic, Chinese, Latvian, U.S., Canadian, and Mexican governments, to the United Nations Institute for Training and Research (UNITAR). He is president of the Institute for the Study of Long-term Economic Trends (ISLET). He is also a former balance-of-payments economist for Chase Manhattan Bank and Arthur Andersen, and economic futurist for the Hudson Institute (no relation). For Scudder, Stevens & Clark in 1990, he established the world's first Third World sovereign debt fund, which became the second best performing international fund in 1991.

Hudson is the author of *Killing the Host* (2015), *The Bubble and Beyond* (2012), *America's Protectionist Takeoff, 1815-1914: The Neglected American School of Political Economy* (2010), *Super-Imperialism: The Economic Strategy of American Empire* (1968 & 2003), *Global Fracture, The New International Order* (1979 & 2005), *Trade, Development and Foreign Debt* (1992 & 2009) and *The Myth of Aid* (1971).

Ross E. Mitchell has led industrial projects and advised on resource-based development over a 30-year career. He has extensive experience analyzing and integrating social and environmental issues and indicators into sustainable business operations, stakeholder engagement, and policy analysis. His specialties include risk assessments, social and environmental impact assessments, public participation, international and community development, and sustainable approaches to resource management. His many publications include an edited book *Thorstein Veblen's Contribution to Environmental Sociology: Essays in the Political Ecology of Wasteful Industrialism* (2007, Edwin Mellen Press). He holds a Ph.D. in Environmental Sociology from the University of Alberta, Canada.

Anita Oğurlu received her PhD in Humanities & Cultural Studies from Birkbeck College, University of London (2016) and BA in Fashion - Communication from Ryerson University, Toronto, Canada (1987). Her research interests include social evolution, culture and globalization, visual communication, film and media studies, European and Turkish interwar period and autobiography. Oğurlu was a lecturer in Film & Television studies at Istanbul Bilgi University prior to pursuing doctoral research in the UK. Before returning to academia in 2005, Oğurlu worked as an Art Director and Creative Director in multi-national advertising corporations in Toronto and Istanbul for over eighteen years.

Ahmet Öncü is Professor of Sociology in the School of Management at Sabancı University where he has been a faculty member with a specialization in political economics since 1998. He received his Ph.D. in Sociology at the University of Alberta and his MA and BA in Economics at the Middle East Technical University. His research and teaching interests include international political economy, social theory and historical sociology. More specifically, his works ground Turkish modernity and capitalism on social theory, analyze class dynamics and their implications for social and cultural change, and reflect on social, political and moral foundations of democracy and citizenship. Öncü's articles appeared in *New Perspectives on Turkey, Journal of Historical Sociology, Cultural Logic, Science and Society, Citizenship Studies, International Review of Sociology, Review of Radical Political Economics* and *Sociology of Islam.* His recent edited volumes include *Neoliberal Landscape and the Rise of Islamist Capital in Turkey* (N. Balkan, E. Balkan and A. Öncü, eds.) and *A Guide to Thorstein Veblen* (in Turkish).

Michael Perelman is Professor of Economics at California State University. He was born in New Castle Pennsylvania in 1939. He did his undergraduate work at the University of Michigan and graduated in 1961. I received his Ph.D. from the University of California Berkeley in 1970. He is the author of more than 20 books, the latest of which is *Sex, Lies, and Economics: The Amazing Story and Relevance of Economics and Economists before Adam Smith* (under review). Perelman's early research revealed how profit-oriented agricultural system created hunger, pollution, serious public health consequences, and environmental disruption, while throwing millions of people off the land. Perelman wrote extensively in criticism of conventional or mainstream economics in all his books, papers and interviews.

Sidney Plotkin is Professor of Political Science, Margaret Stiles Halleck Chair of Social Sciences, at Vassar College. He has written on subjects ranging from land use, political economy, and power, to most recently, the political ideas of Thorstein Veblen. He has served as President of the International Thorstein Veblen Association.

Felipe Rezende is Associate Professor of Economics at Hobart and William Smith Colleges and a research fellow at MINDS – Multidisciplinary Institute on Development and Strategies. His research has focused on money and banking, monetary theory and policy, macroeconomic theory and policy, and economic development. He previously taught at the University of Missouri–Kansas City.

Rezende has authored more than a dozen book chapters and articles, which have been published in a number of journals. He secured a grant from the Ford Foundation to direct a research project titled, "Financial Governance, Banking, and Financial Instability in Brazil: Analysis and Policy Recommendations."

Rezende earned a B.A. in Economics from Federal University, Rio de Janeiro, Brazil, and a M.A. in Economics and Ph.D. in Economics and Mathematics from the University of Missouri-Kansas City.

William Waller is the William R. Kenan Jr. Professor of Economics at Hobart and William Smith Colleges. He received the Veblen-Commons Award from the Association for Evolutionary Economics. He is the past-president of the Association for Evolutionary Economics and the Association for Institutional Thought. He has co-edited three books *Alternatives to Economic Orthodoxy, The Stratified State* and *Cultural Economics and Theory*. His articles on institutionalist methodology, feminist economics, public policy and the work of Thorstein Veblen have been published in *Journal of Economic Issues, History of Political Economy, Review of Social Economy, Forum for Social Economics, Rethinking Marxism,* and *Review of Institutional Thought.*

www.ingramcontent.com/pod-product-compliance
Lightning Source LLC
Chambersburg PA
CBHW081813200326

41597CB00023B/4233